AF834930

Who Killed Linda Vanderveen?

Who Killed Linda Vanderveen?

A True Crime Mystery

Gerald W. Kinsey

COPYRIGHT PAGE

ISBN 13: 978-1-62329-114-3

ISBN 10: 1-62329-114-3

Published in the USA

Photos courtesy of findagrave.com and Reprinted from Bing Search

Dedication

Dedicated to my writer friends, without whose assistance this book would look much worse.

Table of Contents

Albert Lee III being arrested for the murder
of Linda Vanderveen. (Note: the mustache and beard.)

Compare and Contrast

Witnesses' Composite of Abductor

Preface

I enjoy my day job is as editor of a small-town weekly newspaper. But for over fifty years, my calling has been working with prisoners. And for forty-three of those years I was a volunteer in various city and county jails and state prisons.

When my son was sent to prison for a crime he didn't commit, I became involved in the pursuit of justice for the innocent. In the process, I became acquainted with about twenty cases of men who have been unjustly incarcerated.

In 2009, I learned about the widely publicized Linda Vanderveen murder case. From the beginning it was questionable to me whether Albert Lee, who was convicted of the crime, was actually the one who did it. After several years of study, including thirteen years of correspondence with Mr. Lee himself, I became even more doubtful that the right man was sent to prison.

Much of the material for this book came from articles in the Grand Rapids Press and from court cases. There is also information from Albert Lee himself taken from his many letters to me.

With so much interest in this case, it is somewhat surprising no one else has written a book about what happened. It has taken me several years to write this book. At first, I hoped to finish it in time to interest the authorities in releasing Albert, who was dying. However, it is too late now.

Tragically, Albert died in prison of cancer in September, 2022. Nevertheless, here is his story. May he rest in peace.

Introduction

The Linda Vanderveen murder case was one of the most famous cases in the history of the State of Michigan. People all over Michigan, other states, and even Canada sent in tips and contributed money toward the $50,000 reward for the apprehension and conviction of the perpetrator. Parents began accompanying their children to school, and there were many policy changes to ensure the safety of students. The Linda Vanderveen Children's Festival was started in Grand Rapids and continued for many years with attendance reaching 6,000 people.

A Homicide Investigation Team (HIT) was formed, which eventually included up to fifty officers. Hundreds of tips were investigated, and after six weeks a suspect was arrested and ultimately convicted. His name was Albert Lee III. He was sent to prison for life, but his conviction was later thrown out by the Michigan Supreme Court. Rather than release him, the Court sent him back to the same prosecutor who had prosecuted him at the first trial. He was convicted a second time and sent to prison for life. He continued to appeal but was not successful. Albert Lee III died in a prison hospital in 2022.

To his dying day, Lee insisted he was not the one who committed the crime. Either he did, or he did not. If he did, there are still several unanswered questions. If he is not the one responsible, the question remains: who killed Linda Vanderveen?

Who Killed Linda Vanderveen?

A True Crime Mystery

Chapter One – The Crime

On the morning of February 12, 1979, Linda Vanderveen was working as a crossing guard at the Mulick Park School in Grand Rapids, Michigan. She had not been scheduled to work that morning, but the boy who was supposed to work that day was sick, and she was asked to take his place. As she was working, a Black man with a dark colored car stopped and proceeded to force her into his vehicle. A man saw what was happening and approached the abductor. He asked what was going on. The man said that nothing was happening and pushed him out of the way. He then got in the car and sped off. It was apparent that the girl was being kidnapped. The witness then got back into his car and followed the abductor until he lost him.

Of course, the matter was reported to the police. Since the abductor was a Black man with a dark-colored car, the police were stopping all drivers who fit the description. Around noon they stopped a man named Albert Lee, who had recently bought a black Grand Prix and had just gotten his plates and driver's license at the Secretary of State office in Grand Rapids. Since he was a possible suspect, they kept him under surveillance until the body of the victim was found later in the afternoon.

Sometime in the late forenoon or early afternoon a couple men encountered a Black man with a dark colored Monte Carlo stuck in the snow. They helped him get out. When asked later, they were both insistent that the car was a Monte Carlo, and one of them said that he saw the words *Monte Carlo* on the car.

The body of Linda Vanderveen was found in a snowbank nearby around 4:45P.M. There were tire tracks from the vehicle that was used to transport the body, and there were footprints in the snow from the man who carried the body to the snowbank. The police measured the size of the footprints and found that they were size eight to nine and three-quarters. Also, there was a notebook found in a dumpster nearby, and there were fingerprints on it that were later found to match the fingerprints that were found on the neck of the victim.

When the body was turned over, warm air came out of her mouth. The medical experts determined that she had been placed in the snowbank sometime after 2:00 p.m. One way it was obvious that the body had not been there for a long time was that it was not frozen, and the day of the murder was a very cold day.

A homicide investigation team was assembled, which was headed by Lieutenant Gerald Steele. The matter was reported in the Grand Rapids Press, and the public was greatly concerned that the murderer be found. In fact, they contributed close to $50,000 toward the reward for the capture of the perpetrator. At that time the previous record for a reward was $10,000. With so much pressure from the public, the police investigated hundreds of tips. After six weeks, they arrested Albert Lee, who was subsequently convicted and sent to prison for life.

Chapter Two – The Victim

Linda Vanderveen was a cute, blonde-haired, eleven-year-old girl. She was the daughter of Andrew and Shirley Vanderveen. She had one brother named David. Her father was the personnel director for the city of Grand Rapids. He was the one who hired and fired police officers. Linda was a happy, friendly child. She didn't have any enemies.

The only family member who had enemies was her father. As a result of his work as personnel director, he had received numerous death threats. Some have suggested that he was the true target of the Linda Vanderveen murder. At the trial he appeared to have serious doubts about whether or not Albert Lee was the one who killed his daughter.

Six years after Linda's death he was hunting in Osceola County with three other employees of the city of Grand Rapids. They brought him into the Reed City hospital, dead. His death certificate is in the Reed City courthouse. There was no autopsy, and the death was not referred to the medical examiner. There are only two words for the cause of death. It says he died of cardiopulmonary arrest. In other words, his heart stopped beating. It is not clear why.

Linda's mother died in 2002 at the age of 70.

Linda's brother died in 2005 in Montcalm County at the age of 43. His death certificate indicates that the exact date of death is not known, and he died of cardiomegaly, a condition in which the heart gets enlarged creating various health problems. It is common for ages 60 and older.

It seems strange that all four members of the family died prematurely. They are all buried in the Woodlawn Cemetery, 2530 Kalamazoo Avenue S.E., Grand Rapids, Michigan.

Chapter Three – The Suspect

The man convicted of the murder of Linda Vanderveen was Albert Lee. He has consistently denied his guilt from the beginning. Lee's family was originally from Louisiana. He grew up in the Houston, Texas area. As a young man he moved to Battle Creek, Michigan, where his brother worked. He met a woman named Vivian Pride who moved to Grand Rapids. He followed her there and worked for a time in the area. He considered becoming a teacher or a police officer.

On the morning of February 12, 1979 Lee went to Sambo's restaurant in Grand Rapids for breakfast. He ordered eggs, and when they were brought, they were not done to his satisfaction. For that reason he sent them back to be redone. He thought because he had sent his eggs back, the cook would remember him being there that day. When he was suspected of the murder, he asked if the man remembered. This was twisted by the police who said that he asked the man to lie by saying he had spent the entire forenoon at the restaurant. He never claimed to have spent all that time there, and he never asked the man to lie.

He had recently bought a black Grand Prix and needed to get it licensed. He also needed to get his driver's license. The Secretary of State office opened at nine o'clock, and he wanted to be there when it opened. He said he was the third person in line that morning. The prosecutor and police claimed he was lying because they said his license plate number ended in 062, and when they found the people who had numbers ending in 060 and 061, they were at the Secretary of State office around 11:00 o'clock. Therefore, he would have gotten his license around 11:30. Lee agreed, but he explained that he had been there twice that morning because when he first came, he was told he couldn't get his licenses because he had unpaid traffic tickets, which had to be paid before he could be issued the licenses. He then went to city hall and paid the tickets before returning to the Secretary of State office. Again the prosecution claimed he was lying because they had checked at city hall and found no record of any traffic tickets. This does not sound like a story a person would make up, because it would be too easy to disprove. It appears that either someone removed the tickets or simply lied about them not being there.

After receiving the license plate, Lee did what a person would normally do. He put the plate on his car. Again the prosecution claimed he was lying. They said he couldn't have put the plate on the car because it was too cold. It is not clear why a person can't put a plate on a car when it is cold. All it takes is five minutes and a screwdriver.

After attaching the plate, Lee was driving through town and was stopped around noon by the police, because they were stopping every Black man with a dark colored car in search of the man who abducted Linda Vanderveen. As mentioned earlier, since Lee was a possible suspect, the police kept him under surveillance until the body of the victim was found later in the afternoon. Lee knew they were watching him because he could see the police car outside his home.

Lee not only needed to get plates for his car; he also needed a new driver's license. This required a photograph. Since he had his picture taken for his license the same day as the Vanderveen murder, it should be easy to verify that Lee didn't look anything like the man the witnesses described. One of the most obvious differences was that Lee had a beard, but all the witnesses agreed that the man they had seen did not. It is possible for a man to commit a crime, be seen by witnesses, shave off the beard and then be seen the same day without a beard. However, it is not possible for a man to commit a crime, be seen by witnesses without a beard and have a full beard later the same day. Since the picture on the license was important in identifying the abductor, it was shown at the trial. However, the area on the picture where the beard would have been had been defaced so that it was not possible to tell if he had a beard or not. Clearly the defense would want people to know Lee had a beard since all the witnesses agreed the man they saw did not. Only the prosecution would want to hide the fact that Lee had a beard. There is no question that Lee did have a beard. The police saw him that day, and so did several other people. When he was arrested six weeks later, he still had a beard, and his picture was published in the Grand Rapids Press.

Through the entire investigation Lee cooperated with the police because he knew he was innocent, and he was confident that he would be exonerated when all the facts were in. Two other men were considered to be possible suspects, but both of them left the area. Lee is the only one who stayed around. Therefore, he appears to be less suspect.

Lee had no criminal history. All those who knew him would say that it would be totally out of character for him to kill a child he knew nothing about. Lee died in a prison hospital in Jackson as a result of cancer that had spread to his bone marrow and then to his brain.

Do you know this man?

Chapter Four – The Investigation

On Tuesday, February 13, the day after the body of the victim was found, the Grand Rapids police created a special task force to investigate the murder. It was headed by Lieutenant Gerald Steele, who had previously headed another similar task force. The Homicide Investigation Team (HIT) was originally composed of thirteen members, but soon had over fifty officers involved.

The police used the services of a hypnotist the day of the murder, and the day after, to "help people recall details." This proved to be somewhat problematic. The witnesses said that the hypnotism did not put anything in their minds that was not there already. However, it was reported later that they were told under hypnosis to identify whoever the police arrested. They testified at the trial that Albert Lee looked identical to the man they had seen, even though he looked nothing like the man they had described. On two occasions they failed to pick Lee out of a police lineup. On a third occasion they were shown pictures of possible suspects, but they failed to pick Lee. Ultimately, Lee's conviction was thrown out by the Michigan Supreme Court because of the hypnotized witnesses.

By afternoon the day after the murder, people had already contributed $10,000 to the reward fund to find the killer. By March 16 the fund would reach $50,000, which was the ceiling set by Silent Observer. People called in tips from all over the country, as well as Canada.

Initially, it was thought that there might be a second man involved because a woman claimed she saw a girl being transferred to a Ford Country Squire station wagon. However, she later admitted she lied about the incident because she was late for work.

Since LindaVanderveen's father had received numerous death threats as a result of his work as personnel director for the City of Grand Rapids, a search was made of applications to see if they could find someone who might have a grudge against him. They claimed they didn't find anyone.

On Wednesday, two witnesses came forward and reported that on Monday they had seen a car stuck in a snowbank near the place where the body of the victim was found. They said it was a black 1975 to 1978 Chevrolet Monte Carlo with a 1978 license plate. This obviously could not have been Albert Lee's car since he had a Grand Prix, and he had just gotten his license plate that day. The witnesses were very insistent that the car was a Monte Carlo, and one said he saw the words *Monte Carlo* on the car.

Chapter Five – The Arrest

On the evening of March 29, the police arrested Albert Lee for the murder of Linda Vanderveen. He was picked out of a lineup by two witnesses. That is curious because they had failed to pick him out from two other lineups and on a third occasion when they were shown photographs. He also didn't look at all like the man they had described.

Since the police said Lee had been a suspect from the beginning, the natural question was why they had waited a month and a half to make the arrest. Their answer was that they didn't have enough evidence. They didn't indicate what new evidence they had found that justified the arrest. They said that Lee had been cooperative all along during the investigation.

... it had been "extremely difficult" to gather enough evidence against Lee.

After the arrest, Lieutenant Steele indicated that the toughest part of the case was still ahead. That seems strange if they had clear proof of guilt. He also said that it had been "extremely difficult" to gather enough evidence against Lee. If there was a great deal of evidence, why was it difficult to tie it to Lee?

Lee had a different story about the arrest. He said that the police had had his car for a week and found no trace of any evidence in it. The car needed work, and he took it to Goodyear off Wealthy Street in Grand Rapids, where it was for a week. He went there to check on the car on March 28. The proprietor told him the police checked on his car and took a carpet sample. This was because carpet fibers were found on the victim. Lee returned the next day to get his car. Officer Larry Crace met him there and told him that if he passed a polygraph test, the police would not bother him anymore. They went to the Hall of Justice where he was given the test. He passed, but then Lieutenant Steele asked the examiner to see him outside the room. When he returned, he said there was a problem with the test and wanted to do it again. This time he said Lee failed the test. Then Steele told Lee to stand, and he proceeded to handcuff him. He then told Lee he was under arrest for the murder. Since the arrest occurred at the Hall of Justice, it is not clear why the newspaper claimed he was arrested at home.

Lee was first put in the city jail, and then later he was taken to the county jail until his trial. While in the county jail, he was in a four man cell. Each man had his own individual cell. Cell one was for Billy Mansfield Jr. who was extradited from Florida for two rapes he had committed in Kent County. Cells two and three were for two other Black men, and Lee was in cell four, which was next to the shower. The prosecutor tried to get all three of the other inmates to testify against Lee, but both Black men refused. Mansfield agreed because he was facing up to two life sentences for two cases of forcible rape. He was already a convicted sex offender and a parole violator. The two teenage girls he had stripped and raped at knifepoint were available to testify, and they had warned the officials that Mansfield was a very dangerous man who was sure to repeat his crimes. Since Mansfield's only hope was to make a deal with the prosecutor, he agreed to testify that Lee had confessed to the murder. Lee has said that he was never alone with Mansfield. If he had made any confession, the other two Black men in the unit would have heard it. They both said they never heard any such confession, and they also testified that Mansfield was not to be trusted.

Lee remained in the Kent County jail until his trial in October.

Chapter Six – The First Trial

The trial began on October 17. However, before the trial could start, there were several issues that needed to be decided, and it was necessary to select a jury. It was thought this could be a problem because the case had received so much publicity. A change of venue was considered, but the judge said that would have to wait until it was learned whether or not an unbiased jury could be obtained in Kent County. As it turned out, a jury was selected after many prospective jurors were rejected for various reasons.

The main players in the trial were Kent Circuit Court Judge George Boucher, defense attorney William Murphy and assistant prosecutor William Forsyth. Lee also had an attorney named Peter Walsh, but he is seldom mentioned in the subsequent trial.

Before the trial, the judge had to rule on several motions. The most important had to do with whether or not to allow the identification by the hypnotized witnesses, and the supposed confession. The judge agreed to both, but both were later found to be illegitimate.

According to the prosecutor, the police found a barrette, hair samples, feathers, and carpet samples in Lee's car when they searched it on February 26. They also said they could not substantiate his alibi that he had been at Sambo's restaurant and the Secretary of State office the morning of the abduction. It seems like they should have been able to verify his story, since several people saw him at both places. However, the failure to prove his story true does not prove it false. Many people come and go at both places. It is not surprising that one person may not be remembered. The police also claimed it was suspicious that Lee changed his license plates and cleaned his car. Since he had recently purchased the car and had to get new plates, it should not be surprising that he put on the new plates. It also is not surprising that a man might want to clean out his car. Furthermore, it was claimed that Lee's features were similar to those of the man described by the witnesses. It is hard to see how anyone could come to that conclusion when comparing Lee with the picture that was published in the Grand Rapids Press on March 2, 1979. The picture was from a sketch made by the police and was based on the description given by five different witnesses. All were in close agreement about the man's appearance, and all agreed that the man they saw did not have a beard.

The trial began with the testimony of Linda Vanderveen's mother, Shirley Vanderveen. She identified twenty-two items her daughter had with her when she left home the day of the murder.

Then the prosecutor gave his opening statement. He said, "We will prove without a reasonable doubt that she was strangled to death by Albert Lee." The Michigan Supreme Court later decided otherwise. He then summarized the evidence he planned to present. As expected, he said he would show Lee was the abductor and murderer by the identification by the witnesses, the confession and the items found in his car.

The defense attorney waited to make his opening statement until later.

The first day of testimony concluded with witness Jack Hill telling his experience the day of the abduction. He saw a black car parked on the wrong side of the street with a man bent over toward it. He thought the car might be stuck. He asked the man what was going on. The man said everything was all right. Hill then looked into the car and saw a girl waving frantically in the back seat. It was obvious something was wrong. The man jumped into the car and sped off, knocking Hill down. He followed the car until he lost it.

On Thursday, October 18, the second day of the trial, real estate salesman Jim Vos testified that he saw a black Grand Prix speeding near the site of the abduction. He saw a young white girl waving her arms in the back seat. The Grand Prix nearly hit the car he and his son were riding in. He said he was not able to identify the driver of the other vehicle. Jack Hill testified again. He insisted that he was sure Lee was the man he had seen, even though he had said earlier that the man he saw was clean shaven. Lee clearly had a beard, mustache and long sideburns. Hill had also previously said he thought the car he saw was a Chrysler. Lee had a Grand Prix. In addition, Hill said the car he saw had wide white wall tires. Lee's car did not.

The trial resumed on Monday, the 22nd. The prosecution called nine witnesses that day. One was a safety patrol boy named Greg Start. He testified that Lee looked just like the man he saw driving near the abduction site on February 12. However, defense attorney Murphy played a tape recording of the hypnosis session in June in which Start said that he didn't get a good look at the driver. Several other witnesses said they saw a black car driving near the abduction site. There was confusion as to the make of the car. A couple witnesses that day were very insistent that the car was a Monte Carlo.

On Tuesday Billy Mansfield Jr testified. He claimed Lee had said he tried to have sex with a girl and then strangled her and dumped the body in a snowbank near an apartment complex. He gave several other details that were well-known in the case. He said Lee told him about the incident in several conversations while they were cellmates in the Kent County jail. If that were true, the other two cellmates would have heard them since they were close together, and everyone could hear what the others were saying. Mansfield's credibility was highly questionable from the beginning, and he ultimately admitted he lied about the whole thing. Dr. Harvey Wilks, who was a medical examiner and pathologist, testified that Linda Vanderveen was strangled, apparently by her necklace. Nearly everyone agrees that she was strangled, but it is highly unlikely that the necklace was used because it was too flimsy. It almost certainly would have broken.

On Wednesday Grand Rapids police officer Larry Crace testified. He said he had questioned Lee February 16, which was four days after the murder. He said that Lee was sweating and looked nervous when he questioned him. That is not surprising since it was clear that the police considered him to be a suspect. Most people would be nervous in a similar situation. Crace said Lee told him he had been at Sambo's Restaurant on 28th Street between 7:30 and 9:00 a.m. the morning of the abduction. He then went to the Secretary of State office to get his license plates and driver's license. He had to return home twice to get papers he needed to complete the requirements for the licenses. Crace claimed Lee said he was stopped by a police officer about 9:30 or 10:00. It is not clear if Lee actually said that or if there was a misunderstanding. When Grand Rapids Police Detective Phillip Werkema testified, he said he stopped Lee shortly after noon the day of the murder. Crace claimed that Lee said he was the third person to buy plates the day of the murder. What Lee said was that he was the third person there to try to get plates. He always has said he couldn't get his license the first time he went to the Secretary of State office because he found he needed proof of insurance, and he had to pay his traffic tickets. By claiming Lee said he actually purchased his licenses shortly after 9:00 a.m., the prosecution tried to discredit him. The manager of the Secretary of State office, Jesse Colon, said that licenses are normally given out in numerical order. Since Lee's plate number ended in 062, he would have been the 54th or 55th person to get plates that day. Lee has always said he got his plates around 11:00 or 11:30 and then put them on his car. Then he was stopped by the police around noon. Crace also testified that he returned later on February 16 to take a picture of Lee's car. He returned again on February 23 to pull carpet fiber from the car. Then on February 26 he searched Lee's car again.

On Thursday, October 25, crime lab scientist Edward L. Gundy testified that he examined hair samples and carpet fiber found in Lee's car. He said they were similar to those from Linda Vanderveen's body. Of course, many cars have carpets from the same carpet roll. There is also a question about whether the police may have planted evidence. DNA testing was not available until at least 1984. Since the first trial was in 1979, it was not possible at that time to tell if the hairs were from the victim. By the time of the second trial in 1991 DNA testing was available, and when the hair found in Lee's car was tested, it was proven that the hair was not from the victim. Gundy also said that a plastic barrette that was found under the back seat was similar to Vanderveen's. If Lee killed Linda Vanderveen, it is strange the barrette would be under the seat. It would seem like it would be in the open or thrown away. We now know the barrette could not be Vanderveen's because it had the wrong kind of clasp. Gundy also said there were feathers in Lee's car that could have come from the victim's mitten. Naturally, they also could have come from something else. Also on Thursday, witnesses were questioned to try to determine the time Lee obtained his license plate. Those with license numbers ending in 060, 061,063 and 064 all testified that they obtained their plates between 10:30 and 11:30. This confirms Lee's claim that he got his around 11:00 or 11:30. Crace claimed Lee said he had his plates on his car by 9:20 a.m. Lee never said that. Either Crace lied or there was a misunderstanding.

There is also a question about whether the police may have planted evidence.

The trial resumed on Monday, October 29. A fingerprint expert testified that of the 31 fingerprints found in Lee's car the only one he could identify was from Lee's brother, Eugene. He was not able to find any print from Linda Vanderveen. A rubbish hauler named George VanAntwerp told about finding the victim's University of Michigan knapsack in a dumpster two days after the murder. He thought about keeping it for his daughter, but when he found Vanderveen's lunch, mitten, red shoelace, and a book with her name, he reported it to the police. Another witness, David D. Orr Jr., had previously testified that on the morning of the abduction, he had helped pull a car out of an icy spot near the place the body was found. The driver of the vehicle then threw something into a dumpster nearby. The car was a Monte Carlo. Therefore, it could not have been Lee's car since he had a Grand Prix. Raymond L. Kenny from the state police's Holland crime lab was not able to find any evidence of Lee's car being towed. Edward L. Gundy, who was a crime lab scientist, said that he didn't find any fibers from Vanderveen's clothing in Lee's car.

On Tuesday, Earl Finkbeiner, a Grand Rapids police fingerprint expert, testified that he could **not** identify the fingerprint found on Vanderveen's notebook that was found in a dumpster near where her body was found. Since it was highly likely the fingerprint is from the murderer, it was very important that the print be identified. It was **not** from Albert Lee, and over a thousand other Black males were checked without finding a match. The print was also compared with everyone else that the victim may have had contact with. No match could be found. Witnesses also were asked about feathers and carpet samples found in Lee's car. They could not tell if they linked Lee to the victim. Abraham Sidelma, vice president of H. Goodman & Son's Co., testified that the barrette found in Lee's car and those belonging to Vanderveen were made by his company, but it was not possible to know if they were from the same package because his company made 20 million of them per year. It was not mentioned that the barrette found in Lee's car had a different kind of clasp than the ones the victim had. The barrette would become quite important at Lee's second trial.

On Thursday, William Murphy began the case for the defense. Lee testified that he did not abduct or kill Linda Vanderveen. He recounted again what he did the morning of the murder. His story has been quite consistent from the beginning to the present. Of course, William Forsyth tried to discredit him on several points. Mainly he pointed out that Lee's testimony was inconsistent with the notes of Officer Crace. Naturally, that doesn't tell whether Lee or Crace was incorrect. The testimony of Billy Mansfield was brought up again. Lee denied telling him anything. He said he kept finding Mansfield snooping around his cell and caught him reading a transcript of Lee's preliminary examination. Mansfield claimed he had not read the transcript. Forsyth questioned Lee about whether he had asked a cook at Sambo's restaurant to say he was at the restaurant the morning of the abduction. Lee said he only asked the cook if he saw him.

That same day, a witness testified that he had helped pull a black car out of an icy spot near the place where the body of the victim was found. The witness asked the driver for a cigarette, and the man gave him a Kool and offered a light with a Bic lighter. Lee smoked Kools and had a Bic lighter. Of course, thousands of other people do also. Lee's girlfriend Vivian Pride also testified, saying she had used Lee's car to transport children, and some of them were white and probably had blond hair. She also said feathers could have been in Lee's car because her mother had a pillow in the car. Also, Lee had a down-filled jacket he had cut to make a vest. Since the reliability of the hypnotized witnesses was important to the case, Lee's attorney played a tape recording of a witness who was told he would "remember all the details" and "see his (a man's) face." Witness Jack Hill had testified that he had no doubt Lee was the man he saw with the victim the morning of the abduction, but attorney Thomas Schultz testified that at the lineup on March 29 Hill had said Lee only looked "the closest of all."

The trial resumed on Monday, November 5. The only witness that day was a hypnosis expert named Martin T. Orne. He questioned the credibility of some witnesses who were placed under hypnosis, since suggestive pressures to such witnesses can damage their memories. He stated that under hypnosis, innuendoes and other pressures may cause a person to imagine details and later believe they are facts. Especially troubling to him was the hypnosis of a twelve-year-old boy named Greg H. Start. He had picked Lee out of a lineup on June

20 after being hypnotized, and after seeing Lee's picture in the newspaper. Orne said that chances were "exceedingly high" that the newspaper photo made a bigger impression on Start than what he had seen on February 12. Orne said that he believed investigators should exhaust the memory without hypnosis first and then try to obtain additional information by hypnotizing. That is not what was done with Start. It was also pointed out that witnesses Jack Hill and Jack Vos only picked Lee out of a lineup after being hypnotized twice. They had previously passed over him on at least two occasions. Orne believed that they should have been able to pick Lee earlier if their memories were based on what they saw on February 12. The lineup in which they picked Lee was on March 29, which was a month and a half after the abduction, and after they had been hypnotized. Orne asserted his belief that hypnosis is a legitimate tool for law enforcement, but that it does increase the chance that information obtained may be inaccurate.

On Tuesday, Jerome Sueing, one of Lee's former cellmates at the Kent County jail, testified. He said that Billy Mansfield, who claimed Lee had confessed to the murder, should not be trusted. He said that all the other inmates believed Mansfield was a snitch because he had more visits and access to the phones. He also seemed to be well acquainted with the guards. Sueing said Lee could not have made a confession to Mansfield without all the other cellmates hearing it, because "you couldn't even whisper in the cell without everyone hearing." He also confirmed that Mansfield had almost certainly read Lee's preliminary hearing report. The prosecution called Dr. Donald Rossi, director of behavioral science with the Michigan State Police, to testify as a rebuttal witness. However, he agreed with the previous defense witness that memories can be altered by hypnosis. He questioned some claims of the previous expert, but he didn't provide any proof of error.

On Wednesday, the defense called its last witness, Dr. Robert Buckhout, a psychology professor at Brooklyn College in New York. He pointed out that Blacks tend to give less accurate descriptions of whites and vice versus. Lee is Black, and all the witnesses identifying him were white. This didn't prove the identification was wrong, but it does raise a question of its reliability.

The prosecutor then presented his closing arguments. Since he clearly didn't have any proof of guilt, he tried to convince the jury that there were too many coincidences for Lee to be innocent. First, he reminded the jury of the identification by the witnesses. This was a major point of disagreement from the start. It later became a moot point when the Michigan Supreme Court threw out the identification because the witnesses had been hypnotized, and Lee didn't look anything like the man they had described. Then, the prosecutor tried to convince the jury that the car used by the abductor was a Grand Prix, even though there was considerable evidence that it was a Monte Carlo. He pointed out that there were red carpet fibers on the victim, and Lee's car had red carpet. Next, he reminded the jury that a barrette was found in Lee's car, but failed to mention that it had a different clasp than the ones the victim had. Then he mentioned the blond hairs found in Lee's car, which were later proven by DNA testing not to be Linda Vanderveen's. He reminded the jury, "You have heard no evidence at all who else used to own or drive Albert Lee's car." This is incredible, since it was a well-known fact that Lee had recently bought the car, which was why he had been getting new plates the day of the murder. Also, how could he have so quickly forgotten the testimony of Lee's girlfriend Vivian Pride, who plainly told the court that she had used Lee's car to transport children? Next, the prosecutor pointed out that the feathers found in Lee's car were just like the ones from the victim's mitten. Of course, they also were just like the ones from the pillow that had been in the car, and just like the ones from Lee's vest. Then he asked the jury whether it seems odd that Lee had changed his license plates the morning of the abduction when it was 10 degrees. People normally put on new plates when they get them. The temperature makes little difference. Since the supposed confession was a major factor in the case, Forsyth tried to convince the jury that they should believe Billy

Mansfield. He said they should not be misled into thinking Mansfield might have a motive for lying. He clearly did have a motive, since he was facing two life sentences with clear proof of his guilt. He later admitted he lied about the whole story he had told. Forsyth claimed Mansfield was "just the kind of guy Lee would confess to." It is not clear why that would be. They didn't get along. If Lee was going to make a confession, it seems like he would confess to the other Black men in the cell instead of a white man he didn't like. Of course, if he had made any confession, all the cell mates would have heard it. Finally, Forsyth referred to an incident six days before the Vanderveen murder. Two girls were asked by a Black man for some information. He then left without doing anything questionable. The prosecutor claimed Lee was that man, and he intended to kill the two girls. How he got that idea is hard to explain. The girls could not identify Lee as the man they saw, and the man didn't do anything. This incident was also used at the second trial, even though it proved nothing, except the fact the prosecutor was desperate for evidence. Forsyth concluded by admitting the case was mostly circumstantial, but he said he didn't have to prove a motive, even though motive is very important in any case, and especially so when the case is so heavily based of circumstantial evidence. As time went on, most of the evidence presented was proven false.

When defense attorney William Murphy began his closing arguments, he pointed out that even though it was a tragedy that Linda Vanderveen was murdered, it would be another tragedy if the wrong man was convicted of the crime. He then reminded the jury that the case was based on "falsehoods…innuendos…half-truths…similarities…look alikes…can't excludes…and conjectures." In other words, there was no clear proof of guilt.

In his closing statement William Forsyth said, "Albert Lee is not on trial because he's a black man. The man's on trial because he's a cold-blooded killer." That had not yet been decided, and after the jury voted guilty, the Michigan Supreme Court threw out the conviction. To this day there is considerable doubt about his guilt. He was not on trial because he was a "cold-blooded killer," but because he was *accused* of being a killer. Forsyth further stated about Lee, "He thought he had the right to take a life." How did he know what Lee thought? Everyone who has known Lee believes that it is totally out-of-character for him to commit a murder. He has plainly stated that he could never kill a child. He has never given any hint that he "thought he had the right to take a life."

William Murphy concluded his plea to the jury by saying, "We're not in the Deep South in the early 1900s. Justice is not the conviction of a black man for the offense of any black man. Albert Lee is not guilty of this crime."

On Friday, November 9, the jury found Lee guilty after deliberating for almost six hours. One juror explained that "There wasn't any key thing. It was the combination of all the evidence." In other words, there was no clear proof of guilt. Naturally, the defense attorney said he was "disappointed." Equally expected was the response of the prosecutor, who said he was "relieved." What seems somewhat suspect was the overly emotional response of the police officers. After the verdict was announced, Forsyth was surrounded by hugging and hand-shaking officers. It might be understandable that they would be glad their work had paid off with a conviction, but they seemed a little too happy. It should be pointed out that it was suspected from the beginning that a police officer might be behind the murder, since Andy Vanderveen had received many death threats as a result of his work as personnel director for the city of Grand Rapids. When defense attorney William Murphy was interviewed by the *Grand Rapids Press* at his office after the trial, he said that the grounds for appeal were too numerous to name. It was not surprising that the Michigan Supreme Court later overturned Lee's conviction.

The next day the Vanderveens were interviewed at their home. Andrew said the "evidence led me to the conclusion that (Lee) was the man who committed the crime. There was no doubt in my mind."

It is significant that the Vanderveens were shown evidence by the prosecutor, but apparently they had not talked with Lee or his attorney. It should also be noted that they were not present during most of the trial. Lee has stated that he believed Andrew Vanderveen had some doubts about his guilt.

Whether he did or not, we may never know, since he died six years later, before most of the evidence against Lee was proven false.

Chapter Seven – The Evidence

Before proceeding, let us look further at the main evidence presented at the trial.

> *One of the main reasons innocent people are convicted is because of misidentification.*

First, let us consider the identification by the witnesses. One of the main reasons innocent people are convicted is because of misidentification. Sometimes this is deliberate, but often it is an honest mistake. In this case we know that the witnesses were hypnotized, and that was the reason the Michigan Supreme Court threw out their testimony. It should be noted that this is unusual. The Court only looks at one case in a hundred, and the general rule is to let the conviction stand.

The real question was whether or not Albert Lee looked like the man the witnesses actually saw. After the abduction and murder the police interviewed several witnesses. There were five who saw the abductor and gave descriptions. They were in close agreement, which suggests that we have a fairly accurate account of his appearance. The police made a sketch based on their descriptions, and it was published in the *Grand Rapids Press* on March 2, 1979. When Albert Lee was arrested six weeks after the murder, his picture was taken, and it was published in the *Grand RapidsPress*. Anyone can go to the Grand Rapids library and compare the two pictures. It should be obvious that Lee didn't look at all like the man the witnesses saw. Let us consider the details.

The most obvious difference is that Lee clearly had a beard, but the abductor definitely did not. All the witnesses were in complete agreement on that detail. Some thought he might have had a mustache, but they were certain there was no beard. On the day of the murder Lee had a full beard, mustache, and bushy sideburns. Shortly thereafter he shaved off part of his beard but kept a goatee.

Another difference in the two pictures is the general shape of the head. Lee has a fairly round face, but the man the witnesses saw had a thin drawn face.

Lee has a large round flat nose; the abductor had a thin pointed nose.

Lee had a medium to long Afro haircut; the abductor had a very short Afro. No one would describe Lee's haircut as very short.

Lee is a very dark complected Black man. The man the witnesses saw was described as a light complected Black man. No one would describe Lee as a light complected Black man.

The man the witnesses saw was thought to be about five foot ten inches tall. Lee is about two inches taller. That is close, but it appears that Lee was slightly bigger. Both were about 155 to 165 pounds. Of course, many Black men in their twenties are about that weight.

From the footprints in the snow where the body of the victim was left, it appears that Lee's shoe was two to three sizes larger than that of the murderer.

Next, let us consider the car, since it was important in identifying the murderer. The prosecution claimed Lee must be the killer because he had a black Grand Prix, and there were only three Black men in Kent County with black Grands Prix. There are several problems with that claim. If there are three such men, where are the other two? How were they eliminated as suspects? The other two skipped the country when they learned they were possible suspects. Lee did not.

How do we know the car was black? The witnesses variously described the car as blue, green, or black. It may have been black, but we don't know that for certain. A blue car can look black, and a green car can look black, but a black car almost always looks black. It appears that the car was a dark color, but we don't know for sure what color.

How do we know the car was a Grand Prix? The witnesses variously described the car as a Cordoba, a Grand Prix or a Monte Carlo. Two witnesses were very insistent that it was a Monte Carlo. One said he saw the words *Monte Carlo* on the car. The tire tracks in the snow where the body was dumped were compared with Lee's tires, and it was found they did not match. The witnesses said the abductor had wide whitewalls. Lee's car did not. The murderer's car was towed out of a snowbank or icy spot. There was no evidence of Lee's car being towed. The witnesses said they saw the victim through the back window. Lee's car had tinted windows. Some believed the car had bicentennial license plates. Lee had just got his plates that morning. The Secretary of State was not still giving out bicentennial plates three years after the bicentennial. The investigators were not able to find anything from Linda Vanderveen in Lee's car. They claimed to find her barrette and hair in the car, but they were later proven not to be from her.

Why would we assume the murderer was from Kent County? He could have been from anywhere. Just because the murder was committed in Kent County doesn't mean the perpetrator had to be from there. Remember that it was suspected from the start that a Grand Rapids police officer might have been behind the murder. If that were true, he might have hired a hit man from outside the area. There would be less chance of him being identified. The fact is, we don't know where the killer was from.

Let us consider in more detail the alleged confession. This was highly suspect from the beginning. Lee has always denied making any confession, and it is significant that there is only one person who ever claimed to hear it. He was Billy Mansfield Jr. Who was this man the prosecutor insisted was a reliable witness, who was just testifying out of the goodness of his heart? There is a book written about him. It is titled *When Angels Weep*: *The Weeki Wachee Homicides* by W. R. Langston.

There is also a chapter about him in the book *Murders in the Swampland* by Patricia Lieb. Mansfield was a serial rapist and murderer who was facing two life sentences as a repeat sex offender and parole violator.

The Mansfield family started out in Michigan and moved to Florida. The whole family seemed to be vicious criminals. Billy Mansfield Sr. had forty felony charges against him. He served a few years in prison, and when he got out, he disappeared. All the neighbors in Florida were afraid of the Mansfields, which may explain why it took so long to bring them to justice. Since the Mansfields started out in Michigan, they still had ties there. Billy Mansfield Jr. had returned for a time. While he was in Kent County, he forcibly stripped and raped two teenage girls at knifepoint. In 1979 he was brought back to Michigan to stand trial for those two crimes. He was put in the same cell as Albert Lee. It appears that this was by design. The police were trying to find evidence against Lee. Mansfield knew he was in serious trouble. The girls who had been raped were available to testify, and they had warned the authorities that Mansfield was a very dangerous man who was sure to repeat his crimes. His only hope was to make a deal with the prosecutor. It was so obvious that is what happened that the defense attorney put the chief prosecutor, David Sawyer, on the witness stand and asked him about the deal. Sawyer denied that there was any deal. He insisted that Mansfield was a reliable witness and that he would be facing charges for the crimes he had committed. Two weeks after Lee's conviction, Mansfield's cases came up for consideration. Even though he was facing two counts for first degree criminal sexual conduct with clear proof of guilt, he was allowed to plead guilty to one count of fourth degree criminal sexual conduct, which has a maximum sentence of two years in prison. Forcible rape is clearly first degree, and since there were two victims, there should have been two charges. Instead of giving Mansfield the two years he could have been given, the judge gave him one year and said he could serve it concurrently with the two years he was serving for parole violation. Since he had already served most of that two year sentence, he was just released with no punishment at all for the two Michigan rapes. Everyone was appalled by the leniency of the punishment, but the prosecutor explained that they appreciated Mansfield's help in getting Lee convicted.

What did Billy Mansfield Jr. do with his newfound freedom that he clearly didn't deserve? He did exactly what anyone who knew him would have expected. He returned to Florida, where he immediately raped and murdered at least one more woman. Since the police in Florida were starting to investigate all the many cases of women disappearing near the Mansfield property, Billy Mansfield Jr. and one of his brothers decided that it was time to move on to a new location. They went to California, where Billy immediately raped and murdered another woman. She was the mother of three small children. He was arrested and ultimately convicted of the California murder.

About the same time, the police in Florida finally got a search warrant and came to the Mansfield property with heavy equipment and began digging. They uncovered four bodies of women who had been murdered and buried there. Then they stopped digging because they said the time limit on the warrant was running out. Since they had already found four bodies, it would seem like the court would have been willing to extend the time limit. Because they stopped digging, we will probably never know how many women are buried on the property. Most people believe there are dozens. The reason they believe that is because there are dozens of women who disappeared near there. It was a common thing for Billy to wake up his siblings in the middle of the night to bury another victim. He probably doesn't know himself how many women he raped and murdered because he was usually drunk when he did it.

After the four bodies were found, Billy confessed to murdering them. There is some question as to whether Billy or his family members actually murdered those particular women. At the time he pleaded guilty to the murders, he was already going to prison for life for the California murder. It would cost him nothing to confess to the Florida murders because he would be in prison for life anyway. Also, he had a history of confessing to things to protect his family members when it wouldn't cost him anything. Whether he committed those particular murders or not, there is no question that he was guilty of multiple rapes and murders.

In California, a life sentence in considered to be 25 years. Since he was convicted in 1980, in 2005 he was scheduled for a parole hearing. Since he knew there was no hope that he would be paroled, he didn't bother to go to the hearing.

The reason this is all relevant to the Albert Lee case is because when Mansfield was sent to prison for life, there was no longer any reason to keep up the pretense that Lee had confessed to the Vanderveen murder. Mansfield admitted that he had lied to get out of prison. Lee wanted Mansfield to return to testify at Lee's second trial. There were at least three problems, however. First, the prosecution didn't want Mansfield to expose them for the dishonest deal they had made with him. Second, the court questioned why the defense would want to bring a witness who had been a witness for the prosecution in the previous trial. The obvious reason was that Mansfield would testify that Lee had never made the confession and that the only reason he claimed Lee did was because of the deal with the prosecutor. Third, Lee had been in prison for twelve years by that time. He had lost contact with most people on the outside. He had no money, and the only way he could get Mansfield to return to Michigan from California was to pay for an armed guard to bring him. Needless to say, that would be very expensive. What about Lee's attorney? Couldn't he do something to help? Lee believed that William Murphy made an honest effort to defend him at his first trial, but he had a different attorney at his second trial. He was not satisfied with his efforts. The bottom line was that Lee did not have one witness at his second trial that could have been quite helpful.

Before moving on, let us consider the problem of the motive in the Vanderveen murder. This is a question that has been asked many times. Whenever there is a murder, there is some kind of motive. People don't just go around killing other people for no reason whatever. The prosecutor said that we may never know the motive, and he was not concerned about it. He should have been. Motive is always important in any murder case. Why would Lee want to kill a little girl he knew nothing about? No one has ever been able to even suggest a motive Lee could have had.

This is a matter that should be given more consideration. There are several common motives people have for committing murder. The most obvious is revenge. A person may kill another person because that person has done something the murderer doesn't like. This is most likely the motive behind the Vanderveen murder, but it is clear that Lee had no such motive because he knew nothing of Linda Vanderveen or anyone in her family. However, Andrew Vanderveen had enemies who hated him so much that they had made numerous death threats against him. This matter was investigated at the time, but it was the Grand Rapids police who did the investigation, and it was people connected with the Grand Rapids police who had made the death threats.

Another motive for murder is ransom. Since Linda Vanderveen was murdered shortly after being abducted, it does not appear that money was a factor. No one ever said anything about a ransom note.

Another common motive when a girl is murdered is rape. The investigators tried their best to find evidence of sexual abuse, but they could find none. Billy Mansfield had claimed Lee tried to rape the victim, but that is meaningless since we know that he lied about the whole thing. Of course, rape clearly was the motive for the multiple murders committed by Mansfield. It is not surprising he might accuse someone else of doing what he had done many times. At the sentencing, the judge tried to imply that Lee had some kind of sexual motive for the murder, but there was no basis for the claim. The victim was not sexually abused, and Lee had no record of any sex offenses. In fact, he had no criminal record at all. The worst thing on his record was that he had spent 30 days in jail for a disagreement with a police officer over a traffic matter. He had no felonies on his record.

What other motives could there be for Lee to murder a child he didn't know? Since he was Black and she was white, some might suggest that race was a factor, but there is no evidence for such a thing. Lee has shown no hint of any racial hatred.

The lack of any discernable motive continues to be a problem in this case to this day. It is strange that the prosecutor was not concerned about that obvious problem.

Chapter Eight - The Sentencing

After Albert Lee was convicted, his attorney, William Murphy, filed documents seeking a new trial. As he had stated after the trial, there were numerous grounds for appeal. Among the most obvious were the hypnotized witnesses and the alleged confession that Billy Mansfield lied about. Murphy also questioned whether the publicity in the case may have unduly influenced the jury. Judge Boucher did not act on the request until the sentencing, which occurred on February 15, 1980.

It is not clear why it took over three months from the time of the conviction to the sentencing since the charge carried a mandatory life sentence. There was really nothing for the judge to decide other than the request for a new trial, which he had no inclination to grant. The sentence given was life in solitary confinement at hard labor. That sentence is meaningless since Lee has not been in solitary confinement, and he has not been at hard labor. A life sentence in Michigan is considered to be 30 years. Lee could have been paroled years ago if the parole board had wanted to do so.

At the sentencing, the judge made several statements that seemed to have no basis whatever. He claimed that Lee was "an insecure man preoccupied with his own sexual virility ... who has a special affinity for young women and who becomes violent when his will is frustrated." Where did he get that idea? There was nothing on Lee's record to suggest such a thing. The only apparent basis was the testimony of Billy Mansfield Jr., which was highly suspect from the beginning and now thoroughly discredited.

Boucher also urged against an appeal, even though anyone convicted by a jury has a right to appeal. He said, "If this defendant is ever released, he may very well be put into a position where he must kill again." Where did he get that idea? Lee had no previous felonies on his record. There was no reason to believe he had any propensity for violence. Boucher certainly did not know Lee personally. A judge ought to have some basis for his statements at a sentencing besides his own imagination.

At the sentencing, the judge made several statements that seemed to have no basis whatever.

When a person is about to be sentenced, he is given an opportunity to make a statement. Lee spent nearly ten minutes addressing the judge. As usual, the judge did not respond. Naturally Lee denied killing the victim. He has been consistent in his denial from the beginning to this day. He also denied making any confession to Mansfield. As he said, "When I'm in jail with two other blacks, why am I going to pick a hippie white guy to tell? Mansfield was the only one willing to stand up and tell a lie so he could get out of jail." Lee also held up a December *Press* clipping that said the jury foreman was undecided about the verdict until she supposedly received direction from God while praying in the bathroom. She obviously had serious doubts about Lee's guilt. With the information we have now she would have had even more doubts. Lee concluded his remarks by saying, "I can see I won't get any justice here, so we might as well go on. It's evident that this jury, this city, and this county would find me guilty no matter what. I'm finished."

The judge then said, "As for the sufficiency of the evidence, the case against the defendant was overwhelming. There is not the slightest question in my mind that this verdict was correct." Again we have to ask, "Where did he get that idea?" The evidence was not the least bit "overwhelming." There was considerable doubt from the start, and nearly all the evidence was later proven false. He may not have had "the slightest question" that the verdict was "correct", but the Michigan Supreme Court certainly did. They later threw out the conviction and all the evidence.

Murphy again expressed his concern that the jury was not told Mansfield might get a reduced sentence for testifying against Lee. Kent Prosecutor David Sawyer continued to claim that there had been no deal with Mansfield. He said Mansfield "would have testified no matter what, because he was appalled at what had happened." If that was so, we have to ask why Mansfield was not "appalled" at what happened to the multiple victims he himself raped and murdered. Are we to believe it is okay to rape and murder young women but not an eleven-year-old girl? As Sawyer spoke, Lee repeatedly called him a liar.

After the sentencing, Sawyer told the *Grand Rapids Press*, "I'm convinced if Mr. Lee was ever allowed to walk our streets again, he would kill again." Why? The evidence does not support the claim.

Chapter Nine – The First Appeal

Albert Lee began appealing right away after his conviction and sentencing. However, the wheels of justice turn slowly. In 1983 the Michigan Court of Appeals denied his claims, but in 1985 the Michigan Supreme Court sent the case back to the Court of Appeals for reconsideration. They again denied his appeal. For the next five years there was a lot of paperwork sent back and forth. Finally, on January 10, 1990, the Michigan Supreme Court reversed Lee's conviction and sent the case back to the Kent County Circuit Court for a new trial.

During those ten years Albert Lee was in prison, considered to be a cold-blooded murderer by most people. What about other people who were part of the story? Most of those involved went about their lives, and there is little that needs to be said about them. However, two people that are significant in this case had events that are worth noting.

First, Billy Mansfield Jr. continued his usual practice of rape and murder until he was finally caught and sent to prison for life. Remember that Albert Lee was sentenced on February 15, 1980. It was still February when Mansfield was released from the Kent County jail even though he had faced several criminal sexual conduct charges. He lost no time in returning to his life of serial rape and murder. We don't know how many victims he had or the exact time of all the murders, but one victim we know of in Florida was 21-year-old Sandra Jean Graham, who disappeared in April 1980. She was last seen with Mansfield in a bar at Tampa, Florida. Her body was one of four that were found by the police, buried on the Mansfield property in Weeki Wachee, Florida. After his killing spree in Florida, Billy and his brother Gary went to California, where Billy strangled 29-year-old Rene Saling outside a bar at Watsonville, California on December 7, 1980. He was arrested and placed in the Santa Cruz, California county jail. He and another inmate escaped, but they were both recaptured the next day. Mansfield had a trial for the California murder in July 1981, but it resulted in a hung jury because of the difficulty of identifying him. Several of the witnesses had been drinking heavily. At a second trial he was convicted. Then he was flown to Florida to stand trial for the four murders and one attempted sexual battery there. He originally pleaded not guilty, but later changed his plea to guilty to avoid the death penalty. Upon pleading guilty, he stated, "I am pleading guilty because I am guilty of the charges and I have no other reason." In 2012, Mansfield was considered for parole but was denied. At that time he stated, "I have killed a lot of people, both males and females. I [am] starting to have that feeling again, like I did before. Something inside me says, 'kill him.'" Angelica Garcia, the secretary to the district attorney, said that because Mansfield "had committed his crime in an especially heinous, atrocious or cruel manner, and because of his violent past and need for further insight into his crimes," the parole board felt justified in denying him parole. On October 27, 2020, Billy's brother Gary was arrested on drug charges in Hernando County, Florida. While being handcuffed he claimed that there were more bodies "all over" the Mansfield property. The next day the investigators did in fact find human remains. After Billy Mansfield was sent to prison for life, he admitted that he lied about Albert Lee's alleged confession.

The other person that should be mentioned is Andrew Vanderveen. He owned a cabin in the Baldwin area along with three other employees of the city of Grand Rapids. The other three were James Biener, assistant city manager; Robert Spry, assistant city engineer; and Bud Johnson, sewer maintenance supervisor. The four often hunted together. On October 26, 1985, Vanderveen suffered a heart attack and was taken to the Reed City hospital by his partners. They had administered cardiopulmonary resuscitation, but he was pronounced dead at the hospital. It is unclear if he was dead before arriving. He was 61 years old and had worked for the city of Grand Rapids for over 30 years. For 25 of those years he was personnel director. The death certificate says that his cause of death was cardiopulmonary arrest. It was not stated whether he had any previous heart problems. There was no autopsy or medical examination. Since he had received numerous death threats, some might think such an examination would be appropriate.

After the death of their daughter, the Vanderveens founded the Linda Vanderveen Children's Festival, the purpose of which was to celebrate the lives of all the community's children. It continued for many years. In September of 1985 the event drew 6,000 people to John Ball Park. Linda's name was removed from the festival around 2001, but it continued.

Chapter Ten – The Michigan Supreme Court Case

When the Michigan Supreme Court finally took up Albert Lee's appeal, there were two main issues that needed to be considered. The first and main issue was whether the testimony of witnesses who were hypnotized was properly admitted. The second was whether the similar acts evidence was properly admitted. The conclusion of the Supreme Court was that the testimony of the hypnotized witnesses was not admissible, but the similar acts evidence was.

Let us look at these two issues in more detail.

From the very beginning to this day, the biggest question has been whether Albert Lee was the man the witnesses saw the day of the murder. No one has ever been able to make a positive identification of Lee, and he looks very different from the description the witnesses gave. It was only after hypnosis that they identified Lee, and even then they expressed doubt about the identification. Let us consider the testimony of each of the seven witnesses.

The first witness to see the abductor was Jack Hill. He saw a car parked on the wrong side of the street and stopped to offer his assistance. He saw the victim in the back seat and suspected foul play. The driver knocked Hill down and sped off. Hill followed but lost sight of the car. He described the driver as a neatly dressed Black man with a neat haircut and no facial hair. Lee had a beard and a medium-to-long Afro haircut. Hill and others were hypnotized on February 12, the day of the murder. On February 15, three days after the abduction, Hill and four other witnesses were shown mugshots of possible suspects, but no one identified Lee as the man they had seen. Hill and others were hypnotized again on February

23. Afterwards the witnesses were shown photos but failed to identify Lee. On February 26, the witnesses participated in a lineup. There was no positive identification. On March 15, the witnesses were again shown mugshots of possible suspects. Lee was not in the pictures. All but one witness identified someone from the mugshots. There was another lineup on March 29. Some of the witnesses identified Lee; others did not.

When Mr. Hill was pursuing the abductor, he encountered James Vos, who was driving his son, Jack Vos, to school. Mr. Vos was stopped for traffic. He had observed a black car skidding fast around a corner. He described the car as a Grand Prix with fancy wheel hubs and white walls. It should be pointed out that Albert Lee's car did not have white walls. He could not clearly identify the driver since he was focused mainly on the car. He believed the driver was a Black man in his late twenties who was wearing a dark leather jacket. He didn't notice any passenger in the car. Jack Vos did see a girl in the back seat. He said she was a white girl with blond hair and wearing a blue hat and green coat. He also described the car as a Grand Prix. James Vos and Jack Vos were both hypnotized along with Jack Hill on the day of the abduction. They were among the five people who were shown mugshots on February 15 but failed to identify Lee. All five chose someone other than Lee. Jack Vos was among those hypnotized on February 23, but he did not identify Lee from mugshots at that time or on February 26, when there was a lineup. It wasn't until March 29 that Jack Vos and two other witnesses finally picked Lee from a second lineup. Others picked someone else or no one at all. At the trial, Jack Vos said that Lee looked identical to the man he had seen, but he was not sure he was that man.

James and Jack Vos stopped and asked a twelve-year-old crossing guard named Greg Start if he had seen a black Grand Prix. At first, he didn't remember, but then a few minutes later he remembered, because the car had run a stop sign. He saw the vehicle twice. He described the driver as a young Black man with a mustache and an afro hairstyle, but he later stated, "No, I didn't get a good look at him either time." Start was not contacted by the investigating officers until May 2, which was nearly three months after the abduction. By that time he had seen Albert Lee's picture in the newspaper. On June 19 he was hypnotized by Dr. Rossi. The next day he picked Lee in a lineup. Even Justice Boyle, who voted against overturning Lee's conviction, agreed that Start's identification should not be considered reliable. It should also be pointed out that he only saw the driver briefly inside the vehicle, and the vehicle was moving "medium" fast.

A couple hours or so after the abduction, Timothy Wilcome was cleaning snow at the Georgetown Condominiums when he was approached by a Black man who asked for help because his car was stuck in the snow. The two of them tried to free the car but were not able to do so. Then Mr. Wilcome asked his coworker, David Orr, to help with his truck. Mr. Orr attached a tow rope to the rear of the vehicle, and he pulled with his truck while Mr. Wilcome pushed by hand. While Mr. Orr was hooking up the rope, Mr. Wilcome talked with the driver of the car. Wilcome asked for a cigarette, and the man gave him a Kool. He also gave him a light with a Bic lighter. This was considered significant to the prosecutor because Lee smoked Kools and had a Bic lighter. Of course, millions of other people do as well. After freeing the vehicle, Mr. Orr saw the driver throw something into a nearby dumpster. Later that afternoon a rubbish collector found Linda Vanderveen's knapsack in the dumpster. It had fingerprints on it which were not those of Albert Lee. Mr. Orr also testified that the driver left the scene "in a hurry." When Lee's car was examined, there was no evidence that it had ever been towed. Also, both Mr. Wilcome and Mr. Orr were very certain the car was a Monte Carlo. Mr. Orr saw the words *Monte Carlo* on the car while he was hooking up the tow rope. Mr. Wilcome stated during the investigation that the car he saw on February 12 could not have been a Pontiac Grand Prix. Another reason the car could not have been Lee's car was because it had bicentennial plates. Lee was at the Secretary of State office getting new plates during the time the Monte Carlo was being pulled out of the snow. Also, the tire tracks didn't match Lee's tires. It is quite certain that the car pulled from the snow was not Lee's car, and it is quite certain that whoever threw the victim's knapsack into the dumpster was not Lee.

Mr. Orr did not get a good look at the driver, and he never identified Lee. Mr. Wilcome, however, did have ample opportunity to see and talk with the man. Two days after the incident, both Mr. Wilcome and Mr. Orr were hypnotized by Mr. Mazur. Then Mr. Wilcome was shown a mug book and selected someone other than Lee as the man who looked closest to the driver. The next day he was shown another mug book that did not include Lee, and he did not select anyone. About ten days later, after being hypnotized by Dr. Rossi of the Michigan State Police, Mr. Wilcome attended a lineup. He thought Lee looked the closest to the man he saw on February 12, but he wasn't sure. It was the same on March 15 and at the trial.

The last witness that needs to be considered was Jim Bonnema. He contacted the police after reading the newspaper report and seeing a story on television. He did not identify a driver other than that he was a young Black man, but he did believe he had seen the vehicle. He was hypnotized on February 16 and gave a license plate number while under hypnosis. We do not have a record of what that number was, but apparently it was not the number of Albert Lee's car.

...the Michigan Supreme Court ruled that the identification by the hypnotized witnesses was inadmissible.

Thus, we only have two witnesses who actually had an opportunity to get a good look at the abductor, and neither was able to identify him as Lee until after they had been hypnotized twice. Even then, they were uncertain about the identification. It is quite understandable why the majority on the Michigan Supreme Court ruled that the identification by the hypnotized witnesses was inadmissible. It is significant that the majority on the Supreme Court stated their conclusion that "absent the testimony of the hypnotized witnesses, the remaining evidence does not positively link defendant to this crime. Thus we cannot conclude that the evidence against defendant was overwhelming."

Next let us consider the similar acts evidence. The majority on the Michigan Supreme Court voted to allow the evidence, but Judge Cavanaugh disagreed. First, let us look at the basic facts of the matter.

On February 6, 1979, ten-year-old Judy Sanchez and nine-year-old Amy Combs were walking to school when they were approached by a Black man in a black car. They said the man stopped his car and put one foot outside the door. He asked the girls what time it was and how to get to Hall Street. They answered, and then the man motioned for them to come closer. They said the man told them to, "Come here." They were afraid, and Judy ran from the car. Amy stayed longer, and as Judy came back, the man got into his car and left. That was the extent of the incident.

The question that naturally arises is what this has to do with the murder of Linda Vanderveen. The simple fact is that it has nothing to do with it. The only reason it was ever brought up is because the prosecutor claimed that the man was Albert Lee, and he intended to kill those two girls. If that were true, then the incident was an act that was similar to the Vanderveen case.

First, we need to ask if the man was Albert Lee. There are only three people who can answer that question. One is Mr. Lee himself. He said he was not that man. Some might say he would lie because he didn't want to admit he was guilty. That is possible, but admitting he was the man would not show he was guilty because the man didn't do anything but ask a couple question and leave. The only other two people who could tell if the man was Lee were the two girls. Neither of them could say with certainty that Lee was the man they had seen; they only thought he looked similar.

Secondly, we need to ask if the man intended to kill the two girls. He stopped, put one foot out, asked for the time and directions to

Hall Street and asked the girls to come closer. One girl was afraid and ran away. When she returned, the man got back into his car and left. If he intended to kill them, why would he leave when the girl came back? That would be his chance to abduct her. He didn't run after them. He didn't say anything that was threatening. Where is the evidence that he had criminal intent? It seems to only exist in the imagination of the prosecutor.

It is difficult to understand why the Michigan Supreme Court thought this evidence was worthy of consideration, but they did. Let us look at their analysis of the matter.

As a general rule, evidence from other crimes is not admissible, but the similar acts evidence is an exception to that rule. There are four requirements for such evidence to be admitted. First, "there must be substantial evidence that the defendant actually perpetrated the bad act sought to be introduced." There is no "substantial evidence" that Lee was the man in question, and there was nothing "bad" about the incident. The man just asked for some information. Also, one of the girls said the man did not have a mustache, but Lee had a mustache and noticeable sideburns as well as a beard. Second, "there must be some special quality or circumstance of the bad act tending to prove the defendant's identity or the motive …" There was none. Third, "one or more of these factors must be material to the determination of the defendant's guilt of the charged offense." Again, there was nothing in the alleged similar act that says anything about Lee's guilt. Fourth, "the probative value of the evidence sought to be introduced must not be substantially outweighed by the danger of unfair prejudice." It would appear that "unfair prejudice" was all the prosecutor had in this case.

Remember that the main purpose of the similar acts evidence is to show the identity of the defendant. How did the evidence show that Lee was the man who stopped the two girls? Let us look at the reasoning of the court. "The similarity between the two incidents upon which the prosecutor bases its admission are that (1) both incidents involved a black man driving a black car, (2) each occurred in the early morning hours when children would be walking to school, (3) both incidents involved young girls, and (4) both occurred in the same general area." It is difficult to see how this shows that the man who stopped the two girls was Albert Lee. The prosecutor agreed that this "similar act" was not a crime, but he argued that "the acts in effect constituted an attempt, that the defendant intended to kidnap and kill the two girls." If so, he must have been one of the most inept of all kidnappers. He just left when he had the best chance to carry out his scheme.

It is not surprising that Judge Cavanagh wrote a separate opinion. It is common for one judge to write an opinion for the majority and another judge to write an opinion for the minority. It is somewhat less common for a third judge to write an opinion. Let us look first at what Judge Cavanagh had to say.

He agreed that the evidence from the hypnotized witnesses should not be admissible. However, he disagreed with the majority that the similar acts evidence should be allowed. He said, "it was an abuse of discretion for the trial court to have admitted the testimony of the similar acts witnesses at defendant's trial. The similar acts testimony simply does not support the inference that the defendant was about to entice the two young girls into his car, or that he was about to engage them in some other improper or criminal conduct." He went on to say that if the "actor had stalked his victims or sought to attract the two little girls into his car by physically reaching out to them or verbally urging them into his car for no apparent proper purpose, then I might deem such acts to satisfy the requirements" for admission. However, nothing like that happened. It should be pointed out that the girls did not say that the man tried to abduct them. The majority only assumed that. As Judge Cavanagh went on to say, "The circumstances of this incident do not indicate that the man intended to abduct the two young girls, though he may have secretly harbored such an unlawful intent. Moreover, the man's behavior can as well be explained as motivated by a totally innocuous purpose." He further went on to say, "This Court cannot simply take judicial notice of the fact that a Black man who stops young white girls to ask them the time of day and for directions is engaged in acts that are a prelude to a child abduction." The majority considered the similar acts evidence admissible because the man had a black car and Lee had a black car, and Lee didn't go to work on February 6. As Judge Cavanagh pointed out, however, without the testimony of the hypnotized witnesses it may not be provable that the killer was a Black man with a black car. Also, the fact that Lee didn't go to work proves nothing. If he were home sick, naturally, few if any people would have seen him. He doesn't have to prove his innocence. The burden of proof rests with the prosecutor.

In a court case, as in most issues in life, there are two sides to the matter. It is important to look at both sides, and one should not draw a conclusion until he knows both sides. In some cases the decision of the court may be unanimous. If that is so, there may be only one opinion written. However, in this case the justices did not all agree. Let us look at the opinion of Judge Boyle, who wrote for the minority.

Although Judge Boyle agreed that the similar acts evidence should be admitted, she did not agree that the testimony of the hypnotized witnesses should be rejected. She said that the majority ignored the fact that "at the time of the initial hypnosis, the identity of the defendant was unknown to the police officers. Thus, on this record it is indisputable that there was no connection between that hypnosis and the witnesses' later selection of the defendant from a lineup." Saying that something is "indisputable" does not prove it to be true. The fact is that the matter is disputed. Remember that Albert Lee was stopped by the police at about noon the day of the murder. Therefore, he was a possible suspect right from the start. Furthermore, it should be pointed out that the witnesses repeatedly failed to pick Lee as the abductor until after they had been hypnotized twice, and even then they expressed doubt about the identification.

Let us look at Judge Boyle's second point. She said "since the defendant's expert witness, Dr. Martin Orne, testified that hypnosis had no bearing on the identification of the car by the four witnesses who identified it before, during, and after hypnosis as a clean, black Grand Prix, it is indisputable on this record that identification of the vehicle was reliable." Once again, saying that something is "indisputable" doesn't prove it to be true. The truth is that the witnesses were not consistent in identifying the car. They variously described it as blue, green, or black, and as a Cordoba, a Grand Prix or a Monte Carlo. As pointed out in chapter seven, there are several reasons to believe that Lee's car was not the one the witnesses saw.

Judge Boyle's third point was that "Dr. Orne testified that the defendant's ownership of the car was corroborative evidence of the reliability of the identification of the defendant." Once again, the car the witnesses saw was almost certainly not Lee's car.

Finally, Judge Boyle said that "Dr. Orne also testified that the identification of the defendant by Jack Hill and Jack Vos was not the product of the hypnotic sessions." As just stated, neither of these two witnesses identified Lee until hypnotized twice. Also, Mr. Vos did not get a good look at the abductor.

Judge Boyle proceeded to give a lengthy discussion of whether the testimony of hypnotized witnesses should never be admitted, always be admitted, or sometimes admitted. She concluded that it should be admitted sometimes on a case-by-case basis.

In her concluding statement she summarized the reasons she believed Lee's conviction should be affirmed. This is what she said: "The prosecution built an impressive direct and circumstantial case involving over fifty witnesses and six days of trial. The prosecution established that only three cars matching the defendant's car were owned by black males in Kent County. A barrette, matching a second one worn by the victim was found in the back seat of the defendant's car. Feathers, such as those in the victim's gloves, and long blond hairs were also found in the back seat of the defendant's car. Carpet fibers matching those of the defendant's car and negroid type hairs were found on the victim's clothing, and a cellmate of the defendant's testified that the defendant had admitted that he accidentally killed the victim while attempting to sexually molest her. The defendant's alibi was effectively rebutted by testimony that placed him at the Secretary of State's office several hours after the abduction, rather than at the time of the abduction as the defendant testified."

Let us examine this statement one point at a time. The number of witnesses and the length of a trial are not any proof of guilt. There were not fifty people who said they saw the defendant commit the crime. They could not even say with certainty that Lee was the man they saw. The fact that there are only three Black men in Kent County with black Grand Prix's proves nothing since we don't know if the car was black, we don't know it was a Grand Prix and we don't know if the abductor was from Kent County. The barrette was not the victim's because it had the wrong kind of clasp. This will be discussed more later, since it was one of the main pieces of evidence used by the prosecutor in the second trial. The feathers in Lee's car could have come from any one of several sources, including Lee's vest and a pillow that had been in the car. The long blond hairs were later proven by DNA analysis not to be from the victim. This will also be discussed further when we look at the second trial and the subsequent appeal. The carpet fibers prove little since the same type of carpet is used in many cars. The negroid hairs should be examined more. The witnesses agreed that the abductor was Black. We would expect he would leave negroid hairs. Since Blacks are about 13 percent of the population, there are millions of people who could have supplied those hairs. It is somewhat unlikely that they were Lee's hairs because most of his hairs were fairly long and the hairs found on the victim's clothing were short. There was a way to determine if the hairs could have come from Lee. Short rootless hairs contain mitochondrial DNA which can prove that the person providing those hairs is maternally related to the suspect. If he doesn't have the same mother, he is not the same person. It is incredible that Judge Boyle was still claiming that Lee had confessed to the crime when it had been about ten years since Billy Mansfield Jr. had admitted he lied about the confession, and nobody should have believed his lie in the first place. Finally, the defendant's alibi was not "effectively rebutted" as Boyle claimed. The investigators simply did not prove it was true. That does not prove it was false.

In summary, Judge Boyle was wrong on every point. Whether anyone agrees or not, the majority voted to overturn Lee's conviction and remanded the case for retrial.

Before moving on to the second trial, let us look at some of the reactions to the Michigan Supreme Court's decision. When the court's decision was announced, there were two articles in the Grand Rapids Press on January 11, 1990. The first gave the reactions of several people who had been involved in the first trial; the second was an interview of Shirley Vanderveen, the mother of Linda Vanderveen, by Tom Rademacher. Mr. Rademacher later wrote a follow-up article about the case April 1, 2009.

The first reaction mentioned was that of Jack Hill, who was the first witness to the abduction. He said, "I know he did it and he knows he did it." It is difficult to understand how he could be so certain since he had repeatedly failed to identify Lee until hypnotized twice. He also had originally said the car he saw was a Cordoba. His report on what happened is not in question, but his identification of Lee as the abductor is highly questionable.

The next reaction in the article was from Amy Combs, who was one of the two girls who testified about the alleged similar act. As pointed out earlier, the similar act really had nothing to do with the case, but the court had allowed it to be used in the second trial. She simply stated that she was willing to testify again.

The article repeated the claim that Linda Vanderveen was strangled with her own necklace, but it didn't mention that the necklace was so flimsy it would have broken if someone tried to strangle her with it. The article also didn't mention that there were fingerprints on the victim's neck that were not from Albert Lee.

Of special interest was the reaction of the prosecutor and the defense attorney at the first trial.

William Forsyth was the prosecutor at the first trial, and he had become Kent County prosecutor by the time of the second trial. He said that the decision by the Michigan Supreme Court was "an absolute travesty." Of course, that is the reaction one would expect from a prosecutor who has one of his convictions overturned. He went on to say, "You play a baseball game or a football game by the rules existing at that time. Eleven years later they say, 'Gee, we changed our minds. You did it wrong. Now you've got to do it again'." Needless to say, a murder conviction that sends a man to prison for life is much more important than whether someone wins or loses a ball game. If an innocent man is convicted, he should have another chance at justice. It makes no sense to say that if the justice system gets it wrong, they should stick with their error. Mr. Forsyth also complained that the Supreme Court and the appeals court system took nearly 11 years to return a decision. It would seem like a lawyer would know that cases often take many years to resolve. The Michigan Supreme Court did not spend 11 years studying the case. It went to the appeals court, then the Supreme Court, then back to the appeals court and then back to the Supreme Court. Needless to say, this process takes a lot of time. It should also be pointed out that Albert Lee was in prison all this time. Mr. Forsyth was free to go about his life.

William Murphy, who defended Lee at the first trial, was asked for his reaction. He pointed out that the hypnosis controversy "was one of the primary issues raised during the first trial." Mr. Murphy didn't think he should say any more because of his position as a Court of Appeals judge.

The article went on to give the reactions of other witnesses. They basically said that they didn't think hypnosis affected their memories. However, when a person is hypnotized, he may not know what was in his memory before and what was placed there by the hypnotist. Remember that no one identified Lee until after being hypnotized. The Supreme Court made the decision that the memories were not reliable. The article also pointed out that hypnosis is rarely used anymore.

As mentioned, the other article in the January 11, 1990 issue was about an interview with Shirley Vanderveen, who was the mother of the victim. The father, Andrew Vanderveen, was already deceased. Mrs. Vanderveen never saw the abductor, and therefore, had no way of knowing if Lee was that man. Her statement was "you've got to trust the system. Without that-that and faith-you have nothing. Andy and I believed in the law of the land then and I do now." There are a couple of problems with that statement. First, the best experts estimate that two to five percent of the people in prison in this country are not guilty. Therefore, in those cases the system got it wrong. They should not always be trusted. Second, the question is not whether or not we should believe in the law of the land; the question is whether or not Lee was the one who committed the crime. That was the question at the first trial, and it was the question at the second trial. It is still the question today.

On January16, 1990 there was an editorial in the Grand Rapids Press about the Supreme Court's decision. It was titled "Unfair verdict on a fair trial." It was not stated who wrote the editorial.

The first statement made in the article was that revisiting the Linda Vanderveen tragedy would be painful for the community. No doubt that is true, but it was also true that being sent to prison for life was painful for Albert Lee. If he was not guilty, he should have another chance at justice. An innocent person should not be kept in prison just because it is inconvenient for the community to review the case.

The editorial then complains about the Supreme Court's ruling that the testimony of the witnesses was invalid because the police didn't follow state guidelines in using hypnosis. The article states, "The conclusion is strained, even ludicrous. The reason the hypnosis guidelines were not applied in the Vanderveen case is that the guidelines did not exist then. They were established by the high court in cases decided years *after* the Vanderveen trial. The finding would be laughable were the consequences not so dire. It suggests an approach to the law that is recklessly abstract, utterly removed from the real-life problems of police, prosecutors and judges. Beyond that is a total insensitivity to the public safety concerns of ordinary citizens. The picture that emerges is of an institution that is insulated from the people it serves – dangerously so, Mr. Brickley: are there not even windows in your chambers?" It should be pointed out that the Supreme Court explained why it believed the guidelines should be followed. One may disagree, but it was the responsibility of the court to make that decision. It is difficult to see how the *consequences* are so *dire* if a possibly innocent man gets another chance at justice. How is a second trial "insensitivity to the public safety concerns of ordinary citizens?" Is someone going to die because a man has a second trial? What relevance is there to the question of whether there are windows in Mr. Brickley's chambers? Would he see something outside his windows that would change his decision?

The author of the editorial then asks, "If there is a trial, who is to say whether a new result might also be tossed out sometime in the future, based on yet another twist to the rules by this quixotic court?" Of course that is possible, but a verdict should be tossed out if it is unjust. For those who don't know the meaning of the word quixotic, it is defined as "exceedingly idealistic; unrealistic and impractical."

The editorial then states, "Basic sense in this ruling is all on the side of the dissenters." That is the opinion of the author. Others have a different opinion. Remember that the general rule in the justice system is to let the conviction stand. There must be substantial evidence to overturn a verdict. The author then repeats the arguments used against Lee, most of which have been proven false. None are conclusive.

Next the author states, “The essential issue before the high court was whether Albert Lee received a fair trial. Overpowering evidence is on that side....twice, in separate court rulings, the word ‘overwhelming’ was used to describe the case against the defendant.” That is true, but as the Supreme Court pointed out, without the identification by the hypnotized witnesses, the evidence was not overwhelming.

Finally, the editorial concludes, “There is an injustice in this situation, but it’s against this community. And the offenders are not the local police, prosecutors, and former Judge Boucher but four justices on the Supreme Court.” How is it an injustice against the community if a man gets a second trial? Why is it offensive for the Michigan Supreme Court to grant a second trial for a man whose guilt is in question? The prejudice of the author is obvious.

Chapter 11- The Second Trial

In January 1990 the Michigan Supreme Court ordered a new trial for Albert Lee. It took over a year before that trial began. One of the reasons it took so long was because Kent County Prosecutor William Forsyth appealed to the Michigan Supreme Court and the United States Supreme Court attempting to reinstate the original verdict. Needless to say, this all takes time. It is interesting that Mr. Forsyth criticized the Michigan Supreme Court for taking so long to make their decision, considering it was he himself who caused major delays with appeals he admitted had little chance of success. He claimed that he didn't want to put the Vanderveen family through the pain of another trial, and he also wanted to spare the county the expense of another trial. Whether that was his true concern is open to question. He could have simply dropped the charges against Lee since his main evidence had been thrown out by the Michigan Supreme Court. Another reason for the delay was that Lee needed an attorney, and he didn't have one until five months after his first conviction was overturned. He was given a young and inexperienced attorney named John Beason. A man accused of murder has a right to two attorneys from different law firms. The second attorney was James Rinck.

On February 4, 1991, the new trial was to start. On the previous day there was an article on the front page of the Grand Rapids Press entitled "Retrial to start in '79 murder of Linda Vanderveen." It stated that "At least 60 witnesses from as far away as California, Florida and Maryland have been called to testify."

It did not specify who those witnesses were, but we have clues. We know that Billy Mansfield Jr. was in prison in California for the murder he committed there. Also, the Mansfield family lived in

Florida, and the bodies of four murder victims had been dug up on their property. David Vanderveen, the brother of Linda Vanderveen, lived in Maryland at that time. The article also said that this would be the first time in Kent County in which DNA evidence would be used in a circuit court trial. This was quite important because the best evidence the prosecutor had was the hair found in Lee's car.

... the necklace almost certainly would have broken if someone tried to strangle her with it.

The article again repeated the claim that Linda Vanderveen was strangled with her own necklace. As already pointed out, the necklace almost certainly would have broken if someone tried to strangle her with it. Again, curiously, there was no mention of the fingerprints found on her neck, which were almost certainly from the killer. Another interesting quote from the article was from Assistant Prosecutor Tim McMorrow, who handled the appeals in the case. He said, "It is pretty clear to me these witnesses would not have testified any differently if they were not hypnotized."

If that is true it raises the question of why none of them identified Lee until after being hypnotized. It should also be pointed out that this is a statement from a prosecutor. They typically state quite confidently that they are convinced of a defendant's guilt.

The first matter to deal with in a trial is to find jurors who are qualified to serve. Since the Vanderveen case had received so much publicity, many prospective jurors were dismissed because they knew too much about the matter. There were 96 potential jurors to start with. Of the first 15 potential jurors 14 said they had some knowledge of the case. Finally, after two days of questioning, 15 jurors were selected. Judge Benson dismissed 23, and the attorneys dismissed 22. Each attorney was allowed to dismiss 12 prospective jurors. Kent County Prosecutor William Forsyth dismissed ten, and defense attorney John Beason dismissed 12. He said he would have dismissed at least four more if he could. He requested a change of venue because he questioned if Lee could receive a fair trial in Kent

County, but Judge Benson refused, saying the "15 people are as untainted as you will find in the state." That is highly questionable. Lee was a Black man accused of killing a white girl. The only Black person on the jury was Anna Wade, whose daughter was facing charges from the prosecutor for stabbing a man. There also was a man on the jury who himself was facing charges for operating under the influence. It goes without saying that people facing charges from the prosecutor are not "untainted."

As in the first trial, the judge denied most of the motions by the defense attorney but granted most of the motions by the prosecutor. Mr. Forsyth was allowed to ask witnesses a follow-up question as he did in the first trial. If a witness says he cannot tell if Lee was the man driving the car, he could ask if there was anything about him that would lead him to believe Lee was not the man. Mr. Beason objected because he believed that was a "back-door" way of asking an open-ended question. Just because a witness cannot say Lee was not the man driving doesn't prove he was that man. Also, if a man is driving a car, it may not be possible to get a clear look at the man. Judge Benson also granted Forsyth's motion to read testimony from the barrette company representative who testified at the first trial. The man was not able to attend the second trial due to health problems. He had testified that the barrettes found in Lee's car and those belonging to Linda Vanderveen were both made by his company. He also had pointed out that his company made 20 million of them per year. Since the barrette was one of the main pieces of evidence in the second trial, there will be more about it later.

One thing that was concerning was that the jurors were told that the case had been tried before, but they were told not to be concerned with why it was being tried again. Naturally, they would be curious to know why the first conviction was thrown out. Since the general policy of the justice system is to let a conviction stand, there had to be a very compelling reason for the Michigan Supreme Court to overturn a conviction. Also, since the defense attorney based his argument on the claim that there had been a conspiracy by the prosecution and the police, knowing the arguments and opinions of the Supreme Court would have strengthened his case. The law places restrictions on what information a jury is allowed to have. Therefore, they often do not have all the information that might affect their decision. Basically, a jury only knows what the judge and attorneys want them to know. Normally, jurors do not ask questions; they only listen.

On Wednesday, February 6, the trial began. Prosecutor William Forsyth in his opening statement told the jury that his case was based on circumstantial evidence. In fact, he made the statement, "No one is going to come into this courtroom and say that this is the man I saw put Linda Vanderveen in a car."

He said that his evidence would include 16 blond hairs and a barrette the police said they found in Lee's car. One piece of new evidence that was not available at the first trial was a hair from a black man that the investigators had recently found when they turned the sock inside out that had been used to gag the victim. This is not surprising since all agree that the abductor was a Black Man. The question was, "which Black man?"

Mr. Forsyth said that he would provide witnesses who saw a 1979 black Grand Prix in the area where the crime took place. As previously stated, there are multiple reasons to believe Lee's car was not the one the witnesses saw. He concluded by saying, "I'm confident when you are done you will be convinced without question the person responsible is defendant Albert Lee."

Needless to say, that is the sort of statement a prosecutor always makes.

Next, the defense attorney spoke. He believed Lee was the victim of a police setup. He said, "A little, white female child was murdered. Someone had to go."

He also suggested that the police may have planted evidence in Lee's car. He asked if the police really found what they claim to have found or not.

On the next day of the trial, 16 witnesses testified. No witness could say Lee was the man who was seen the day of the murder, but the claim was that he fit the description and owned the kind of car in question. Both claims were false. Lee looked considerably different from the man the witnesses had described, and the car didn't fit the description given by the witnesses. One of the witnesses was Jack Vos. He said he saw the blond girl in the back of the fleeing vehicle. He stated, "Her mouth was open as if she was screaming and she was waving her hands. The look on her face was probably the most prominent thing that sticks in my mind…It was a look of terror."

This is one of the most compelling reasons to believe the car in question was not Lee's car. His car had tinted windows. The witness would not have seen the victim through the back window. That crucial piece of information was not mentioned.

Another witness that day was Gregg Start who was a sixth grader at the time of the murder. He said he saw a black Grand Prix drive by twice. He said he saw the letters on the car's fender, and that is why he was sure of the make of the car. As stated previously, another witness who saw what was believed to be the same car saw the words, *Monte Carlo* on the car. Either one witness was wrong, or there were two different cars. Either way, the car Mr. Start saw could not have been Lee's car.

On February 14, 1991 the *Grand Press Rapids* had an article titled, "**Nine witnesses contradict murder suspect's alibis.**" The article states, "Albert Lee III was not at a Southeast Side restaurant as he claimed when school crossing guard Linda Vanderveen was kidnapped, employees testified Wednesday, including one worker who said Lee asked him to back his alibi. Lee approached the restaurant cook one day after police questioned Lee at headquarters and told him the account of his whereabouts that morning didn't jibe 'He said he needed someone to say he was in the restaurant at a certain time,' said Lucius Daryl Madden. 'I told him I couldn't say he was there because I hadn't seen him.'"

There are two things to note here: First, the witnesses did not say Lee was *not* at the restaurant as he claimed. They simply didn't remember him being there. Second, Lee asked the cook if he remembered him being there. Why would a customer expect the cook to remember him? The cook normally would be in the kitchen, where he would have limited ability to see the customers. It would be the waitresses who would be most likely to see the customers. The reason Lee thought the cook might remember him that day was because when his eggs were brought, they were not done to his satisfaction, and therefore he sent them back to be redone. This would be sufficiently out of the ordinary that the cook might have remembered him. Unfortunately he did not.

The article goes on to say that Lee claimed he was at Sambo's restaurant from about 7:30 to nearly 9:00 a.m. when he went to the Secretary of State office in the mall. It says he claimed that he bought new plates by 9:20 a.m. However, Lee never said he bought the plates by 9:20. He said he went to the Secretary of State office to get his plates and driver's license, but he was told he had to pay his traffic tickets first. He came back a second time and got his plates and license around 11:30.

The article also says that investigators believed the body of the victim was dumped behind a snowbank at Regency Park Apartments sometime before 10 a.m. That is unlikely since other experts said the body had only been there since sometime after 2 p.m. If the body had been in the snowbank since before 10 a.m., it would have been frozen, since February 12, 1979 was a very cold day. When the body of the victim was turned over, warm air came out of her mouth. She clearly had not been there for a very long time. Why would the prosecution want people to think the body was dumped in the snowbank before 10 a.m.? One possible reason was because the police were watching Lee from noon onward. They know he could not have dumped the body any time after that.

Officer Larry Crace of the Grand Rapids Police Department testified that he interviewed Lee four days after the murder. He said Lee was more nervous than he expected. One would expect a murder suspect to be nervous when questioned by the police. That is especially true if the suspect is Black. Everyone who knows the statistics is aware that Blacks are more likely to be convicted than Whites with the same amount of evidence. On February 23rd Lee repeated the same account of his actions as he had given before. When Officer Crace said Lee's story didn't jibe, he asked Lee to go to the police station for another interview on February 26. There Lee repeated the same story. The police again said his story didn't match statements by other people. It should be noted that Lee was consistent with his story. If he lied about his actions, it would seem like he would vary his story somewhat after several repetitions. After the interview at the police station Lee approached the manager and the cook at the restaurant to ask if they remembered him being there the day of the murder. They did not. The cook said Lee did not ask him to lie, but that was his impression. Needless to say, his impression could be wrong.

Three former waitresses at the restaurant testified that Lee occasionally ate at the restaurant both before and after the murder, but they didn't remember him being there that particular day. Obviously, they don't keep a record of every customer every day. Since that day did not become significant until later, it would not be surprising if Lee was there and they didn't remember seeing him.

On February 15 there was another article in the Grand Rapids Press about the trial. The notice on page A2 said, "**Witness says fibers from victim match ones from Lee car.**" Carpet fibers found on the clothes and in the hair of Linda Vanderveen, killed in 1979, match the ones police removed from the car of her attacker, Albert Lee III, according to testimony Thursday. The blond hair found in Lee's car also is similar to Linda's hair, according to testimony." Notice that it assumes Lee was the attacker. That was what the trial was about. It should not be assumed.

In the actual article on page C1 it indicated that Lee was only the "alleged assailant." Hopefully, the readers will read the whole article and not just the earlier notice which made it appear his guilt was established.

Edmund Gundy from the state police crime lab testified he examined the reddish-orange fibers taken from Linda Vanderveen's clothes. He said he used a special microscope to compare them with the fibers from Lee's car. He said, "The fibers are identical in every aspect. I found no difference between the two samples." Gundy also said he found two long blonde hairs on a snow brush he found in the back seat of Lee's car. He also found in the crack of the seat 14 more blonde hairs, feathers, and a barrette that Vanderveen's mother identified as her daughter's. Gundy said he could find no differences between the hairs from Lee's car and those from the victim's head.

The article also says that Secretary of State employees contradicted claims of Lee's whereabouts between 8 a.m. and 10 a.m. Quoting from the article, "Police say Lee claimed he was third in line that day to purchase license plates when the Eastbrook Mall office opened at 9 a.m. and that he had the plates installed by 9:20 a.m. But the Secretary of State records and witnesses indicated Lee couldn't have purchased the plates before 10:30 a.m. According to Jesse Colon, manager of the Eastbrook Mall branch, license plates are sold sequentially. He said the first plate sold that morning was FNZ-008; Lee's plate was FNZ-062, some 54 customers later. Witness Dorothy Kloosterman testified she bought license plate FNZ-061 – the plate sold just before Lee's – about 10:30 a.m."

Once again it should be pointed out that Lee did not say he bought the plates and had them on his car by 9:20. He said he went to the Secretary of State office to get the plates, but he couldn't get them because he had to pay his traffic tickets first. He returned a second time and got the plates and driver's license. Since he didn't get his plates the first time he was there, naturally there would not be a record of him being there. Thus, the employees did not "contradict" his claim; they simply could not confirm it.

When the trial resumed on the following Monday the court heard testimony from Robert Holcombe, who was the laboratory director with JPS Industries of Greenville, S.C., a manufacturer of auto carpeting. He had examined the fibers and he said, "In my opinion they are identical. They came from the same common source or one identical."

However, when asked by Lee's attorney how many carpets were made with the lot that Lee's car carpet came from, he said he didn't know. Presumably, there are thousands of cars with the same kind of carpet. In spite of the prosecutor's attempt to make it sound like the carpet fibers found on the victim had to come from Lee's car, the truth is that his car is only one of a large number of cars that could have provided those fibers.

When Mr. Gundy was asked by the defense attorney about the hairs he found in Lee's car, he said he could not say they were from the victim. He could only say that if they were placed next to Linda Vanderveen's hair, it would be impossible to tell them apart. Unlike carpet fibers, the hair can be examined by DNA testing to determine with certainty if they are from the victim or not. Since these hairs were crucial in the trial and the subsequent appeal, there will be more about them later.

On Tuesday, David Orr testified. He was the one who helped pull a car out of the snow. He had testified earlier that the car was a Monte Carlo, but after being hypnotized he claimed it was a Grand Prix. It should be pointed out that he originally had been very insistent that the car was a Monte Carlo. He said the hypnosis didn't taint his memory, but it is difficult to see why his story changed if that was true. He said, "It (hypnosis) just helped me remember things. What I could and couldn't say today makes a world of difference."

Mr. Orr was plowing snow at Georgetown Condominiums behind Grand Rapids Christian High School when his co-worker, Tim Wilcome asked him to help pull a car out of the snow. After pulling the car out, the driver drove to some nearby trash bins and threw something away. Two days later George VanAntwerp, a self-employed rubbish removal worker was emptying the bins and found a yellow bag. In it he found a book, notebook, one red shoelace and one red mitten. Inside one of the books he saw the name Linda Vanderveen. It is believed that the yellow bag is what Mr. Orr saw the driver throw into the bin.

Also on Tuesday Sgt. Stephen Kuiper testified. He had checked to see how many black Grand Prix were made in 1976 and 1977. Of the 4,788 cars made in those years 344 were registered in Michigan and twelve in Kent County. Nine of those were owned by white people and three by Blacks. All were eliminated as suspects except Albert Lee. It was not stated how the other two Blacks were eliminated. It also was not mentioned that both of them had left the area when they learned they were possible suspects. Since both Mr. Orr and Mr. Wilcome had been insistent the car was a Monte Carlo, it would seem like statistics should have been obtained for that model as well. Also, it should be pointed out that there is no reason to think the abductor was from Kent County just because the murder happened in Kent County.

... the fingerprint found on the victim's notebook was not from Albert Lee.

The next day of the trial a former fingerprint expert named Earl Finkbeiner testified. He said the fingerprint found on the victim's notebook was not from Albert Lee. In fact, after comparing the print with those from over 300 people, no match was found. Defense Attorney John Beason pointed out to Mr. Finkbeiner that if the print had been identified they wouldn't be there. At that point Judge Benson interrupted and said, "The attorneys are watching too much TV."

What that has to do with the case is unclear, but Mr. Beason withdrew the question. Since the print is most likely from the murderer, it would seem Mr. Beason's point was well taken. It should also be asked if the print was from the same person whose prints were found on the neck of the victim since that print is almost certainly from the murderer. The crucial point here is that the print was not from Lee. If it had been, that would have been the main evidence against him. The print was also run through the new Automated Fingerprint Identification System which had prints from 750,000 people convicted or arrested in Michigan. That was in 1991. Today there are over 50 million fingerprints in the police database. It should also be noted that the murderer may not have been from Michigan although that is likely. None of the witnesses reported seeing an out of state license plate.

On the same day of the trial Lt. Raymond Kenny from the state police crime lab testified that he had examined Lee's car and found indentations on a section of the left rear frame that could have come from a tow hook. Mr. Orr had testified that he had put an orange-colored hook under the left rear side of a black car to help free it from the snow where it was stuck. Kenny did not find any orange paint on Lee's car frame. He said the indentations could have come from a hook, but he was not sure. Mr. Beason asked him if he had contacted the previous owner of Lee's car to see if it had ever been towed. He said the police had not.

On Thursday, Douglas W. Deedrick testified. He was the FBI agent who analyzed feathers, hair and fibers found during the investigation of the murder. He said he saw no difference in the hair found on the victim's socks and those from Lee. He said, "Albert Lee is a likely source."

However, when questioned by the defense attorney, he said he could not say the hair from the sock was from Lee. He also said he didn't know how many people have similar hair. He also said that chicken feathers found in Lee's car were similar to those from the victim's mittens. But he said there were duck feathers in Lee's car, and there were no duck feathers in her mittens. It was known that Lee had cut the sleeves off a coat to make a vest. It was also known that Lee had a pillow in his car. Feathers could have come from either of them or from any one of a number of other sources. Mr. Deedrick also agreed with other experts who said the carpet fibers found on the victim were similar to those from Lee's car. Of course, they were also similar to those from thousands of other cars.

When the trial resumed the following Monday, Dr. Edward Blake, founder of Forensic Science Associates of California, testified. This was the lab that conducted the DNA tests on the hair. He said he could not tell if the hair found in Lee's car was from the victim, but he did say it "is genetically comparable to Linda Vanderveen and about 5 percent of the Caucasian population."

Much of the time that day was spent explaining how DNA is extracted from hair and blood. In this case a total of 16 hairs had been found in Lee's car. Of those, 14 were found behind the rear seat and two were found on a snow brush. One hair found on the brush had a root. This was the only hair that contained nuclear DNA, which is necessary to positively identify the owner. The other 15 hairs did not contain roots, and therefore, they would only provide mitochondrial DNA. This does not prove the identity of the owner, but it does tell if that individual is maternally related to another person. It was said that the scientists couldn't do DNA tests on the hairs found on the sock used to gag the victim or the hairs found on her body because they did not have root ends. However, they could have tested the mitochondrial DNA to see if Lee was maternally related to the person who left those hairs. Conspicuous by its absence was any mention of the previous DNA tests that proved the hair found on the snow brush were not from the victim. There was also no mention of the fact that the parent's DNA was also tested, and the test confirmed the results of the former test. It was also not mentioned that the judge had said the DNA evidence would not be used if the last test did not agree with the former tests. It is amazing how the DNA evidence could be so greatly distorted when DNA testing is such a powerful tool to prove guilt or innocence. Not surprisingly, it was a major issue in the appeal that followed Lee's second conviction.

The following day another genetics expert testified. She was Dr. Bonnie Blomberg who was a geneticist and associate professor at the University of Miami. She explained how the DNA process works and agreed that the hair from the snowbrush could have come from the victim. It also could have come from any one of nearly 15 million other people. DNA testing is very exact. Since the first tests proved with virtual certainty that the hair on the brush was not from Linda Vanderveen, it is amazing so much time could be spent at the trial on a later test that gave indecisive results.

In the February 27, 1991 Grand Rapids Press issue dealing with the trial there was an article titled, "**Cellmate who testified Lee admitted strangling won't attend retrial.**" Once again we see that information important in the case was withheld from the jury. Let us examine several statements made in the article. It was stated that "Kent County Prosecutor William Forsyth…declined to discuss his reasons for not bringing back inmate Billy Mansfield to testify."

It is not hard to figure out his reasons. Mansfield had already admitted he lied about the confession. If he had been called to testify, he almost certainly would have admitted he made a deal with the prosecutor to help get Lee convicted. That would have proven Prosecutor Sawyer lied under oath when he testified that there was no deal with Mansfield. It is no wonder Mr. Forsyth didn't want Mansfield there.

The article goes on to say, "Mansfield was awaiting trial on sex charges at the time, but since then has been convicted of killing five people in two states and is imprisoned in California."

The two states referred to are Florida and California. Most people believe there were many more victims. In fact, Mansfield himself has said he killed many people, both males and females. We only know about the females. A number of the victims were killed in 1980 when Mansfield would have been in prison if the Kent County prosecutor had done his job properly. Again we see why the prosecutor would not want Mansfield at the trial.

Defense attorney Beason was critical of Forsyth's decision not to bring Mansfield back to testify. He stated, "My defense is that there was a conspiracy to get a person in this crime, and Mansfield was a part of this. Why not bring him back?"

Not only did Forsyth not want Mansfield to testify, he even got an order from Judge Benson to bar Beason from raising the Mansfield issue during questioning of the police witnesses. As Beason pointed out, Mansfield was an important witness at the first trial, and he was important to the defense claim that there had been a conspiracy to convict Lee. The judge agreed with the prosecutor that mentioning Mansfield could be construed as being prejudicial to Beason's client. If that were so, why would Beason want to do so? Did he want to lose the case? The only conceivable reason he would want to lose the case would be if he had made a deal with the prosecutor to throw the case. If he had done that, the prosecutor would be in favor of bringing Mansfield to testify. The judge said that if Beason wanted Mansfield to testify, it could lead to an appeal on the grounds that Beason provided "ineffective counsel" that could be damaging to his client. That would make little difference since Lee would appeal anyway if he lost the case. Denying Beason the right to mention Mansfield would be another ground for appeal. Notice that once again the judge is siding with the prosecutor against the defense attorney.

As Beason pointed out, "Why they didn't bring him back causes me concern. Why should I bring him? I didn't make the deal with him. The question is why the prosecution didn't bring him back."

Beason could have subpoenaed Mansfield himself, but he did not. The natural question would be why he didn't. One problem was that Mansfield was serving a life sentence in California, and it would have required having an armed guard to transport him to Michigan and back as well as watching him all the time he was in Michigan. Needless to say this would be very expensive as well as being rather cumbersome. As previously mentioned, information crucial to the defense position is withheld from the jury.

On Wednesday, February 27, the prosecutors called their last witnesses. They were Judy Sanchez and Amy Combs. On February 6, 1979, when they were ten and nine years old respectively, they were walking to school when a Black man with a black car stopped, opened his door and stepped out. He asked where Hall Street was and what time it was. Sanchez said he motioned several times for Combs to come closer, but she did not. He said, “She’s scared of me isn’t she?”

Combs testified that the man motioned to her and he was “almost reaching for me but not touching me.” She continued, “I didn’t move. He was kind of laughing…I guess I was shocked. I didn’t know what was happening.”

Upon urging by Sanchez, Combs backed away. Then the man got into his car and drove away “real fast.”

The obvious question is what this has to do with Albert Lee? The prosecutor claimed the man in question was Lee. Lee said he was not that man. Two weeks after the incident Sanchez was shown six photos by the police. At first she picked another man, but after a second try she picked Lee. The article in the Grand Rapids Press about her testimony said that in her first attempt she picked the “wrong man.” How could anyone know he was the wrong man when the identity of the man was unknown? When Sanchez was asked to identify the man she had seen in a lineup, she picked both Lee and another man. She said Lee was the “closest description”, but the other man “sounded” like the man she had seen. Combs did the same with the photos, but in the lineup she said Lee was the “man I saw that morning.” Obviously, there was some uncertainty about the identification.

Whether Lee was the man the girls saw or not, it is unclear what the incident has to do with the murder of Linda Vanderveen. The claim of the prosecutor was that the incident shows that Lee had a history of attempting to abduct and kill young girls. This seems like quite a stretch since it is not known the man was Lee, and even if he was, he made no attempt to abduct or kill the two girls. The only thing we learn from this testimony is that the prosecutor was grasping at straws because he had no real evidence. This desperate attempt by the prosecutor would be laughable if it were not so serious. It should be remembered that Lee had no criminal record.

In contrast to the nearly 60 witnesses called by the prosecutor, the defense only called one witness, and his testimony was of little value. The man was Sgt. Tom Rozema. He was the officer who investigated the case. Beason asked him if the other men in the photographs took part in the police lineup at the Kent County Jail on March 29. Rozema said Lee was the only one in the photographs who was in the lineup. This raises the question of whether the police were trying to influence the girls to identify Lee. Why was the man Sanchez originally identified not in the lineup?

Unlike the first trial, Lee was not called to testify. It is unclear why Mr. Beason didn't call any other witnesses. Perhaps that is part of the reason Lee didn't feel Mr. Beason did an adequate job of defending him. The trial consisted almost entirely of the prosecutor's case against the defendant. There was much evidence the defense attorney could have presented.

- Why didn't he mention that Lee didn't fit the description given by the witnesses?
- Why didn't he point out all the things about Lee's car that didn't fit the description given by the witnesses?
- Why didn't he point out that the barrette found in Lee's car had a different clasp than that of the victim?
- Most important, why didn't he point out that multiple DNA tests proved conclusively the hair found in Lee's car could not have been from Linda Vanderveen?
- Why didn't he raise the obvious question of the motive? There had to be some reason Linda Vanderveen was murdered. Lee clearly had no motive.

Since the judge had shown a prejudice in favor of the prosecution, it could naturally be asked if that had an influence on Beason's lack of adequate defense. Regardless of how that may be, Mr. Rozema was the last witness to be called. The attorneys gave their closing arguments the next day.

Mr. Beason spent an hour and a half on his closing arguments. His claim was that Lee was the victim of a police conspiracy, which included planting evidence. Mr. Forsyth said Beason's claim was like "an octopus releasing its ink bag to create a screen and slide away when it's under attack. If you look at the facts, it points to his client." What were those facts? The evidence the prosecutor offered included a barrette found in Lee's car, blond hair found in his car, carpet fibers found on the victim that were similar to those from Lee's car and testimony discounting Lee's alibi. Mr. Beason responded by suggesting that the barrette was planted and that the hair and carpet fibers were inconclusive. He also questioned the recollections of the witnesses who discounted Lee's alibi. He pointed out that the police were under a lot of pressure from the public to find the killer. He said that he believed the police made a mistake in their effort to find the man responsible. However, if they did what he suggested, it would not be an honest mistake. It would have been deliberate. He said the case was based on innuendos, half-truths, and falsehoods. This is similar to the statement by William Murphy at Lee's first trial. He concluded by saying, "It's put together too well. Either they're the luckiest police department or someone put it there." This was in reference to the barrette.

What was Mr. Forsyth's response to this claim? He said he was offended by the suggestion that the police, his office, and other authorities planted evidence. Of course, whether he is offended or not tells us nothing about whether the claim is true. He said, "If this is such a conspiracy, why do we do it in this fashion? If he didn't do it, what good are we doing the community?"

Again, the question that should come to mind was that of motive.

Obviously, they were not doing the community any good, but it is questionable if that was really his main concern. Again, the question that should come to mind was that of motive. Lee clearly had none. Mr. Forsyth said, "(You) have to stretch your common sense a long way to conclude it was someone else other than the defendant."

As the defense attorneys in both trials pointed out, the case was built on "innuendos, half-truths and falsehoods." How then does one have to stretch his common sense to question if Lee was the killer? Forsyth spent three hours on his closing arguments. He said, "Lee cannot account for where he was on … the day Vanderveen was killed. The physical evidence tells you where he was. He was strangling Linda Vanderveen to death. That's where he was."

Let us examine this statement. The prosecutor said that Lee "cannot account for where he was…" That was not true. Lee told the police repeatedly where he was. His story was always the same. He went to Sambo's restaurant for breakfast. Then he went to the Secretary of State office to get his plates and driver's license. He was told he had to pay his traffic tickets before he could get his licenses. He went to city hall and paid his tickets. Then he went back to the Secretary of State office and finally got his licenses around 11 or 11:30. He put the plates on his car and returned home. He was stopped by the police around noon. The police then kept him under surveillance until after the body of the victim was found sometime around 5:00 p.m. This was his story when first questioned by the police, and it was his story to the day he died. The police did not disprove his story. They simply did not confirm it. It should be pointed out that no one ever claimed to have seen Lee anywhere other than where he said he was. None of the witnesses ever identified Lee until after they were hypnotized twice by the police.

What about the physical evidence the prosecutor referred to? There was a barrette that was not the victim's barrette. There was hair that was not her hair, and there were carpet fibers that were the same as carpet fibers from thousands of other cars. It is hard to see how this "tells you where he was." It is hard to see how this proves, "He was strangling Linda Vanderveen to death." If he was strangling Linda

Vanderveen, why were someone else's fingerprints on her neck? Why did the prosecutor and the police keep claiming she was strangled with her necklace when it certainly would have broken if someone tried to strangle her with it?

Every jury is told that they are to presume a defendant to be innocent until the prosecutor can prove beyond a reasonable doubt that he is guilty. It is hard to see how the prosecutor in this case proved Lee guilty beyond a reasonable doubt.

What about the defense attorney? He did not have to prove the defendant innocent. In fact, he didn't really have to say anything. It is sufficient that the prosecutor cannot prove the defendant guilty. However, it is the duty of a defense attorney to act in the best interest of his client. It may be questioned if Mr. Beason did the best he could to defend Lee, but he did offer a defense. His defense was that there was a police conspiracy to convict Lee. The first question that should come to mind is why they would want to do that. Did they have something against Lee, or was there some other reason they would want to get him convicted? It does not appear that the police had anything against Lee. He was new in town, and he had no criminal record. Other than a few traffic tickets, which the police denied existed, he had not had any run-ins with the police. In fact, the police said that Lee was very cooperative when questioned. Therefore, it is reasonable to assume that the police didn't want to convict Lee because of anything they had against him. Why then would they try to get him convicted? Mr. Beason answered that question. Linda Vanderveen had been murdered, and the public was insistent that the murderer be found and convicted. They had contributed about $50,000 to the reward for the conviction of the murderer. The police were under a lot of pressure, and they had to convict somebody. Lee was a Black man with a dark colored car, and he couldn't prove his innocence. Therefore, he was the one the police chose to convict. That was the defense attorney's claim. Was he right or wrong?

Let us look at the evidence. First of all, it should be pointed out that the whole reason the case was being retried was because the Michigan Supreme Court had thrown out Lee's first conviction. Why had they thrown out his conviction? They plainly stated their reason: It was because of the hypnotized witnesses. Who had hypnotized the witnesses? It was the police. That in itself might suggest a police conspiracy. Remember that no one identified Lee until after being hypnotized. Lee claimed that the witnesses were told under hypnosis to identify whoever the police arrested, and they arrested Lee. No doubt the police will deny Lee's claim, but since the claim was made, it should be investigated. It may not be possible to prove or disprove it, but the claim is consistent with what we know. If the witnesses were not told to identify whoever the police arrested, then why did they identify Lee after being hypnotized when none of them did before being hypnotized? It was stated repeatedly in the newspaper that the witnesses were hypnotized to help them remember. It seems strange that not one witness could remember that Lee was the one he saw the day of the murder until after hypnosis. Then they all remembered that he was the one even though he looked quite different from the man they had described. This certainly suggests a police conspiracy.

If that were all the defense attorney could offer, it might be inconclusive. However, there was more. Remember that early in the trial the prosecutor had persuaded the judge to ban the defense attorney from mentioning Billy Mansfield Jr. Mr. Beason had pointed out that his defense was that there had been a police conspiracy, and he believed Mansfield was a significant part of that conspiracy. Since that was his defense, why was he not allowed to present it?

The mere fact that the judge would not allow the defense attorney to present his defense contributes to the claim of a conspiracy. A judge is supposed to be neutral in a trial. His job is to see that each side has an equal opportunity to present its case. By refusing to let the defense present its case, he was showing a clear prejudice in favor of the prosecution. If Mansfield had testified, he probably would have said that the reason he lied about Lee's supposed confession was because he had made a deal with the police to help get Lee convicted. After he was sent to prison for life there was no reason to maintain that lie. By admitting that he had made a deal with the police, he would have shown that there was in fact a police conspiracy.

There are several other reasons to believe that there was a conspiracy by the police. Officer Crace claimed Lee said he got the plates and had them on his car by 9:20 a.m. the day of the murder. Lee's story was always the same. He never said he got his plates and had them on the car by 9:20. He always said he had to pay his traffic tickets before he could get his plates, and that he got the plates when he went to the Secretary of State office the second time. Since Lee always told the same story, Officer Crace must have lied when he said Lee claimed to have gotten his plates by 9:20. This is another evidence of a police conspiracy.

What about the claim by the police that Lee lied about having to pay the tickets? When someone wants to lie, he comes up with a lie that will sound believable. Lee could have simply said he was shopping at the mall that morning. In a large city like Grand Rapids a person could easily shop for hours without seeing anyone he knew. Why would Lee say he had to pay tickets when he would certainly know that the police would check to see if he had done so? Such a lie would not be a believable lie. Why then did the police say Lee did not have traffic tickets? It is almost certain that he did. It is possible but unlikely that the police simply failed to find the record of the tickets even though they were there at city hall. It seems more likely that they were there and the police lied about them being there, or someone removed the records to keep anyone from finding them. If either of those things happened, it would have been a police conspiracy to discredit Lee.

What about Mr. Beason's suggestion that the police planted the barrette in Lee's car? This is one point where he seems to be in error, but the claim of a conspiracy is still valid. Since the barrette was one of the prosecutor's main evidences, it should be given more consideration. It was stated at the trial that Linda Vanderveen's mother identified the barrette as being her daughter's barrette. This is something that should be questioned. How did she know the barrette was Linda's barrette and not just one that looked like it? The company that made the barrettes made 20 million of them per year. Since there are millions of identical barrettes all over the country, what distinguished this barrette from all the others? As far as we know the barrette didn't have Linda's name or initials on it. There was no distinctive bend or scratch or stain. There was nothing unique about Linda's barrettes. Therefore, even if it were Linda's barrette, there was no way of knowing it. However, we don't need to guess because there are a couple of reasons that we know it was not her barrette.

> *How could a barrette become corroded in such a short time?*

The barrette the police found in Lee's car was corroded. Linda had received the barrettes for Christmas. She was killed on February 12. That is about six weeks after she received them. How could a barrette become corroded in such a short time? If a company produced products of such poor quality, it seems like the company would soon be out of business.

Since this problem was such a significant challenge for the prosecutor, he had to find an explanation. His explanation was that Linda Vanderveen had a habit of sucking on her barrette, and that caused it to corrode more quickly than normal. That was certainly a fanciful explanation, but since he made the claim, it should be considered. There are at least two problems with his claim. First, if Linda Vanderveen could suck on a barrette and cause it to corrode more quickly, it would seem like other people could as well. It is doubtful that she is the only one ever to suck on a barrette, and it is doubtful she had any unique saliva that no one else had. Even if we concede that Linda Vanderveen was such a unique individual, we don't have to guess if her barrette corroded quickly because she supposedly sucked on it. There is a simple way to resolve the issue. Remember that Mr. Forsyth was a lawyer; he was not an expert on barrettes. The expert on the subject was the representative of the company that made the barrettes. He was asked about the prosecutor's claim, and he said that the barrette definitely would not corrode that quickly because someone sucked on it. Therefore, the prosecutor was definitely wrong.

However, that is not the best reason for saying the barrette was not the victim's barrette. We know with certainty it was not hers because it had the wrong kind of clasp. Some barrettes had metal clasps and others had plastic clasps. Since the clasp was different, it could not be Linda's barrette, and therefore, it was worth nothing as evidence. Why was it even mentioned? Did Mr. Beason know the clasp was different? Since the barrette was one of the prosecutor's main evidences, the defense attorney should have known about it, unless this information was kept from him. If so, this would be more evidence of a conspiracy. However, the conspiracy would not be that the police planted the barrette since they would have planted a barrette that was identical to the victim's barrette. If there was a conspiracy, it would be in withholding crucial evidence from the defense attorney.

Another evidence of a police conspiracy that was not mentioned at the trial was the arrest of Albert Lee. The police had been investigating Lee and his car since the day of the murder. Officer Crace told Lee that if he would come to the police station and pass a lie detector test, he would be dismissed as a suspect. Since Lee knew he was innocent, he agreed. He was given the test and passed it. Then Lieutenant Steele, the head of the Homicide Investigation Team, spoke privately with Officer Crace. When he returned, he said there was a problem with the test, and he wanted to do it again. This time he claimed that Lee failed the test. Lee was then arrested and was held in custody the rest of his life. This sounds very suspicious. Lie detector tests are not a hundred percent reliable, which is why they are not permissible at a trial, but they are highly reliable. It would be unusual for a person to pass a test and then not pass it. If that happened, the matter should be pursued further. If the results were inconclusive, that would not justify an arrest. Notice that Officer Crace said Lee would be dismissed as a suspect if he passed the test. That must mean there was no real proof of guilt since they could seek a conviction on other grounds without the lie detector test. As stated, the test would not even be admissible in court.

After Lee was arrested, He was kept in the Kent County jail until after he was convicted and sentenced. Here again we need to mention Billy Mansfield Jr. Why was he put in the same cell as Albert Lee? Lee and the other inmates in that four-man cell were Black. Mansfield was White. They didn't get along well. Wouldn't the police be inviting trouble by putting inmates together who were charged with violent crimes? Lee believed Mansfield was put there purposefully to help get him convicted. Again this suggests a police conspiracy.

Another evidence of a conspiracy was the claim that the hair found in Lee's car was from the victim. Multiple DNA tests proved conclusively that the hair was not from Linda Vanderveen. One inconclusive test showed that the hair was like the hair of five percent of the population. The judge had said that evidence would not be used if the last test did not agree with the earlier tests. It did not agree, and they did use it. Not only did they use the test that the judge said they would not use, the earlier tests were not even mentioned. This shows that the judge was dishonest and clearly prejudiced in favor of the prosecution. Since the DNA tests were a major issue in the subsequent appeal, there will be more on this subject later.

As mentioned earlier, the police had gone to considerable effort to find how many Grands Prix were made, how many were registered in Michigan and Kent County, and how many were owned by Blacks. Since some witnesses were very insistent that the car was a

Monte Carlo, why were no statistics gathered for those cars? It appears that the police were trying to convict Lee instead of doing an honest investigation.

There were many other reasons to believe there was a police conspiracy.

- Lee claimed that the police told the crime lab scientist to put the body of the victim into Lee's car.
- Why did the prosecution claim Lee could not have put his plates on his car because it was too cold? This was a feeble attempt to discredit Lee.
- Why didn't the police admit they were watching Lee during the time the body was being dumped in the snowbank?
- Why did the police do an illegal search of Lee's car?
- Why didn't they admit the blood and saliva found didn't match Lee's?
- Why did the police violate Lee's Miranda rights?
- Why was Lee not allowed to have an attorney present at his polygraph test even though he continually requested one?
- Why did the police lose Lee's alibi statement and then editorialize what was in it?
- Lee had his picture taken for his driver's license the day of the murder. Why was the area on his face where his beard would have been defaced so that it was not possible to see if he had a beard?

Lee claimed that there were a couple of police officers who wanted to tell the truth about the case, but they were intimidated by their fellow officers. It is well known that police support their fellow officers. This is sometimes referred to as the "Code of Silence." In a few cases honest police officers have been known to buck the system with great risk to themselves. Others have simply resigned to avoid danger. Hopefully, most police officers in this country are honest, but in every occupation there are some who are not. With all the evidence of a police conspiracy Mr. Beason's claim had sufficient support to be taken seriously. Unfortunately, he was not allowed to present the full case.

On Friday, March 1st the jury returned a verdict of guilty. After the court was adjourned, several of the key players were interviewed.

Linda Vanderveen's mother Shirley said, "We are very happy it's finally been put to rest. Not just for our sake but for the whole community. We feel bad we had to go through this again. It's a good feeling."

The case was not put to rest. Lee next proceeded with another appeal. To his dying day he insisted he was not the one who committed the crime. To this day the fingerprints have not been identified. All the members of the Vanderveen family and Mr. Lee are now deceased, but the case is not put to rest because there are many questions still unanswered.

As in the first trial the jurors said it was a combination of evidence that led them to their conclusion. One juror said he was convinced after all the evidence was in. He claimed the jury went over all the evidence to be sure their decision was correct. The problem with that statement was that all the evidence was not in. The defense attorney either failed or was prohibited from presenting all the evidence. The evidence the prosecutor presented did not prove Lee guilty. It is hard to see how any juror could vote guilty if simply given all the relevant facts. Three of the jurors said they were convinced of Lee's guilt immediately. After five hours of deliberations all twelve jurors voted guilty.

Not surprisingly, Mr. Forsyth said, "I'm ecstatic about the verdict. I hope the Supreme Court is happy."

The jurors had not been told why the case was being retried. When they were told, they said they felt better about the verdict. Their reaction should have been the opposite since the reason the case was retried was because the first conviction was thrown out by the Michigan Supreme Court because the police had hypnotized the witnesses to get them to identify Lee. This supported the defense attorney's claim that there had been a police conspiracy.

As would be expected, the defense attorney John Beason was disappointed with the verdict, but he said he "gave it my best shot." He thought the jury was overwhelmed by all the evidence that was presented. That would have to be in reference to the evidence presented by the prosecutor since he presented very little. He said, "The jury has spoken. I can't say too much about that."

What was the evidence that convinced the jury? Those who spoke said the main evidence that persuaded them were the carpet fibers, the blond hair and the testimony that discounted Lee's alibi. The jury foreman Joe McMahon said, "He lied about his alibi. His whereabouts could not be established. The second most important factor was the barrette and hairs in the back of his car."

As previously pointed out, it was not proven that Lee lied about his alibi. It simply was not confirmed. Also, the barrette and hairs were not from the victim. Mr. McMahon said that some jurors were not convinced at first, but after all the evidence was weighed, everything fell into place. It is hard to see how that could be. Again there was no mention of motive. Why not? Motive is very important in a murder case. One juror said, "The guy feels no sympathy for what he did. It is so sad."

How did she know how he felt? Maybe he didn't feel any sympathy because he didn't do it. The jurors said they considered the defense claim that there was a police conspiracy but later dismissed it. McMahon said, "They could have done a better job if they were going to plant evidence."

That hardly seems like an adequate assessment of all the evidence in favor of the defense attorney's claim. However, as pointed out, he was not able to present all the evidence.

On March 27, Lee was again sentenced to life without parole. Later he did have a parole hearing, but he was not paroled. Shortly before his passing he was again considered for parole, but, sadly, he died before being released.

Chapter 12 – The Next Appeal

When Lee was sentenced on Wednesday, March 27, he filed another appeal. Defense attorney John Beason said the appeal would be based on various issues including DNA results. Since DNA testing was fairly new at that time, its reliability was not yet established.

It was stated at the time of the sentencing that the cost of the retrial was nearly $80,000, and it was expected to continue to rise. Mr. Forsyth had said before the trial that he was concerned about the cost to the taxpayers. It was not stated what the individual costs were, but presumably the nearly 60 witnesses called by the prosecutor were a significant part of the cost. Since the defense attorney had only called one witness, it is doubtful he had cost the taxpayers very much money. It should also be pointed out that it costs $30,000 to $40,000 per year to keep a person in prison. If the man is not guilty, all this money is wasted.

Lee's appeal was finally submitted April 13, 1995, and it was decided July 21, 1995. Notice that this was over four years after Lee started the appeal process. One has to ask why it takes such a long time to submit an appeal. As in previous cases the advantage was given to the prosecution. The attorneys in opposition to the appeal were Frank J. Kelley, Attorney General, Thomas L. Casey, Solicitor General, William A. Forsyth, Prosecuting Attorney, and Timothy K. Mc Morrow. Lee's only attorney was State Appellate Defender Charles J. Booker. The opinion in the case was given by Stephen J. Markman, who later became Chief Justice of the Michigan Supreme Court.

In the summary of the case Judge Markman repeated some of the same false information that had been given previously. He stated again that the victim was strangled with her own necklace. It appears that the reason the prosecution continued to make that claim was to distract attention from the fingerprints on her neck. Mr. Markman also claimed that there was evidence of sexual assault. That was not true. The experts that examined the body said that there were marks that could be interpreted as sexual assault, but it was not certain that she was sexually assaulted since similar marks could have been received simply because she was resisting her attacker. She definitely was not raped. Where would the judge get the idea that the victim was sexually assaulted? He did not say. We do know that Billy Mansfield Jr. had claimed that Lee killed the victim while attempting to rape her, but Mansfield had already admitted that he lied about the confession. We also know that the judge who originally sentenced Lee implied he had a sexual motive even though there was no evidence to support the claim.

Judge Markman stated that Jack Hill, the first witness, said that the abductor was about five feet, eleven inches tall with neatly trimmed hair. A few minutes after the abduction James Vos saw a Black man with a black car run a stop sign at an excessive rate of speed. Vos said the man had a short Afro hairstyle. A boy named Greg Start saw the man and said he had a short Afro hair style. Since all three witnesses gave the same description of the abductor, it is virtually certain that Albert Lee was not the man they saw since he had a medium to long Afro hair style. No one would describe his hair style as short or neatly trimmed. It should also be pointed out that when the police made a sketch of the man seen by at least five witnesses, it showed him with very short hair. It should have been obvious that Lee was not the man the witnesses saw.

The judge went on to relate that Jack Vos, the son of James Vos, saw the victim in the back seat of the abductor's car. She was waving her arms and had a look of terror on her face. As pointed out in the previous chapter, this shows that the car was not Lee's car since he had tinted windows. This is something that is easily verifiable, and it is crucial to the case. Why was it not mentioned?

The report then goes on to repeat some of the same claims that were presented at the second trial about the barrette, hair, carpet fibers and feathers. None of these proved the guilt of the defendant, and we know the barrette and the hair were not from the victim.

The defense raised **five issues** in the appeal. The **first** was about the admissibility of some testimony. The Michigan Supreme Court had ruled that witnesses could only testify about facts that were recalled and related prior to hypnosis since there was significant evidence that some memories may have been affected. There were a number of variations in the testimonies of the witnesses from the first trial to the second trial. This was to be expected since the two trials were twelve years apart. Naturally, memories tend to fade over time. The appeals court ruled that the variations were more the result of time than of hypnosis, and the changes in testimony were so minor that they would not be likely to affect the decision of the jury.

The **second** objection of the defense was that the prosecutor had improperly referred to a prior incident involving the defendant. This was the similar acts evidence that the prosecutor had used at the first trial. The Michigan Supreme Court had ruled that it could be used at the second trial. The appeals court said, "The prior bad acts evidence was admitted for the limited purpose of showing that defendant committed the crime at issue in this case." It is hard to see how "showing the defendant committed the crime" was a "limited purpose" since that was what the trial was all about. The Court claimed that the prosecutor had made arguments that showed the defendant's "manner and circumstances of stalking and attracting victims." The two girls involved in the alleged similar act were not victims since they were not harmed in any way. It also was not shown that the defendant committed the similar act since it was not known that Lee was the man in question. Since a knife was found at the scene of the abduction, it was assumed that it was used in the abduction. The Court said, "The jury did not need to determine why defendant would use a knife to commit this crime since it had sufficient information available to it that defendant, in fact, had used such a weapon." A knife was found at the scene. There was no evidence that Lee had such a weapon. It was not determined that the knife belonged to Lee or that his fingerprints were found on it. It is likely that the abductor used the knife, but there was no evidence that it was Lee who did so. The Court should not assume Lee was the perpetrator since that was the matter that was at issue.

The **third** complaint was that Lee did not get a fair trial because the jury was not impartial. There were three problems that were stated. The defense had to use peremptory challenges to excuse jurors who should have been excused for cause, the trial court refused to grant additional peremptory challenges and it also refused a change of venue. A peremptory challenge is a request to remove a juror without stating a reason. It should have also been stated that at least two of the jurors should not have been on the jury because one was facing charges from the prosecutor and one had a daughter who was facing charges. It is incredible that this was not mentioned in the appeal. We need to ask why those two jurors were not referred to. Since it had been over four years since the trial, there should have been enough time to investigate the twelve jurors. Lee himself was in prison all that time, and therefore, he was able to do little investigation. He seems to have had only one appeal attorney. Was that attorney aware of the two jurors who were clearly not qualified for jury duty? Since the claim that the jury was not impartial was one of the main issues in the appeal, this is something the appeal attorney should have studied thoroughly. It is unknown why he didn't mention those two jurors.

There were three jurors who were questionable.

There were three jurors who were questionable. Their names were not given in the appeal court's opinion to protect their privacy. They were referred to by their initials. They were Juror N, Juror O and Juror F. It may be worthy of note that all three were white women. Since this was a case of a white girl killed by a Black man, the issue of prejudice may be considered. It is significant that there were no Black men on the jury.

Juror N had expressed concern about her ability to keep in mind that she was supposed to presume the defendant to be innocent. However, she did promise to keep an open mind and decide the case based on the evidence. The court did not dismiss her, and the defense attorney did not use one of his peremptory challenges to do so. The claim of the defense was that the court should have dismissed her. The appeal court disagreed.

Juror O had followed the first trial and remembered that the defendant had been convicted. She was concerned at the time because she had two small children, and she was relieved when the defendant was convicted. She claimed she would not let an earlier jury decision sway her. It was also mentioned that she was married to a Grand Rapids police officer, and she knew some of the police witnesses. It would seem like this should have disqualified her as a juror since it was believed by some that it was a Grand Rapids police officer who was behind the murder. It should be recalled also that the defense at the second trial was that there had been a police conspiracy to convict Lee. As pointed out in the last chapter, there was considerably more evidence of that conspiracy than the defense attorney was allowed to present. Juror O certainly should have been dismissed by the court, but she was not. Instead the defense attorney had to use another one of his limited peremptory challenges.

Juror F had followed the first trial closely and thought the defendant was guilty. It would seem like that should have been sufficient cause to dismiss her from the jury, but the trial court did not. The claim was that she could set aside her previous opinion. That is questionable. The defense attorney had to use another peremptory challenge to dismiss her. It is interesting that she said that she thought the new trial was possibly because "there was another man involved that said that he admitted he was guilty." It is unknown where she may have heard that.

After the jury had been selected the defense attorney had stated, "If I would have had additional challenges, I would have removed a lot of the jury members that are now seated in this jury, and we would ask the Court to change the venue of this trial. I feel it is not a fair and impartial jury to Mr. Lee."

The appeal court said that the request for additional challenges and the motion for a change of venue came too late. Therefore, that part of the appeal was denied. Whether one agrees with the decision of the appeal court or not, one thing that is clear is that the defense did not believe the jury was impartial even before the trial began. When the evidence offered is considered, it is difficult to see how an impartial jury could conclude that Lee was proven guilty beyond a reasonable doubt. In defense of the jury it should be pointed out that a great deal of evidence relevant to the case was not presented. This is especially true of the evidence of a police conspiracy.

The **fourth** complaint was filed in propria persona. That is a legal term that means the defendant filed the complaint himself without an attorney. This immediately raises the question of why he didn't have the assistance of an attorney when filing something with the appeal court. This would certainly put him at a great disadvantage. The court complained several times that Lee didn't provide sufficient evidence to support his claims. How can a man without legal assistance who has been incarcerated for sixteen years come up with all the documentation the court demands? Again we see how the justice system gives all the advantages to the prosecution.

Lee stated several objections. The first ones had to do with prosecutor misconduct. He claimed the prosecutor effectively told the jury that reasonable doubt is doubt for which they could give a reason. This could mean that the prosecutor did not have to provide proof beyond a reasonable doubt. The appeal court rejected this claim and pointed out that the trial court did explain what constitutes reasonable doubt.

Next Lee said the prosecutor argued facts not in evidence when he offered theories to explain the testimony of Wilcome and Orr. They had testified that they helped pull a car out of a snowbank in the late forenoon the day of the murder. Lee was getting his licenses at that approximate time. It was believed that the driver of that car was the murderer since he threw something in a nearby dumpster, and Linda Vanderveen's knapsack was later found in the dumpster. Naturally, the witnesses did not note the exact time of the incident since they were busy and didn't check the time. The prosecutor had suggested that the driver may not have been the killer or that Orr was mistaken about the identification of the car. It is also possible that it was not the knapsack of the victim that the driver threw into the dumpster. The appeal court agreed that the prosecutor cannot argue facts not in evidence, but he can "argue the evidence and all reasonable inferences from the evidence as it relates to (his) theory of the case."

Lee's next complaint was that the prosecutor claimed the hair found in Lee's car was from a female. The reason he made that claim is because Edward Gundy, the crime lab scientist, had stated his opinion that the hair probably came from a female because of its length. Since about half the population is female, this is not very helpful in determining who supplied those hairs. Not surprisingly, the appeal court rejected this complaint.

The next complaint was that the prosecutor vouched for the defendant's guilt when he told the jury that Lee was there because he was guilty. It is certainly true that the prosecutor did plainly state that Lee was guilty. It is the jury that is supposed to decide if a person is guilty. The prosecutor is supposed to present his evidence and let the jury decide if guilt is proven beyond a reasonable doubt. Once again we see that the defendant is assumed guilty or declared guilty when that is what the trial is all about. The appeal court said that there was nothing inappropriate about the prosecutor's remarks.

Lee then argued that he was effectively denied his right to a defense when the trial judge told the jury that "you cannot acquit or convict based upon what the attorneys say." As Lee pointed out, the defense attorney presented almost no evidence. Therefore, the only defense the jury could consider was contained in the defense attorney's closing argument. The appeal court disagreed with Lee's claim and pointed out that the trial court's instruction was standard, and it accurately stated the law. That is true, but Lee's complaint in this regard brings up a larger issue. Why did the defense attorney present almost no evidence? As stated in the previous chapter, the defense attorney said that his defense was that there had been a police conspiracy. He was prohibited from presenting some of the evidence, and he either failed to offer or was ignorant of other evidence. He had only called one witness, and he didn't ask him any questions of significance. The defense offered was extremely weak even though there was extensive evidence of a police conspiracy. We need to ask why the defense attorney presented such a weak case. It is understandable why Lee was not satisfied with his attorney.

Lee's next complaint further demonstrates why he was dissatisfied with his attorney. He claimed he was denied his right to confront witnesses because some witnesses from the first trial were not able to testify at the second trial. Billy Mansfield, Jr. was specifically mentioned. As previously pointed out, the trial judge had banned the defense attorney from referring to Mansfield. He also said that if the attorney had called Mansfield to testify, it could be considered ineffective assistance of counsel since Mansfield had been a witness for the prosecution at the first trial. However, Mansfield had admitted that he lied about Lee's supposed confession. The apparent reason he had done so was because he had made a deal with the prosecutor and police to have his charges reduced. This would have supported the defense claim of a police conspiracy. Again it was pointed out that Mr. Beason, the defense attorney, could have subpoenaed Mansfield himself. Why didn't he do so? The reason he stated at the time was rather weak. We don't know what may have happened behind the scenes to influence his decision. What we know is that crucial evidence for the defense was not presented to the jury. The appeal court said that Lee was not denied his right to confront a witness because Mansfield was not called to testify, and therefore, there was no testimony to confront. That is true, but the fact remains that a major element for the defense was never presented to the jury.

Lee then argued that the prosecutor failed to prove all the elements of felony murder. The appeal court stated that "Felony murder consists of (1) [t]he killing of a human being (2) with the intent to kill, to do great bodily harm, or to create a high risk of death or great bodily harm with knowledge that death or great bodily harm was the probable result (3) while committing, attempting to commit, or assisting in the commission of any of the felonies specifically enumerated in MCL 750.316; MSA 28.548." Kidnapping is one of the felonies enumerated in the laws cited. Since Linda Vanderveen was a human being who was killed, and since the killing was obviously deliberate and done in conjunction with a kidnapping, it is clear that the crime was a felony murder. There is no question that a felony murder did occur; the question was whether it was Lee or someone else who did it. The court complained that Lee incorrectly stated that the elements of felony murder were "who, what, whom, when, why and how." Once again we see that Lee was at a serious disadvantage because he was filing his supplemental brief without the assistance of an attorney. Lee may have been incorrect in stating the elements of felony murder, but it is true that the prosecutor did fail to answer several of the questions cited. He did not prove Lee was the one who committed the crime. He could not come up with a timeline that fit the known facts. He could not even suggest a motive Lee could have had. He could not prove the victim was strangled with her necklace. Instead of dealing with the issue Lee brought up, the court avoided the issue by citing the technical definition of felony murder. The court then went on to say, "In reviewing the sufficiency of the evidence, this Court must view the evidence in the light most favorable to the prosecutor and determine whether a rational trier of fact could find that the essential elements of the crime were proven beyond a reasonable doubt." Why must the court view the evidence in the light most favorable to the prosecutor? Why not view it in the light most favorable to the defense? Better yet why not give equal consideration to both sides? Also, it should be repeated that no one questions whether the elements of felony murder were proven beyond a reasonable doubt.

The question was who did it? Finally, the court said, "substantial testimonial and physical evidence was presented at trial in support of the defendant's conviction." What substantial evidence? There was a barrette that was not the victim's barrette. There was hair that was not her hair, and there were carpet fibers that were the same as carpet fibers from thousands of other cars. There was also a supposed similar act by an unknown person who made no attempt to harm the alleged potential victims.

The last claim Lee made in his supplemental brief was that some witnesses were inconsistent in their descriptions of his car and of himself. That is to be expected since there had been 12 years between the two trials. It is true that there were significant differences between what witnesses stated at the first trial and the second. The court complained that Lee didn't provide enough specifics. Again it should be pointed out that Lee did not have the advantage of a lawyer to help with his supplemental brief. Of course, the court made no attempt to do any investigating themselves. It appears that they never talked directly with Lee. As has been pointed out before, there were significant differences between Lee's car and the car described by the witnesses. Even more significant was the description of Lee himself. He said the witnesses described the assailant as "clean shaven, no facial hairs." Lee definitely had a beard. The court complained that "Defendant has not shown by whom or when these descriptions were given, nor has he pointed to any such identification at trial."

If they want to know who gave the descriptions, all they need to do is go to the Grand Rapids Press and look at the police sketch that was published there. It should be easy to ask the police who gave them the information they used to make the sketch. Obviously the five people who gave the information were the five people who had the best opportunity to see the man. Their names have been given repeatedly in both trials and in the appeal the court was commenting on. All the witnesses were in complete agreement that the man they saw had no beard. There is no question that Lee did have a beard. If anyone wants to question that fact, he can go to the Grand Rapids Press again and see the picture that was taken of Lee when he was arrested six weeks after the murder. He had a beard. There are also a multitude of witnesses who saw Lee before and after the day of the murder. That includes the police officer who stopped Lee around noon the day of the murder. It is an easily provable fact that Lee had a beard. Since all the witnesses agreed that the man they saw did not have a beard, Lee could not be the man they saw. It is amazing that this crucial information could be so largely ignored at both trials and by the appeal court. Instead they blame Lee for not providing more information that is readily available to anyone who wants it.

The **last** issue raised in the appeal was whether the trial court should have admitted DNA evidence that supposedly linked hairs found in Lee's car to the victim. As previously stated, the judge had said the last DNA test would not be used if it disagreed with the former tests. It did disagree, but it was used anyway. In fact, the former tests were not even mentioned. Obviously, for the judge to say the evidence would not be used if it did not agree with the former tests there had to be some former tests. It is interesting that the appeal court spent six pages in their opinion dealing with the DNA evidence, which was nearly half the entire length of their opinion, but the former DNA tests were never mentioned once. How can that be? Were they not aware that there had been multiple tests that proved conclusively that the hair found in Lee's car was not from the victim? Didn't the defense attorney know about the former tests? If he did, didn't he make any mention of those tests? As we have seen repeatedly in this case, crucial evidence is totally ignored.

Let us look at what the appeals court had to say about the DNA evidence. First, they pointed out that the DNA test that was under consideration in this case was different from other DNA tests that had previously been approved for admission in other cases. In this case the method under consideration was the polymerase chain reaction (PCR) method. The court had previously determined that the restriction fragment length polymorphisms (RFLP) method was admissible. This immediately raises the question of why the RFLP method was not under consideration since it is very exact, but the PCR method is not. This question was not addressed in the appellate court opinion. Instead they spend all their time dealing with whether the PCR method had general acceptance in the scientific community. If it did, then it would be admissible as evidence.

The appeals court dealt with the DNA issue in **seven sections**. In the **first** section the court pointed out that since there had not yet been a determination if the PCR method was admissible, there had been a hearing to decide if it should be used in Lee's case. The hearing was conducted in September and October of 1990. This may explain in part why it took over a year from the time the Michigan Supreme Court dismissed Lee's first conviction until his second trial. The question at issue in the hearing was the general acceptance of the PCR method. As usual, the advantage was given to the prosecution. They called four expert witnesses. They were Dr. David Ginsburg, Dr. Paul Coussens, Dr. Bonnie Blomberg, and Dr. Julian Adams. The prosecution also called Dr. Edward Blake, who was the forensic serologist who performed the DNA testing in the case. A serologist is a specialist in serology, which according to the Merriam-Webster Dictionary is "a medical science dealing with blood serum especially in regard to its immunological reactions and properties." The defense only called one expert. He was Dr. Ashok Bhagwat. After giving the names of the experts at the hearing, the appeal court gave a description of the structure of the DNA molecule. Since that description is readily available to anyone who is interested, we will not repeat it here. All the experts agreed that the PCR method was accepted as reliable for medical and biological research. The only area of disagreement was whether it was reliable enough for forensic use.

Dr. Bhagwat raised two concerns. He argued that test results may not be reliable because of errors caused by the enzyme, Taq polymerase. Also, he claimed there could be contamination at the crime scene or at the laboratory. After stating the concerns of Dr.

Bhagwat, the appeals court pointed out that the PCR method was devised in 1985 and quickly became widely accepted. By the time of the hearing in Lee's case in 1990 it was one of the most widely used techniques in medical and biological research. The particular gene that was of interest in this case was the DQ alpha gene. It has six identifiable forms, which are called alleles or traits. They are identified by the numbers 1.1, 1.2, 1.3, 2, 3 and 4. Each person has two of these alleles, one from each parent. That means that there are 21 possible combinations. Linda Vanderveen's blood showed that her genotype was 1.3, 4. The hair found in Lee's car had the same 1.3, 4 genotype. Lee himself had the genotype 3, 4. Therefore, we can conclude that the hair found in Lee's car could have come from the victim. It also could have come from any one of several million other people. We can say with certainty that the hair could not have come from Lee since he has a different genotype. Of course, we already know that since Lee was a Black man, and he obviously didn't have blond hair. Dr. Blake said that the 1.3, 4 allele appears in the Caucasian population at the rate of 4.3 percent and in the Black population at 8 percent. Since the hair in question was blond, it certainly was from the Caucasian population.

In the **second** section of the court's analysis the PCR method is explained. There are three steps. In the first step the sample to be studied is purified. In the second step it is denatured and amplified. Each cycle doubles the amount of DNA. Normally a sample is cycled thirty to thirty-two times. In the cases in question the sample was cycled thirty-five times, which produced sixteen- billion copies of the DNA to be tested. The third step is to place the sample onto a nitrocellulose filter which has the allele-specific DNA on it. When washed with an enzyme, the DNA strip should turn blue if there is a match. If not, it will be blank. Therefore the procedure is called the reverse-dot blot procedure or the blue-dot procedure.

In the **third** section of the court's analysis it was stated that the prosecution's experts said that the reverse dot-blot method that was used in this case is generally accepted as reliable, and the one defendant's expert did not contest that claim. There are advantages and disadvantages to the PCR method. The advantages are that it is quicker to use and it can be used on smaller samples. The disadvantage is that it can only be used to exclude a person; it cannot be used to identify a particular person. With the RFLP method the probability of a match is between one in two million and one in sixty-one million. In other words it is nearly complete proof that a sample is from the person in question. However, with the PCR method we can only learn if the sample is from one of twenty-one genotypes. In the case in question the DQ alpha genotype is consistent with five percent of the Caucasian population or one in twenty people. That does not mean there is a one in twenty chance that the hair found in Lee's car was from the victim. Five percent of the population is about ten to fifteen- million people. Therefore, the probability that the hair was from the victim is one in ten to fifteen-million. This is not very helpful. If the hair had been a different genotype, we could say with certainty that the hair was not from the victim. Since it was the same, we have no idea if it was from the victim or not. Again we note that the earlier tests that showed conclusively that the hair was not from the victim were not even mentioned.

In the **fourth** section of the court analysis there was discussion of other courts' rulings on the admissibility of the PCR method. Since the procedure was fairly new at the time, there were only a few cases to consider. In all the cases that the appeal court referred to, the courts in question had approved the PCR method for forensic use. The appeals court stated, "The potential problems of contamination and errors caused by Taq polymerase have not been judged serious enough to undermine the reliability of the PCR method." In 1992 the National Research Council (NRC) of the National Academy of Sciences prepared a report that raised some questions about the reliability of the PCR method. Since this was after the 1991 trial, the report was not considered at that time. However, the appeals court did consider it since they wanted to use the most up-to-date information available. The court concluded that the NRC's report did not alter the result in the case. The report did not claim that the PCR method was unreliable. It only said that certain safeguards needed to be followed. The court quoted the NRC report as saying, "as a general matter, so long as the safeguards we discuss in this report are followed, admissibility of DNA typing should be encouraged. There is no substantial dispute about the underlying scientific principles." The appeals court said that the NRC report did not alter their decision in this case since proper safeguards were followed by the lab doing the testing.

The **fifth** section of the court's analysis dealt with Dr. Bhagwat's first objection. He had said that the PCR method might not be reliable because the enzyme, Taq polymerase, might cause copying errors during the chain reaction, and therefore, results could be false. Dr. Ginsburg and Dr. Blomberg agreed that Taq polymerase could cause errors, but they said the error rate was about one in 10,000. Dr. Bhagwat believed the error rate was higher, but he admitted that for the results to be affected the error would have to occur at a certain point in a cycle. He said that the probability of that happening would only be one in 2,410,000. In spite of this very low probability, he thought the error rate could still be significant because of what he called unknown hot spots and because errors could be multiplied due to the cycling process. He recommended that multiple tests be run to confirm the results. In Lee's case there was a second test run, which confirmed the results of the first PCR test. There had been an agreement that if the test results were the same, the second test would not be admitted at the trial. If the results were different, the defense could present that as evidence. Again the agreement was not followed. The results were presented to the jury. This would give the impression that the guilt of the defendant was confirmed. However, all the second test confirmed was that the genotype of the victim was the same as the person who supplied the hairs found in Lee's car. Since there are only twenty-one genotypes altogether, this is not very significant. Millions of people have the 1.3, 4 genotype. The appeals court concluded, "we do not believe that the error rate associated with Taq polymerase undermines the reliability of the PCR analysis as a forensic method."

The **sixth** section of the court's analysis dealt with Dr. Bhagwat's other objection, which was that contamination of a sample could produce false results. The potential problem is that a cell from another person might get into the sample to be tested. Cells from animals would not pose a problem. Also, environmental factors would not be a concern. If another person's DNA were to get into the sample, the test could falsely exclude the defendant since the PCR method can only exclude a person; it cannot identify a person. The essential issue is whether adequate safeguards are used to prevent contamination. One safeguard is to perform the tests in two different laboratories. Also, control samples are used containing known DNA or no DNA. In the case in question Dr. Blake, who did the test, said that the lab he used had ten procedures that were used to prevent contamination. The other experts agreed that the safeguards were met. Therefore, the court concluded that the defendant had not shown that contamination made the PCR method unreliable.

The **seventh and final** section of the court's analysis had to do with the defendant's claim that there had not been enough validation of the PCR method through independent studies. In 1990 that was true because the method was fairly new. By the time the appeals court reviewed the case in 1995 many studies had been made. One source listed over a thousand articles on PCR analysis. The appeals court concluded, "We are aware of no more recent independent validation studies that have called into question the reliability of the PCR method." The court, therefore, concluded that that method of DNA analysis should be admissible as evidence. There were just two cautions. First, care must be taken to avoid contamination, and second, the jury must be advised that the PCR method can only be used to exclude an individual. Other DNA tests are needed to identify a person. It would appear that the prosecution was trying to imply that the hair found in Lee's car was from the victim simply because it had the same genotype. There are only 21 genotypes, and millions of people have the same genotype as Linda Vanderveen. Therefore, it is inappropriate to use the PCR method to suggest that the hair found in Lee's car was from the victim. The probability of the hair being hers is one in several million. Again we note that the court made no mention of the former tests that proved conclusively that the hair was not from the victim.

The appeals court's final statement was, "Linda Vanderveen was kidnapped and murdered on February 12, 1979. The defendant came under suspicion on February 23, was arrested on March 30, and was convicted on November 9. This was sixteen years ago. It is long overdue that this case be concluded and that justice be obtained for the victim, her family and friends, her community, and the defendant."

There are a couple of problems with that statement. First, Lee was considered a possible suspect from noon on the day of the murder when the police stopped him because he happened to be a Black man with a dark colored car. Because he was a possible suspect, the police kept him under surveillance until the body of the victim was found around 5:00 p.m.

Second, it is true that Lee was convicted November 9, 1979, but that conviction was dismissed by the Michigan Supreme Court. The conviction the court was dealing with was from 1991. It is certainly true that it was long overdue "that justice be obtained for the victim, her family and friends, her community, and the defendant." However, justice was not obtained because there was no proof of guilt, much evidence was ignored, and many questions remain unanswered.

One of the main questions that remains unanswered is whose fingerprints were on the neck of the victim and on her notebook.

Another question that many have to this day is what the motive was. Lee clearly had none. Yes, this case needs to be brought to a conclusion, but it won't be until the relevant questions are answered and the murderer and those who perverted justice are identified.

Chapter 13 – The Newspaper Article

Up to this point the information that has been shared has been mostly from articles in the *Grand Rapids Press* and court cases. From now on the story will be more personal because I became acquainted with Albert Lee myself.

In 2009 I was a carrier for the *Grand Rapids Press*. Normally, I didn't read the paper; I just delivered it. However, on April 1, 2009 there was an article on the front page that caught my attention. It had been 30 years since Lee was arrested, and Tom Rademacher of the *Grand Rapids Press* had decided to do a follow-up story on the Linda Vanderveen murder case. He interviewed both Albert Lee and William Forsyth.

Lee was incarcerated at that time at the Michigan Reformatory in Ionia. Mr. Rademacher started his article by saying that there were two things he wanted to do when he met with Lee. He wanted to show him a picture of Linda Vanderveen and ask why he killed her. That certainly was a very pertinent question. To this day no one has been able to suggest a motive that Lee could have had. The prosecutor and the police said that they were not concerned about the motive. They should have been. Motive is very important in a murder case. In fact, if a person has no motive, it is questionable if the homicide could be considered first degree murder or some lesser charge. Not surprisingly, when asked why he killed Linda Vanderveen, Lee answered, "I did not commit that crime. I did not know that victim. I'm puzzled just like everyone else."

Mr. Rademacher's response was, "Actually, everyone else isn't puzzled. But when you're surrounded by 1,200 other men who also claim they were imprisoned unjustly, maybe that's how you rationalize spending the rest of your life behind bars."

That statement shows ignorance of our justice system. After working with prisoners for over half a century, I can say with certainty that not all prisoners say they are innocent. I have talked extensively with hundreds of prisoners, and I could count on one hand the number who have told me they were innocent. Mr. Rademacher then went on to point out that Lee was convicted not once, but twice. To some that might suggest that he was doubly proven guilty. However, for a person to be convicted twice he had to be tried twice. That is quite rare, and for a person to be tried twice, the first conviction had to be overturned. That would not happen unless there was a serious problem with the first conviction.

> *Saying that all or most prisoners claim to be innocent is one of the biggest lies the justice system tells the public.*

Lee tried to point out some of the faulty evidence in his case, but he was stopped. Instead Mr. Rademacher asked him if he planned any more appeals. He said he did, but when he was told that all the Vanderveen family were dead, he was very disappointed. He had hoped with the new DNA evidence he might be able to get justice.

When Mr. Rademacher interviewed Kent County Prosecutor William Forsyth, he said, "In all the years he's been locked up, I've never lost any sleep over the fact he's in prison."

Why is that? Is it because he is convinced Lee is guilty, or is it because he has so little conscience that he doesn't care if he sent an innocent man to prison for life? Lee was cut off when he tried to point out the flaws in the evidence against him, but Forsyth was given opportunity to tell the evidence he used to convict Lee. He said, "Forensics proved that a barrette and blond hair found in Lee's car were likely Linda's. They found hairs belonging to Lee on Linda's clothing."

Was it proven, or was it likely? They are two entirely different things. As pointed out in the last chapter, the barrette was not her barrette, and the hair was not her hair. What about the claim that

Lee's hair was found on her clothing? What they found were short rootless African hairs on her clothing. They did not contain any nuclear DNA, and therefore, it was not possible to determine whose hair they were. Since the witnesses all agreed that the abductor was Black, we would expect the hairs on the victim to be from a Black person. Since there are several million Black men in this country, the only way those hairs could be of any value as evidence would be to check the mitochondrial DNA to see if Lee was maternally related to whoever supplied the hairs. Apparently, no one has ever done that. Therefore, it is inappropriate for Mr. Forsyth to say those hairs were from Lee. When he was told Lee insisted that he was framed, Forsyth scoffed at the idea. He said, "I fully expected he would tell you what he told you. I don't believe him anymore today than I did thirty years ago." Of course, this is exactly what we would expect the prosecutor to say. It tells us nothing.

Mr. Rademacher said that Lee told him that his visit was the first from someone on the outside in about twenty-five years. Most of his family were deceased, and some of the few who remain live in Texas.

In his article Rademacher stated, "During our interview, he pulled off the dark sunglasses, so I pulled a black and white photo of the girl he strangled with her own necklace." As we see, people are still being told the victim was strangled with her necklace, which is highly unlikely since it probably would have broken if someone tried to strangle her with it. The fingerprints on her neck are still ignored and still unidentified. When Lee was shown the picture, he asked, "That's the victim?"

Rademacher said it was and then asked, "Does it affect you?"

Lee replied, "Nah, it don't. No." Then he said, "I don't see how anybody could do such a thing like that."

When Rademacher was about to leave, he gave Lee his name and work number in case he ever wanted to confess. Lee said, "I would risk my life to save a child." These do not sound like the words of a cold-blooded killer.

In another article by Mr. Rademacher in the same issue of the paper, Mr. Forsyth stated, "In all the years I ever worked here, I never saw a task force labor so intensively to find (a killer). They pretty much were stopping anyone driving a black car."

Were they really trying to find the killer, or did they already know who he was? What they should have been doing was to look for a light complected black man with a Cuban accent and no beard who was driving a dark colored car with wide whitewalls and without tinted windows. It probably was a Monte Carlo and may have had bicentennial plates. They also should have tried harder to identify the fingerprints found on the neck of the victim and on Linda Vanderveen's notebook. At the second trial the defense claim of a police conspiracy should have been taken seriously since there was extensive evidence to support it.

A couple of days after reading the article I sent an email to Mr. Rademacher pointing out some of the problems I saw with the case. Since I didn't receive any reply, I decided to make a copy of the email and send it to Mr. Lee with a brief note saying that it was one of the responses that Mr. Radmacher was sent about his article. The article said that Lee was at the Michigan Reformatory in Ionia. With the Offender Tracking Information System (OTIS) it was easy to get Mr. Lee's prisoner number and address. As the article said, Lee had not received a visit in twenty-five years, and he gets little or no mail.

No doubt Lee was surprised to get a letter from someone he didn't know. He sent back a reply, which began thirteen years of correspondence.

After a couple short paragraphs of introduction Lee wrote about his case. He said, "As for the newspaper article I too read them for what they don't say..e.g; the prosecutor made the statement 'IF NOT for the man who 30 years ago dragged her kicking and screaming into his black Grand Prix' is he talking about the same trial no one testified to that!"

Actually, the article said that; it does not say the prosecutor made that particular statement. It is true that no one ever said he saw her being dragged kicking and screaming, but it is clear that she was forced into the car. We don't know that the car was a Grand Prix. Mr. Hill, who was the only witness to the actual abduction, originally thought the car was a Cordoba. He did not see the girl being forced into the car. He saw her in the car and concluded that she had been forced into it.

Lee went on to say, "(the prosecutor) did not say my name, because he of all the people know that I was not the guy that committed this crime, based on the investigation. They needed a fall guy, and I made the perfect suspect, I was from out of town, knew no one there, had no support, etc."

After studying this case for several years I believe Lee was right. They needed someone to frame, and Lee was the unfortunate man who was picked.

Quoting again from Lee's letter, "This case was overturn because the witnesses was post hypnotic suggested too. The prosecutor was not suppose to use those witnesses but he did anyway. He also use DNA that was tested. He was suppose to dismiss the case, but he refuse to. The DNA came back saying that it was not her hair; the prosecutor was again suppose to dismiss the case, but refuse too. He order a second test which clearly is a lie. Billy Mansfield Jr. wanted to come back and testified that he lied on me in the first trial, but the prosecutor would not bring him back." (grammatical errors in the original)

Lee went on to say that he did not believe he would have been found guilty in another county. Of course, we don't know what would have happened in another county, but we do know that his defense attorneys in both trials requested a change of venue because they did not believe Lee could get a fair trial in Kent County. One of the reasons Lee stated for why he thought he would not have been found guilty in another county was because he said the crime lab scientist testified that he was told to put the victim in Lee's car. The only reason one would do that would be to plant evidence.

Next Lee pointed out some of the evidence that was used to convict him. He said it was:

"A) a old rusted corroded barrette

"B) string of blond hair (from my friends possibly)

"C) feathers from an old pillow that was in my car, that they claim from the victim's glove

"D) Those African American hairs were missing a root and the stem was too short to be tested by the microscope and DNA-PCR. But let them tell it those lil hairs they say came from me."

As already pointed out, those African American hairs found on the victim could not be proven to be from Lee, but with the newer DNA tests it could be proven whether they were from someone maternally related to Lee.

Lee went on to point out that the prosecutor could never put him and the victim together. He said, "AND WHEN YOU CAN NOT PLACE US TOGETHR THEN THAT MEANS THAT I could not have killed her!"

Lee concluded his letter by saying, "This was good therapy for me, I got a lot off my shoulder. Thanks:" He then added a P.S. saying he would like to hear from me again. He did…for thirteen years.

A couple weeks after Mr. Rademacher wrote his first article, on April 14 he wrote a follow-up article telling about some of the responses he had received. Some had questioned why he would want to "stir up old wounds." He said he had two reasons to believe it was the right thing to do. He stated, "One reason relates to readers who refuse to forget a little girl who affected the very way in which they grew up. And the other revolves around men, women, and children who only now are telling their stories publicly."

One of the witnesses who wrote in was Jim Bonnema. He is quoted as saying, "With Linda in the back seat of his car, Albert Lee almost ran me off the road, a block from Mulick Park School. I've lived for thirty years thinking that, instead of moving over and getting out of his way, WHAT IF I had hit him, stopping him from fleeing…Linda might be alive today. I've never gotten past that. That's been heavy for a long time." Notice that he assumed that Lee was the one who almost ran him off the road.

Someone deliberately targeted Linda Vanderveen

One response that is significant was from the mother of the boy who was scheduled to work at that corner that day. He had been sick, and Linda took his place. She said, "To this day, my forty-year-old son recalls with horror how bad he felt, that she had been there and not him." The reason this is important is because it appears that someone knew that Linda Vanderveen was going to be there at that time. Who would have known that? Obviously, someone scheduled the crossing guards, and only certain people would have known who would be where at that time. It is highly unlikely that this was a random killing. Someone deliberately targeted Linda Vanderveen.

One of the main witnesses was Jack Hill. He was the first to see the abductor, and he talked with him. Unfortunately, he passed away five months before Mr. Rademacher wrote his article. His daughter Kim Gill responded to the article. She said that her father carried to his grave the vision of "Linda waving her arms at him (from) the back seat of Lee's car." As pointed out earlier, this shows that the car was not Lee's car since he had tinted windows. She went on to say, "One of his biggest regrets was that he was unable to save Linda." She also indicated that her parents visited Linda's grave often.

Mr. Rademacher stated that one of the longest responses he received was from Pete Walsh, who was one of the defense attorneys who represented Lee at his first trial. Even though his response was long, the only quote that was stated in the article was, "Honest to God, I never thought his guilt was proven beyond a reasonable doubt."

It would be interesting to know what else Mr. Walsh said in his message to Mr. Rademacher. Of course, we would expect a defense attorney to say his client was innocent, just as we would expect a prosecutor to say he knows the defendant is guilty. Mr. Forsyth was given an opportunity to state his evidence, but we are not told what Mr. Walsh said in support of his claim of innocence.

William Murphy was the main defense attorney at the first trial, but he was not supposed to comment publicly on the case because he was at that time a state appellate court judge. He did say though, "We'd be awakened during the middle of the night, and (callers) asked, 'How could you possibly represent somebody like (Lee)'" Of course it was his job to represent him. A defense attorney is required by law to act in the best interest of his client. It should also be pointed out that at the time Lee had not yet been found guilty, and therefore, he should have been presumed innocent. A man accused of a crime has a right to a trial and an attorney who will do his best to defend him. Perhaps these anonymous callers could explain why they think a man accused of a crime should not have a lawyer.

Next the retired Grand Rapids police officers Tom Rozema and Steve Kuiper were mentioned because they had been the lead investigators. Mr. Rozema was quoted as saying, "There is no doubt (Lee) killed her, and any new DNA tests would only confirm that." How does he know what a new test would show until the test is run? Remember that the first tests on the hair found in Lee's car proved conclusively that the hair was not from the victim. Those tests were ignored, and the only test that was later mentioned was the PCR test, which cannot identify a person; it can only eliminate a person. All we learn from the PCR test is that Linda Vanderveen is one of several million people who could have provided those hairs. Saying that a DNA test that has not been run would prove a person guilty is a rather weak argument. If Mr. Rozema has any real evidence, we would like to hear it. Remember that the Grand Rapids police were suspected from the beginning because of the death threats Andy Vanderveen had received, and the stated defense at the second trial was that there had been a police conspiracy. Therefore, a statement by a Grand Rapids police officer that there is no doubt about Lee's guilt is meaningless.

Another person who responded was Robert Schuleit, who was a co-worker of Linda's brother David, who died in Montcalm County in 2005. He stated, "David was a tortured soul and we had many dark discussions on his sister's death and the pain incurred by the family. I trust, hope and pray that by your article, this person will never be released. The cost has been too great." His prayer was answered because Lee was never released. He died in custody. However, it would have been better if the guilty parties had been penalized instead of an innocent man.

After receiving the letter Lee sent in response to my letter, I sent another email to Mr. Rademacher. Several times I received a reply, but every time the contents of the email were blank. I kept sending an answer back saying I really wanted to know what it was that he was trying to tell me. Finally, while I was away, my son received a phone call that was supposedly from Mr. Rademacher. The caller indicated that he was not interested in looking into the matter any further. This seemed strange, but it was only the first of many indications that someone didn't want word to get out about Lee's case.

Chapter 14 – The Visits

In July, Lee sent me another letter. I had asked him several questions. He said that he did not want to answer in a letter because he knew that all letters and telephone calls are monitored, and some might misuse the information. In his letter he said, "You know I can sort of like need a friend. I haven't talk, wrote or visit anyone in 25 yrs. That's when my brothers passed away. So your writing to me (made me) realize how lonely I was. I had just shut everyone out. You look on this stamp that I found in my bag, I purchase it in April and just now using it, nobody to write. I did not have any money to buy one, but I remember I had a stamp somewhere in this junk… bear with me, I haven't had someone willing to write to me in over 25 close to 30 years, so I don't know what to say or how to say it."

He then asked if I could get him an NFL football schedule. Through the years he made that request several times, and several times I printed off a schedule and sent it to him. Then he asked if I would be interested in visiting him. He explained that I would have to fill out a visiting form. After receiving his letter I sent him five dollars because I wanted him to be able to write to me.

In August Lee wrote again and sent a visitor application. In the letter he said, "As for Mr. Rademacher I wouldn't put to(o) much faith in him, the man lives there, work's there…(there would be trouble) I know because of what they did to my first lawyers…Rademacher did not print all that I said, but his boss and the prosecutor probably edited before being printed? Because if I was any where else they would not find me guilty! Which is why I was denied a change of venue during both trials? The people in that city are unbelievable, to find me guilty when the evidence says I'm not, unbelievable!"

Later in the letter he said, “Five years ago I put $20.00 down and never got to use it, send me your phone number and I’ll (call) you and pay for it. I can’t get the money back! I can only use it on phone calls. So I might as well call you?” I did send him my phone number, and he tried calling me a couple of times, but he never did get to talk on the phone. There will be more on that later.

A few days later I received another letter telling why there was a delay in getting the application to me. First the letter was too heavy. Then he mistakenly put the wrong city on the address. It finally got to me, and I filled out the application and sent it in. A few days later I received a letter back from the Michigan Department of Corrections. They rejected my application because they said I was not on Lee’s visitor list.

Lee was put in segregation from August 30 until September 28. He didn’t want to write while there because he knew some guards “have the tendency to read your mail, and some time choose not to mail your letter.” When he did write, he said, “I’ve already put you on the visitor list, so you can come up any time you feel like it! I tried to call you, but the operator say that’s not a valid number every time I dial it. Your number is ***-***-**** right? I know it work that one time, it won’t now! I was calling to see if you wanted to add any one else to ride along with you. If you do let me know or they won’t let them in if they are not on the list. That was in case you wanted to bring your family or a friend etc.” He ended his letter by saying, “Well I’ll end this here so we will have something to talk about when you get here. But before you do, what is up with the phone number, did you change it? Any way that one time we did talk, it felt good to hear another person voice.”

We did not change our number, and he did have the correct number. The person he talked to that one time was not me. Obviously, someone intercepted the call and pretended to be me. Again we see the deceitfulness of some in the justice system. Somebody didn’t want Lee to talk to me.

In October I finally did visit Lee at the Michigan Reformatory in Ionia. One of the first things he mentioned was how nice it was talking to me on the phone. I told him he had never talked to me on the phone. He thought he did. I told him I certainly would know if he had talked with me, but he definitely had not. We checked the number and verified that he had the right number. I asked what this person on the phone had said to him. He didn't seem to have any definite information. As it turned out, I never did speak with him on the phone, but we did correspond through mail and JPay, and I did visit him several times. One of the first questions I asked him was whether he chose the seat where we were sitting. The reason I asked that was because I had seen so much evidence of deceit on the part of the justice system, and I wondered if they might be spying on us. We had a nice visit, and on November 1 he sent a letter telling how nice it was having a visit after so many years.

In the letter he said, "It had been a while since I was out on a visit. That's the closest thing I felt in a long while to being a part of society. A whole lot of heaviness is lifted off your shoulders that you did not know was there.

In here, you always got to walk around as if you got a chip on your shoulder, never letting your guard down.

But to sit out there for a lil while, relax, not worrying and having a peaceful good conversation felt good, no pressure. Hey, it sure was easy to talk to you, you wasn't argumentive (sic), you listen and answer well. I really felt comfortable w/you."

He then went on to ask if I could check on a nun who had visited him while he was in the Kent County jail. I did and found a phone number. If still living, she would have been about 70 at that time. He also said that his religion was Moslem. However, in his later letters he closed them with "Your Brother in Christ." Normally, a Moslem would not say something like that. Then he asked me to check the newspapers from the 1980's and 1990's to read what the papers said about his case. He also wanted to know what I could learn about Billy Mansfield, Jr. I did as he suggested, and that is how I obtained much of the information presented earlier.

Shortly after writing to me after our first visit Lee was transferred to the St. Louis Correctional Facility in St. Louis, Michigan. In fact, it seemed like nearly every time I visited him he was transferred. There was never any explanation why he was transferred. I had to wonder if they were just trying to make it hard for me to visit. If that was their intent, it backfired on this occasion. Anyone can go on the Offender Tracking Information System (OTIS) and find where a prisoner is incarcerated. I checked him out and found where he was. As it turned out, I had been a volunteer at the Mid-Michigan Correctional Facility in St. Louis for many years. It is right next to the St. Louis Correctional Facility. I could just go early to St. Louis to visit Lee and then go to our weekly counseling program at Mid-Michigan.

After our first visit there I received a Christmas card and letter from Lee dated 12-24-09. He said, "Hey, you truly surprise me this time? I did not know who was visiting me.

"Well this is closer and maybe you can stop by a lil more, when you are in the neighborhood.

"I enjoyed the visit. But I was left feeling sorry for the Vanderveens.

"For them to expire so quickly in life. When life is to live as long as you can, and to reproduce your DNA thru generation after generation. And for the whole family to expire so quickly makes you question divine intervention (was it because they lied about the barrette, knowing it was not the victim's).

"Yet, it put a innocent man in prison, but the prosecutor who told the most lies, I imagine he has a heavy burden to knowing a innocent man sits in prison. So it must have been a divine destiny that cause all of this to happen.

"However, this whole experience has me questioning life and the things that happen in one's life.

"True, I could carry and handle a heavy burden, but its so strange the Creator would have a innocent carry burden of one guilty's load.

"It seems he would want to (sic) guilty to bear its own burden, unless the guilty had another manifestation destination.

"But I knew the prosecutor was up to no good when he made a deal with the devil "Billy Mansfield" it cost 4 innocent females their life where their children grew up without a mother and grandmother.

"The prosecutor made another deal with Satan when he had the police hypnotize the witnesses not once but twice.

"The prosecutor made another deal with Lucifer when the DNA-PCR came back and it was not the victim's hair, but the 2nd test claims she is one out of 5 % of a large segment of G.R. population with blond hair. The carbon paper is yours to read.

"Well I close for now, but Merry Christmas and a Happy New Year to you and all those you love. Take Care.

"Your Brother In Christ Love. Al"

The carbon paper Lee referred to had information on two of the jurors from the second trial that should not have been on the jury. It said, "Jurors - James Bouwhuis - OUIL – Operating Under Influence of Liquor. Retrial was schedule for 9??? A.M on 2-21-91. He work at Holland Community Hospital. His attorney was Gaylord Cardinal. He was in 61st Dist. Court. He was arrested before on this.

Anna Wade. Her daughter name is Janelle Cramp charge with a knife assault on boyfriend name Anthony Harden. PreLim set for 2-11-91at 3 o'clock

Find out what happened after they went to court, what was the final decision. Any deal made."

I did not follow through on Lee's request for more information on these two jurors, but it is obvious that people facing charges from the prosecutor do not belong on any jury.

Lee was at St. Louis for nearly three years, and I visited him a few times while he was there. He wrote to me about every other month during that time.

On March 20, 2010 he wrote a short letter. In it he mentioned the drawing of the abductor that was published in the Grand Rapids Press. He said, "That composite drawing is the second drawing and you can see the face structure is different, mine is round and oval shape and drawing is narrow and pointed chin. I'll send you the first drawing, it looks nothing like me either.

Once again thanks, I just finished filling out the papers for the University of Michigan Innocence Clinic, and I will be mailing it to them and let you know what happens."

As it turned out, nothing happened with his request for assistance from the Innocence Clinic. They have received thousands of requests, and only a very few cases are taken.

Lee wrote again April 11, 2010. He had tried sending me some information on his case. In his letter he wrote, "Man, I'm truly sorry about getting this package out to you. Makes me feel like you do, to the point of questioning everything; got me feeling paranoid. I've tried to mail this to you several times and each time it comes back, with some lame excuse, wrong zip code, return to sender, NSF (Non-Sufficient Funds).

Every time, I try to mail this, it's like someone doesn't won't (want) you to receive it."

He went on to ask for a newspaper article from the Grand Rapids Press. He said, "since you are looking things up in the library that's on microfilm, could you look up this starting with the date, August 19, 1979 it's a article about all the victims in that area of Grand Rapids. They were happening before I moved there and while I was in the County Jail and after I was convicted of a crime I did not do."

I did find the article in question, and it was true that there had been several victims in the Grand Rapids area. Lee clearly had nothing to do with any of those cases. If anyone believes Lee was the true killer of Linda Vanderveen, it is clear that this was an inexplicable one-time offense. That is in spite of the prosecutor's feeble attempt to present evidence of similar acts at the second trial.

It was a while before I wrote to Lee. When I did, he sent back a reply on May 16, 2010. He indicated that he was relieved to hear from me since it had been a while. He said that he didn't like to be kept in the dark. He said his relatives had ceased to write to him and that concerned him. By 2010 most of his family were deceased. In fact, when he was sentenced in 1991 both his parents and seven of his siblings were listed as deceased. In the letter he also said, "I always thought it was the police that did this, based on one of them being fired and losing a family member that was terminal ill, and they could not afford the medical expenses? I don't know, that was just a guess, because when they say a black man do anything of this nature, the city, community and the police department go hog wild and be blinded by who really did this?" As Lee said, this was just a guess, but he was not the only one who suspected that the police were behind the murder. That would explain why they were so determined to frame someone for the crime. From the very beginning of the case the police were suspected. It was reported that they did a diligent search to find someone who may have had a grudge against Andy Vanderveen. They claimed that they could not find anyone, but it was the police investigating the police. An independent investigation may have come to a different conclusion.

Lee wrote again June 2, 2010. I had visited him, and he thanked me for the visit. He also thanked me for a newspaper clipping I had gotten for him. He used it in his request for a pardon from the governor. His letter ended, "I'm hoping everything is alright with you and everyone, so take care and I'll look for you when you can make it again. You really has made a difference in my life, for I was feeling bitter towards everything and everyone. Thanks for letting me feel human again, during those visit. Once again Thanks:"

He wrote again June 20. He said he was still working on his request for a pardon or commutation. For those who may not be acquainted with the difference, a pardon is forgiveness for a crime and is often granted after a person has served his time. A commutation is a reduction, in full or in part, of a sentence. A person who is pardoned is then considered not guilty, but a person whose sentence is commuted is still considered guilty. In Lee's letter he said, "It's not about guilt or innocence, it's about forgiveness and remorse." This is a common problem in our justice system. It seems that those in the system cannot comprehend that a person may be innocent. Their reasoning is that they cannot begin a prisoner's rehabilitation until he accepts responsibility for his actions. There may be some legitimacy to that claim if the prisoner is guilty, but a person is not responsible for something he did not do. Apparently, the thinking is that if a person were sent to prison for something he didn't do, all he would need to do would be to file an appeal, and the injustice would be corrected. Albert Lee's case is one of the best examples of the futility of filing appeals. He sought justice from our justice system for over 40 years and died in custody without ever getting justice. In his letter Lee also said that he had not heard from the University of Michigan innocence clinic. With the thousands of requests they receive, there is little hope for any one person getting help.

It was a while before I heard from Lee again, but I visited him again later in the year. After our visit he wrote again on December 11, 2010. As always he indicated how much he appreciated the visit. He suggested I contact his attorney for his second trial as well as Billy Mansfield Jr., who was in prison in California. At our visit I had mentioned the book "Actual Innocence" by Barry Scheck, Peter Neufeld, and Jim Dwyer. This is one of the best books on the subject of justice for the innocent, and it was written by some of the best experts on the issue. They started the Innocence Project and have obtained exonerations for hundreds of prisoners. I also mentioned a couple books about Billy Mansfield Jr. I helped him get those books, and on December 20 he wrote, "I got your letter and the books. Man, thanks! I'm going to read them over and over. I was quite surprise to see the book about Mansfield….Thanks for everything Jake, I was at my lowest and in my darkest hour sometime…you inspire me, you lift me up, my days are not so bad, not so lonely.

"Once again thanks, may God bless you and your loved ones. I actually feel somewhat human, and because I'm innocent of this crime, there was a time I was angry at those who convicted me of this.

"But because of you, I'm beginning to not feel so untrust worthy. Man, I had truly turn myself off to those who claim to have authority.

> *I was at my lowest and in my darkest hour…*

"But because of you I can forgive but not forget maybe in time I will forget."

Lee tried to send me a Christmas card, but he experienced a delay. On January 16, 2011 he wrote, "Sorry, it has taken me so long to write back. Even though it is the system (M.D.O.C) finding ways to return my mail – Just so I couldn't send out my Christmas cards on time.

"It's their way of denying one the enjoyment of Christmas. Nonetheless, I will still mail it to you.

"I did receive the books. And I consider them my Christmas present from you.

"Wow, I did not know Mansfield was doing all of that. What gets me? Is that the Michigan prosecutors knew as well as the Florida prosecutors.

"The Mich. Prosecutor knew this guy was an opportunist. And the put him in the cell w/ me to lie.

"But that lie cost them the life of four innocent women. How do they live w/themselves.

"Knowing that they participated in four murders, because had they not accept Mansfield's lie, four women would be alive today. And two of the women were mothers. And their children had to grow up w/out their mother.

"We realize that these people w/ authority were German, Dutch and Hollanders, but to put a innocent man in prison, simply because they say it was a black man is a bad example for humanity."

On February 12, 2011, Lee wrote again. In his letter he said, "Sorry I haven't written sooner. But it is the institution, and the way they find ways to detain your mail, whether coming in, or going out…

"Nonetheless, after reading these two books. This scenario, keeps pop(p)ing up in my head. And although you and I talk about this before. To contact the author and see if he will do a book on, me or his publishing company; use the money to get an attorney and whats left donate it to you for being there when I needed a friend.

"Plus, if I beat this case, I'll sue for false arrest and, prob(ably) settle for millions, which I will also donate a million to you. Thi(s) is what I been thinking lately, can't get it out of my head.

"You can say that I'm a male victim of Mansfield's scheme, to plot to free himself from the judicial system to continue his murdering ways…surely that should get their attention. I sure wish you could contact that publisher to contact that author. What do you think? Give it some thought and let me know?"

I did not contact the author or publisher as he suggested. Lee never did get justice, but if he had, according to the law he was entitled to $50,000 for each year he was imprisoned unjustly. Since he was falsely imprisoned for 43 and a half years, that comes to $2,175,000.

Lee wrote again April 13, 2011. He didn't give any more information about his case, but he did tell about some of his family who died from cancer. Most of his siblings died in their forties. He died nine days after his 71st birthday. He believed that he lived longer than the rest of his family because he refused chemotherapy. He did die from prostate cancer that spread to his bone morrow and then to his brain, but his siblings all died within three months of starting chemotherapy.

I visited Lee again in August of 2011. Afterwards he wrote to me and asked again if I could locate Billy Mansfield Jr. I did, and I sent the information to him. Since then Mansfield has been moved to another prison, and he has been denied parole several times. In April, 2022 he voluntarily waived his right to another parole hearing for three years.

In late August we purchased our local newspaper, the *Lakeview Area News*. It had been shut down for about a month. The first issue under our ownership was September 15, 2011. When I asked Lee if he would like a subscription, he replied, "Oh man, wow, you have access to print what you want! Wow, I'm flabbergasted, freedom of speech and press. Now that's power. Thats what I'm talking about! You are the man. You can make or breake (sic) a politician with power of speech and press.

"Yes, Yes Oh God Yes! I would love to get a subscription. You can send it, there won't be any problem. I'll even try to get some of the inmates here to subscribe…"

He did try to get other inmates to subscribe, but none did. As time went on we gave free subscriptions to several prisoners that requested them. His claim that I could make or break politicians was a bit exaggerated, but we have been able to have some influence. There will be more on that later.

Lee wrote again on October 12, 2011. I had suggested the book *The Innocent Man* by John Grisham. In his letter Lee said, "I read it and it made me think of my own situation. That I'm not the only one that get accused of a crime that you are innocent of!

"The story was heart rendering and I felt sad for Ronald Keith Williamson. But that letter he wrote on page 351 is exactly the way I feel. 'What was the reason for my birth?'"

He then philosophized about the meaning of life and the need for sacrifice. He questioned if God had allowed the injustice in his life because God wanted him to sacrifice.

Later in the letter Lee said, "I for one know, it has nothing to do with the victim, for I've never seen the victim. I don't know, she could be alive, I know this, I could never kill a child even if I was in a war, less known during peace time. That's not me..."

In December Lee sent a Christmas card, and I was able to visit him once. He sent a letter December 31, 2011. In it he said he really enjoyed the visit. He also said, "The newspaper really makes a difference in my life. Even though I'm not from there it is still informing, helps my vocabulary and lets me share in someone else accomplishments. I truly enjoyed reading them."

He wrote again in March and August. In his August 5, 2012 letter he said that he had written earlier but the letter had come back to him. He enclosed the earlier letter. There didn't seem to be any reason that it was not sent. In it he said that he had put my wife's name on his visitor list. Then in September he wrote again. He said, "I'm so sorry that (my wife) was denied a visit. But I got with 'em and showed them my receipt of when I sent it in (Visiting List). Which was on 5-3-12 the month of May. That's the only reason they claim... that (my wife) was not on the visiting list. When I showed them that she was, you know what they claim next, you won't believe this. Oh you have too many people listed, you are only allowed 20 and she made 21. I couldn't believe it. You'll turn someone down because of a quota. That is ridiculous. So now I'am writing a letter to the warden expressing my dislike and the inconvenience of wasting gas, time, babysitting pay, etc. They still should have let her in. Before you and (my wife) drive all the way call first and see if she will be allowed in."

Shortly after Lee sent the September letter I went to visit him again, but I was told that he had been transferred. While I was talking to the guard at the front desk, I asked about Lee's visitor list. The guard said that there were only two people on the list. There was just me and one woman who was a relative. I mentioned that we had been told that there were 20 people on the list. The guard suggested that someone may have misread the 2 as a 20. That seems doubtful. It was obvious that there were not 20 people visiting him. I was the only one who visited him, and that was not often. It certainly looked like someone didn't want Lee to have visits. It is also curious that he was transferred shortly after he said he was going to make a complaint to the warden. We have a copy of my wife's visiting application. She signed it August 24, 2012, and it was received August 30, 2012. The application was denied by the warden, and the stated reason was that she was not on the list. As Lee had pointed out, he put her on his visitor list back in May.

When Lee wrote again, we found that he had been transferred to Oaks Correctional Facility in Manistee, Michigan. He sent a letter on October 30, 2012. In it he said, "Say hello to (my wife) for me. I know she's pretty angry at me, but it's not my doing. I turned in her name a long time ago and I don't understand why they denied her.

"Nonetheless, I've turned in her name again at this place hopefully she won't get denied here. I'm even sending a slip of the visiting list, just to show her what it looks like that supposed to be on file. I have no reason to deny her.

"I just turn in another one with the ARUS and he's taking it up front to be process. So she should be able to visit me next time.

"I was so surprised when they told me to pack up I'm riding out. I hated to leave but I had been there to(o) long, it was nothing but young children there and I'm getting to(o) old."

Actually, my wife was not angry with Lee. It was obvious that he was not the problem. It was the justice system. Also, I was not surprised that Lee was transferred. It is quite common for a prison to transfer an inmate if he makes a complaint. The reasoning is that he is a troublemaker, and the solution is to remove him. If he truly is a troublemaker, transferring him just passes the problem to someone else. If he has a legitimate complaint, it should be dealt with properly instead of penalizing him for making a complaint.

In Lee's letter of December 29, 2012 he said, "Again, I ask about (my wife) visiting and it looks like they will not put her on until May. I ask why and they would not give me an answer, all they would say, is be happy she's allowed to visit in May." We later heard that their excuse was that they update the visiting lists every six months, and May would be the next time for the update. Why couldn't they just tell him that? Before May he was transferred again. This time he was sent to Kinross Correctional Facility in Kincheloe in the Upper Peninsula. We had to wonder if he was sent there just to make it harder for us to visit him. Of course, no explanation was given for the transfer. He was there for about three years. We tried to visit once when we were going through the Upper Peninsula, but there was road construction, and we ran out of time.

Even though we were not able to visit, we continued to correspond. In Lee's letter of May 24, 2013 he said, "What I want (to) share w/u is I WAS TRYING TO GET THE Courts to use the mit in this case; it is supposed to be better than the PCR (Polymearse Chain Reaction) test.

"The victim's hair and the mom's hair should be the same and by testing the mom's hair along with the sample evidence hai(r) and the victim's hair to see if they all match?

"But they refuse because the PCR test says that is not the victim's hair, that she falls into a 5% blond population that has that type of hair.

"When I read that it made me think about how even DNA prove my innocence, and they still will not let me go, hypnosis and the fact that Mansfield is now saying he lied on me to get his freedom. The prosecutor just don't want to look bad after all these years of having convict the wrong person.

"Also, the people that own the car before I purchase it; had two blond haired daughters. Who the hair could have come from, also one of these daughters could have lost the corroded barrette.

"The victim's mom testified, she bought the barrettes in October for Xmas present. The victim did not get them until the 25th of December of 1979 (sic). And by February 12, 1979, that the barrette that was allegedly found in my car was allegedly said to belong to the victim. This type of evidence the prosecutor would not let the jury hear or be a part of the trial. As you can interpret the system is not fair.

"The prosecutor ask for the second test and it said the victim's hair falls in a 5% population of blond hair people that has the same hair as the evidence hair sample. This was just a lot of bull to coverup the truth, the hair does not belong to the victim."

In Lee's letter of October 1, 2013 he told of some of his misfortunes in life. I had mentioned that my wife had some work done on her teeth. Lee wrote, "I lost my gold tooth. The dentist was fondling and accidentally pull out a tooth next to my gold cap tooth, it weaken and fell out weeks later.

"I had placed my gold cap tooth in a sewing kit, planning to have put back in, however, they do a major shakedown of cells, this prison guard Murdock stole my tooth, lie and say he did not. I file grievance and they claim 'Oh our guards will not do that!' So reimbursement they will not do.

"This chump Murdock, walks around laughing and saying 'yep, I wonder how much one can get melting down a real, heavy gold tooth.

"My parents had purchase that tooth as a xmas present back in 64…I was 13 yrs old, gold was real then and heavy."

Later in the letter he went on to say, "I know what its like to come from a big family, there is much love there, even more so when you are poor, because you really get to bond together.

"I had three brothers Doug, James and Eugene…they are all dead now…Doug had a stomach ulcer which became cancerous, James died of throat cancer (thyroid) and Eugene died of a sawed-off-double barrel shotgun.

"I had five sisters, Carolyn died of breast cancer, Marcil got rape by a gang of white guys, she lost her mind and died of that, she was a park ranger in Yellowstone. Mary has her leg amputated do (sic) to diabetes. My other two sisters Imogene and Jean are very old and is suffering with breast cancer.

"My feancee (sic) at the time of this mistaken identity for this crime, died of breast cancer, her name is Vivian. Cancer is no joke. I suffer with prostate cancer, but my arthritis is what really is killing me and there is no cure for bones and joints depreciation, I think the prostate is what is spreading.

"Sometime getting up takes 30 minutes to get the joints working. The pain is excruciating Wow, it hurts, this stiffness.

"Speaking of pain, I got to go get my mediation, I'll write more later, my fingers is stiffing on me."

It is interesting to compare Lee's report on his siblings with the report of the court when he was sentenced. The court record lists seven siblings and says they are all deceased. First it lists James age 46 and Eugene age 44. Then it lists Jane Brownloo age 43, who seems to be the same as Jean. She is listed as deceased, but Lee's letter seems to indicate that she was still alive in 2013. Next the court record lists Emma Jean Whitley age 42. She seems to be the same as Imogene, and again Lee's letter seems to indicate she was still alive at that time. Then the court record lists Marcil as a brother age 40. Lee clearly says Marcil was a sister. Lastly, the court record lists Caroline DuVall age 38 and Mary Lee age 37. Both brothers listed are said to be from Battle Creek and all the sisters are listed as having Houston, Texas as the last known address. Lee's brother Doug is not listed in the court record. The question that naturally arises here is why there are so many discrepancies between the court record and Lee's letter. Presumably Lee knew his siblings. One thing we can conclude is that something is not necessarily true just because it is in an official record.

July 7, 2014 Lee wrote to me and requested that I try to get some court papers he needed to try to get his case back in court. He said, "The problem is the circuit judge that I'm under refuse to give the papers to me. Because he states that they gave them to me once as a indigent defendant. And he will not do it again!

"Now, as a member of the public and a citizen of the community. Those papers can be gooten (sic) by anyone because the case is for the public…

"They cannot deny a citizen or a member of the public, who wants to know about the trial of Albert Lee III…

"Enclosed is a letter that I typed for you to mail in or if you are in G.R. (Grand Rapids) you can stop by the courthouse, plus, you being a newspaperman, I doubt if you'll have any problems.

"The reason for needing those papers, is to try and get my case back in court again! Who knows the third time, may be the winner.

"The ones I had got lost during a transfer. But I really need them!"

Later in his letter Lee said, "You know I use to think, that if a person was convicted of a crime, that they had something to do with it? I don't anymore.

"People can actually be convicted for a crime that they had no involvement in. You can be wrongly arrested, wrongly convicted. This can happen to anyone, for it happened to me!"

Lee was correct. His case is one of the best examples of a man being convicted of a crime when he had nothing whatever to do with it. He had no connection of any kind with anyone related to the case.

The papers Lee wanted were the following: 1990 felony warrant, felony complaint, 1990 arraignment, 1990 indictment/information, 1991 verdict form with signature of foreman, 1990 motion for direct verdict, 1990 motion for judgment notwithstanding verdict, 1990 motion for a new trial for the case of People vs Albert Lee, LCN-7924278-FC.

I emailed the request for the records to Mary Hollinrake at the Kent County Courthouse on September 12, 2014. She emailed back the same day saying, "Circuit Court records are not subject to FOIA. Most of the records in a court file are already public. Our court clerk's staff will let you know the cost of the records requested and if they are available to you."

On September 16, 2014 Hilary Arthur of the Kent County clerk staff emailed me the following message, "I have searched the record in this case for the documents that you request, listed below in your email. The record search shows that no such documents or pleadings were filed in this case."

This raises the question of whether the purpose of a court clerk is to keep court records. If not, then what is the purpose? This was a major court case. Why is there no record? If no record exists of Lee's conviction, then maybe he should be released since there is no evidence he was convicted of anything. Once again we see that Lee was prevented from obtaining what he needed to further his case.

September 26, 2014 Lee wrote again. In his letter he requested that I obtain three documents. They were the 1991 felony complaint, 1991 felony arrest warrant and 1991 felony information. He said they only cost a dollar a piece, and they are supposed to be on microfilm with the clerk of the court, either in the 61st District Court or the 17th Judicial Circuit Court. Unfortunately, I did not get the documents.

I didn't hear from Lee again for a while. He had been in the hospital for some blood clots. When he wrote again in October, 2015, he had been transferred to Chippewa Correctional Facility, which was also in Kincheloe. In his letter he told how painful the blood clots had been, and he said he would have to wear a catheter the rest of his life.

Later he was transferred to Macomb Correctional Facility near New Haven, which is a little north of Detroit. He wrote on June 6, 2016. In his letter he mentioned that he needed to file a pardon or commutation with the governor. He also said he hoped my wife and I could visit him that summer. We did eventually get to visit him there, but it would take nearly two years before that happened. There will be more on that later.

Lee wrote again in October, 2016 and then on January 1, 2017. I had sent him an article about the State of Michigan giving exonerated prisoners $50,000 for each year of incarceration. He thanked me for the article and said he would not mention any more about the new bills since I was already familiar with them. He then went on to say, “What I will do is write them speaking on the great thing this House Bill will do, its not about the money, its more about the awareness of people like me, innocent, but doing time because of my skin color.

“Which is so wrong. But hate because you are different is even more devastating. I never dream that because of my skin color people could hate to the point that my life…a life that has not harm another life, and only wanted all life to enjoy there inalienable rights to life, that my life because of a color, that is different from the majority of light, white color people in the world, would be so devalue that it doesn’t matter, doesn’t matter.

“Doesn’t matter if it rots in prison away from God’s beauty. Doesn’t matter if its shot down in the streets, or ran over by a car, drag down the road, or hanging from a tree or set on fire, and it was only done because of the color of their skin. That is deep and mind boggling, huh.

“But I’ve learn not to let it become me, because the hate will drive you crazy. I don’t know how those that do hate, can live with themselves.

“If I raise my voice at a person, my conscience eats me up…I could never take the life of another, which is why I did everything in my power to (get out of) the draft during the Viet Nam War…Maybe I should have went, I probably would have lost my life and would never had to go thru this."

I responded to Lee's letter, and on January 22, 2017, he wrote back again. In his letter he said, "I truly enjoyed the article you did on the House Bill. Something needs to be done about life and natural life without possibility of parole.

"No one should be in prison after 30 yrs. Everyone, should be given a chance to live in society again and if he/she misuse that chance after doing 30 years. Then, that's when he/she lives the rest of their life in prison.

"I had never been in trouble with the law on a serious felony. I did not do this crime or know anything about it.

"And to take away my youth, my life for a crime that you hypnotize people to lie on me, DNA proves the blond hair in my car did not belong to the victim, I pass the polygraph test that I did not commit this crime, the jailhouse informant you use to lie on me wants to recant his story, not any of the circumstantial evidence link me to this crime.

"I've done 37 years in prison, and you still will not release a innocent man…simply because of his color. No way would they have done this to a white man."

Actually, there are a lot of white men in prison for crimes they did not commit, but it is true that Blacks are more likely to be convicted than Whites with the same amount of evidence.

Chapter 15 – The Visit with the Lieutenant Governor

In late 2016, I met with James Lower, who had recently been elected as our state representative. I had asked for a half hour of his time to address my concern for justice for the innocent. He listened to me for two hours. He asked what could be done legislatively to help with the problem. Since he was about to begin four years as our representative in the state legislature, this was an appropriate question. I told him that there needed to be more accountability for lawyers and especially for prosecutors. When a prosecutor deliberately breaks the law to pervert justice, there are no consequences. If he is sued, the court rules that a prosecutor has absolute immunity. No one should have absolute immunity. More accountability for prosecutors would not solve all the problems with innocent people being sent to prison, but it would help a great deal since the main reason for this injustice is what is called "official misconduct." Close to 70 percent of cases of innocent people in prison are there because some in our justice system have deliberately perverted justice.

After presenting my information to Mr. Lower I asked him to set up a meeting for me with Lieutenant Governor Brian Calley. He knew Mr. Calley fairly well since he had headed up his campaign when he was running for the legislature. Mr. Lower was quite diligent in making sure I did get the meeting. A meeting was scheduled for March 6, 2017. On that date I drove to Lansing and went to the capitol building. I told a guard that I had a meeting with Mr. Calley at 9:00 o'clock. He took me to the lieutenant governor's office in the capitol building where I waited a long time. I finally found another guard and told him I was supposed to meet with Mr. Calley at nine. He said the lieutenant governor had another office across the street in the Romney building. I wish someone had mentioned that earlier since that was where we were supposed to meet. By that time it was too late for a meeting since Mr. Calley had other appointments.

I talked with his assistant, and she said I should call when I got back home to reschedule. After a few attempts we were able to schedule a meeting for April 11. That meeting was postponed and rescheduled for May 15. That meeting was again rescheduled for May 23.

I finally did get to meet with Mr. Calley. A half hour was allotted for our meeting. The first ten minutes he was talking with someone on the phone, which meant that I only had about 20 minutes to present my information. I told him I wanted to talk about justice for the innocent, and then I briefly told about a number of cases I knew personally. Most of the time I spent on Albert Lee's case because I believed that was the first case that needed attention. I told him that what I needed was one honest, competent police investigator, and I needed to work with him because I knew this case. Mr. Calley listened. When we had to finish because our time was up, he said that we have procedures to deal with such cases. Of course, that is true, but if those procedures worked, I would not have been talking with him. Albert Lee followed the standard procedures for over 40 years and never got justice. I appreciated Mr. Calley meeting with me and listening to me, but I was disappointed he didn't take my advice. If he had, Mr. Lee may have been exonerated before he died. What I proposed was not the least bit dishonest or illegal, and it would have cost almost nothing in time or money.

Chapter 16 - The Later Correspondence

Lee wrote nearly every month in 2017. In his letter of July 9 he referred to my first book. He said, "Man, that is truly beautiful to write a book and have it published. That will be around when one is long gone. A book lives on.

"I wish I could get my life story publish, do you think your publisher is interested? Or how about you write it as the author, something to think about, Let me know if your interested?"

Later in his letter Lee referred to the young people graduating. He said, "Whatever they choose in life, they should make the best of it, and stay away from prison. There is nothing good about one losing his freedom.

"Liberty should never be lost, if I had to do it all over again I would choose death, rather than be in a place like this."

On August 26, 2017, my wife and I drove to Macomb Correctional Facility to visit Lee. It is about a three-hour drive from our home. When we arrived, we were told Lee was not allowed visits. We asked why, but the guard said she could not tell us. In fact, she could not tell us anything. Needless to say, this was very disconcerting. We had not been able to visit for a long time, and we had taken the whole day to drive there. Of course, this was of no concern to the guard or anyone else in the Michigan Department of Corrections. No one had given us any indication that Lee's visits had been stopped. When we returned home, I wrote to Lee and told him that we had tried to visit, but we were told he was not allowed visitors.

On September 21, 2017, Lee wrote back. He explained that he had run out of stamps and had to wait three weeks to get more. In his letter he said, "In prison they don't really wanting you communicating to friends, family members or relatives. They want to treat one as if he's in a concentration camp.

"As for my visit, they were taking for a year simply because a nurse lied and said I wasn't taking my pain medication.

"The pain meds is like a narcotic pill, it's a upper. This nurse who I fell out with lied on me, saying she thinks I'm selling the pill.

"Of course they believe the lie and took my visit for a year. Just to show you she lied, at the time she lied on me, there were cameras showing I was else where, the camera even had the time on it so I could not be in two places at the same time. I was still found guilty and my visit were taking for a year.

"Which started on 6-24-16 to 6-24-17.So when you and (my wife) came on 8-26-17. My visit were suppose to be reinstated.

"Also, if they took the visit, they were suppose to let you all have a non-contact visit, which is behind a glass, talking thru a wall phone, just like they do in the county jail. Nor did they notify me that you all even came to visit.

"I found that out when I got your letter. Now, they claim my visit were not due to be reinstated until Aug. 17, 2017.

"Totally lying, they still have not reinstated my visit. I'll let you know when they do.

"Sorry you had to go thru that, they try hard to discourage people from visiting. But you should suit them.

"You were not on any punishment and should have been allowed a no-contact visit. For they violated you(r) civil rights.

"You spent time, money, bought oil and gas, wear and tear on your car tires. You took a chance on your life, you could have been robbed, car jacked, met a aggressive police officer.

"A lot of bad things could have befallen that trip and they did not reinbust you for anything. which is why you could file a law suit against them.

"I got the NFL football schedule, you sent me. Thanks when I got it …it felt lil as if it was Christmas. Thanks, I truly appreciate it. More than you will ever know."

Lee wrote again on October 1, 2017. He said, "Well, it's the same old crap around here. Anyone with authority all they want to do is pass the responsibility around, no one is held to accountability.

"I still have not been restored my visiting rights. They should have been restored on June 24, 2017.

"That just goes to show you how they do things to tick you off…so they can charge or penalize you for something they are creating.

"I'm truly sorry, knowing that you place yourself at risk to come visit me (car accident) spent your time and gas money to come here and they refuse to give you a visit.

"They were suppose to give you a non-contact visit, if not a contact visit. They were not suppose to deny you both of them.

"And because they did, that gives you grounds for a law suit to reimburst you for the wear & tear of your car, gas money, pain & suffering of mental anguish of not being allowed to see me.

"They were wrong and still is because they have not restored my visit and if I had some money I would file suit myself.

"But I will file a grievance and write the Director again. And if they don't respond I'll write the Governor who's over the Director and prison, because they are not doing their job.

"They are in violation of Policy & Rules that the legislators implemented.

"They were quick to take my visit, how come they are not quick to restore them. And this suppose to be a place that shows you correct behavior, I don't think so."

Lee wrote again on October 21, 2017. He had been in the hospital, and he said that he almost died. The problem was that his prostate, which had cancer, was so enlarged he was not able to urinate. He said he needed another operation, but he said, "The M.D.O.C will not pay for the operation they stop the cancer urologist from doing it, saying that I'm too old. I need that operation.

"Also, that they have already spent enuff money on me…

"So they have been taking care of me, its getting to the point, I'm becoming to(o) expensive to house with my illness...

"I lost my visit do(sic) to substance abuse. They claim I abused my medication. They are guessing, assuming I was not taking my meds but was selling them. I was taking them, the pain is killing me.

"All of that is a lie. When they give you the meds, there is a male officer there, a nurse, a camera, etc.

"The nurse and I was arguing and she lied on me and they took her words over mine and punish me by taking my visit for a year.

"Now, if they would have believe me, nothing would have happen to her. That's unfair in and of itself, but that's what we have to live with in prison."

Later in his letter Lee said, "Like I still need a operation…

"The state (MDOC) doesn't want to pay for it. Which is crazy, they don't want to set me free and don't want to pay for it. So in the mean time I sit here suffering.

"I wouldn't let an animal suffer like this, they would put that animal out of misery. I wish they do something with me.

"Either give me the operation or put me out of my misery. I've lived long enuff, so they will do me a favor either way."

On November 23, 2017, Lee wrote again and wished us a happy Thanksgiving. He said, "Man, I just know (my wife) is probably going to cook you a meal, I can only dream about and imagine the taste.

"I can hardly wait until you write and tell me about it. I really would like to know, because that's how I will eat. fantasizing about food.

"I know it sounds crazy but when you live in a cage and fed process turkey meat that even a dog pass up. What can you do.

"So to hear about the meal will fill me up. There is this question that is circulating, it goes, 'What are you thankful for?'

"I'm thankful, that you and family have shared your life with me. The two of you have given me so much to be thankful for.

"To mention of a few, when I was depress and wanted to take my life. Your simple compassion up lifted me.

"And made me rethink. There were times my cancer had me so ill, and because you cared, gave me strength to care about my pain and suffering not to give up. I'm so thankful that the two of you share your time, moments, your trips, the Lakeview Newspaper with me.

"You have always been there walking with me thru the valley of my darkest hour. And whenever I ask a favor, you don't let me down."

Lee had to stop before finishing the letter because of his pain. He wrote again on December 10, 2017. He explained that he had been in the hospital again for more operations. He said he had to endure the extreme pain because he was allergic to anesthesia. In his letter he said, "Every time I feel sorry for my predicament I just say to myself, someone else is worst off than me. It helps me to give blessing to others when I'm hurting and the hurting isn't so bad after all."

It is a little hard to see how anyone could be much worse off when we consider that he was in prison for a crime he didn't commit with little chance of ever getting justice. He was away from loved ones. He was in nearly constant pain and had to endure repeated operations without anesthetic.

In his letter he mentioned again his desire to have his visits reinstated. Then a few days later he wrote again and asked me to contact the prison to see about getting his visits restored. This had been going on for several months, and it appeared that he was getting no response. On December 25, 2017 I wrote a letter to the warden.

This is what I wrote, "Dear Warden Haas:

"I am writing you regarding my friend Albert Lee (160282), who is a prisoner at your facility. There are three things I would like you to do.

"I would like for you to reinstate his visits. His visits were suspended for one year because of alleged Substance Abuses. The one year is long since over.

"I would like for you to investigate to determine if he was truly guilty of the offenses for which his visits were suspended. He says he is not. I recommend that you speak to him yourself to get his story.

"Mr. Lee says he is being told that he will be denied medical care because they supposedly have spent enough money on him already. As you are aware, the law requires that prisoners receive the same level of medical care as the general public. You may be aware that two prisoners recently died at the G. Robert Cotton Facility because they were denied medical care. I have been informed that attorney Geoffrey Fieger is filing a lawsuit in those cases. I would like you to be sure Mr. Lee is receiving the care he needs.

"Please inform me of your response to these requests so that I may determine what further action I should take. Thank you for your assistance.

"Sincerely,

"Gerald Kinsey"

I did not receive any response to my letter, but shortly after sending it Lee's visits were restored, and he was taken to Lansing for medical care.

Lee wrote again January 29, 2018. Most of his letter told about his operation. He also referred to an article I had written in our paper.

He said, "I also read your article about some people don't appreciate your stand for the innocent. To them everybody is guilty until they go thru the system to see how unfair it is. You hit it right on the nail head with your views. I am really proud of you. Thanks for caring. Thank you, thank you.

“Because those that are innocent needs a voice and the poor needs help, which is why prison are so full of the poor. Its not about guilt or innocence any more. Its about a head count, it’s a business now for careers in law enforcement. I’ve been here long enuff for them to retire and their children take their place Thats a long time, 39 years. Children become adults.”

Lee had forgotten to enclose a copy of the letter that told about his visits being reinstated. He wrote again January 31 with the letter. In his letter he also referred to another article I had written about my grandmother’s Bible.

He said, “Hey, I enjoy the Kinsey Report (sic) about Grandma’s Bible and poem. I can recall when I came to prison… my aunt sent me my Mom’s Bible.

“It was a maroon leather King James Bible with everything in it, even had a zipper and maroon draw string to place where you left off.

“It took (sic) was like a concordance, with maps, questions, dictionary, how to interpret the bible and parables, etc. etc.

“But, the M.D.O.C. lost it or a staff member decided to keep it. Nonetheless I was hurt by their theft, but I figure God will find means to bring the good out of it.

“Maybe, the one who stole it, needed it more than I. And hopefully, its traveling from one soul to the next delivering the word of God, to those in need of uplifting.

“I’m hoping that’s what its doing…”

In his letter of March 29, 2018, Lee apologized for being slow in responding. He said he had been in and out of hospitals. His health was very bad, and he was in nearly constant pain. In his letter he said, “But other than health wise I’m doing okay. Oh yeah, I filed a commutation and Governor Snyder turn down my medical commutation. So I guess I'll have to wait on the next governor to see if I can get some action.

"So I'm feeling pretty low on that, its so crazy…they know I did not do this, and I watch other cases where the guy commit the crime of murder; and they let him go; or a guy get the Innocent Project to win his freedom on DNA.

"And I say ain't that crazy. I've written to them and they said okay but have not gotten back with me. DNA proves my innocence.

"And who sends a person to prison when they do illegal hypnosis…placing post hypnotic suggestion in people head. It's crazy the way they just stole my youth, my life."

Later in Lee's letter he said, "I've been here going on 40 years for a crime I never committed, I can not imagine doing that.

"But hey, I could have been a young black male shot 20 to 40 times for driving behind a wheel of a car, or just walking across the street.

"Sometimes I say to myself, I don't even want to be out there, because of the way society view a black male. I know had I remain out there, I would be dead just like my three brothers and four cousins I grew up with.

"None of them was ever in trouble with the law, they died of natural causes, all except one brother he was killed with a shot gun blast to the chest during a card game (gambling)."

In his letter he also asked how my book was coming along. He said he wanted to read it and asked me to remember him when it was published. It took nearly a year before I was able to get him a copy of it. When he received the book, he said he read through it six times.

In April, we were finally able to visit Lee. On April 25 he sent a message telling how much he enjoyed the visit. As it turned out that was the last time I saw him in person, but we continued to write to each other. In his message he said that he had met a relative of the Vanderveen family in June of 2011 when he was in Oaks

Correctional Facility. He also said he was sending a Mothers' Day card to my wife. He said, "mom's are very special and appreciated. I truly miss my mother. I can relate to lossing (sic) a child I lost two of them, both at birth, one a boy and then a girl by different females."

Lee wrote again June 2, 2018. Once again he expressed his appreciation for my efforts. He said, "I see you are still going strong on those who are wrongfully convicted.

"I truly appreciate your efforts and all those who are in the same situation as I am.

"Without good men like yourself we would be in trouble. The innocent would not stand a chance in life as we know it. I will always be in debt to you."

Later he repeated some of the evidence of his innocence. He said, "Where in my case evidence prove that footprints by assailant were smaller than mine, tireprints did not match my car tireprints, the victim and I could never be put together for a time of death, could never be place at a place where death could have occurred, DNA prove the hair wasn't the victim's hair, witnesses were hypnotize not once but twice to say I look like the guy they saw, fingerprints found on the victim's body were not mine, how many reasonable doubts do they need to say I wasn't the guy who committed this crime?

"Just because of the color of my skin I lose my youth, my life in the pursuit of happiness to please a system that maybe one of there own committed this crime against the city personal manager?

"What a sorry judicial system that exist in Grand Rapids, Michigan. For those in authority know this was wrong and they let it happen and let it continue to happen. When all it should take is one reasonable doubt to show that person may be innocent.

"Well enough of that every now then I have to say those things to keep my sanity or go crazy in here."

Lee and I corresponded through the rest of 2018. On January 22, 2019 Lee wrote again. In his letter he said, "My lack of writing is do to the fact that I and another inmate file a lawsuit against the administration. Well they don't like that.

"So, they took my visits, my penitentiary job, which was passing out games to the wheelchair, handicap guys, my personal property, increase my Level II status to level IV, took the foot pads to my wheelchair and a lot of other stuff.

"They call themselves retaliating against me, creating retaliatory acts to make me miserable, but that won't bother me.

"The lawsuit is about getting a single person cell in Level II, because they only house multiple living cells in Level II. They claim Level IV and Level V have single living cells. So I'm being penalize and punished for it.

"I got another question for you. Like every five (5) years I get to see the parole board. And as you know I know no one else in Michigan except you.

"Well, I was asked by my counselor, if I got a parole where would I go live at. I said I would prefer to be paroled to Houston, Texas.

"They said, here in Michigan, if I had no where to go in Michigan they would place me in a community placement living.

"Well, I did not mention you, but I got to thinking I wouldn't mind being placed in your care. I could live in the barn, work the garden, deliver the papers, maybe even learn how to set the ink for the newspaper, for room and board.

"So let me know if that would be alright with you. I know you probably can not do it, for you already have an exchange student living with you. So that's probably out, it was just a thought.

"Hey, how about the book? Hopefully, it is doing great. I kind of like the concept Rich Man/Poor Man. I can hardly wait to read it, since I love reading your article in the paper 'The Kinsey Retort' anyway."

Later in his letter Lee again mentioned the possibility of being paroled to stay with me. He said, "Nonetheless, if someone contact you about sponsoring me for I know no one else in Michigan. So I did give the newspaper phone number, the one that goes like this 989-352-8146.

"You can always turn it down, it will not take anything from our friendship. Because I know you got a lot to do in keeping the newspaper going."

Lee then told about more trouble he had with the administration. He said they had taken his visits again because they claimed that he had marijuana in his urine. That is hard to believe. As He said, "But I had just gotten my visit back, and you know I would not do that, where will I get it from. I do not have any money to buy it.

"And I know no one who will give it to me for free.

"There reason for doing this is because myself and another inmate file a lawsuit requesting a single man cell in Level II.

"They don't do single man cell living in Level II. They do in Level IV and V.

"So they sent me to Level IV, increasing my status. They took my personal property, because in Level IV you cannot have certain property that you are allowed to have in Level II.

"They took the lil 11.00 dollar penitentiary prison job, my visit, they are just retaliating against me. Plus, they know I see the Parole Board for a lifer review, and doing what they did may make the Parole Board not grant me a parole.

"So you see I'm a lil upset, depress and trying to keep my composer and not do anything stupid.

"Without you to talk to thru writting I probably would have went crazy. But everytime I get to that stage, I just ask myself… What would Jake do in a situation like this.

"And the reality is that you would pick yourself up, dust the dirt off and keep on doing what you do. You would not let them see anger, you would not blame others for your trials and tribulation.

"You would just leave it up to God to take care of your enemies or bring them to the realization that their evil will not trump over goodness.

"So I'm ignoring them in hopes that in the long run, I'll win, where it is good to have patience."

He then mentioned more about his serious health problems. At the end of his letter he mentioned again the possibility of staying with me on parole. He said, "Well take care and let me know how you feel if they were to grant me a parole, could I come and pay for room and board, share my welfare food stamps and disabilities, even work for you.

"Because community placement don't sound to(o) good for me. That would be like I'm still in prison."

On March 29, 2019 Lee wrote, "Well, I think I already mention it to you? The Parole Board turn me down again, enclosed is a copy of what they are saying.

"Yes it hurts, but with you in my life I can manage, even though I'm feeling depress as a headache. Because I'm doing life with parole. Which suppose to be 17 years. And they can parole you.

"I've done 17 yrs twice and some years. This system is totally unfair to me. Considering I've killed no one. And the people that do, they let go., and they come back with another murder case. I do not understand.

"They want me to admit to something I did not do. And I can not. That would eat me up telling a lie to win my freedom, to give in to do them, to lie on myself by admitting to something I did not do.

"Well, I'll end here, my leg swollen on me, my kidneys are hurting, I haven't had a bowel movement, got a blockage. And these people are refusing to take me to a hospital.

"Nonetheless, God is with me, so I'll be alright. Take care will write more next time. I did get the book. Love it. I read it about 6 times now."

As Lee said, he enclosed a copy of his letter from the Michigan Parole Board. Here is what it said, "Dear Mr. Lee:

"Thank you for contacting the Michigan Parole Board. Our records indicate you are currently serving a life sentence for Murder 1st Degree. You are not eligible for parole, but may be considered for reprieve, commutation or pardon as set forth in MCL 791.244. Our records indicate that an Application for Pardon or Commutation was received in our office on October 5, 2017. On January 15, 2018, it was sent to the Governor's office for his consideration. On March 5, 2018, we received a response that the petition was denied. You may reapply in October 2019.

"Further, prisoners serving life sentences are interviewed after serving 10 calendar years of their life sentence. The Parole Board is only required to review each prisoner's file every 5 years thereafter. Subsequent interviews will only be conducted as determined by the Board. Our records indicate you were recently eligible for a 5-year review. A file review was conducted on your case and the Parole Board closed your case in February of 2019 with no interest.

"When the Board reviews a life sentence, the members consider many factors, including but not limited to, how many years have been served, the severity of the crime, whether a death resulted, any physical or psychological injury to the victim, whether the crime is a sexual offense or involved sexually assaultive behavior, any prior convictions and the nature of those convictions, the prisoner's current age, physical and mental health, institutional adjustment and involvement in educational, vocational or therapy programs.

"The Parole Board does encourage you to participate and successfully complete any self-help programming that would be beneficial to you that you can enroll into without a referral. You may want to contact your counselor at the facility for information on self-help/self-enrolling programs that are available to you.

"Again, thank you for your letter.

"Sincerely,

"Michigan Parole Board"

This letter raises several questions.

First, was he eligible for parole or not? The letter said he was not, but he claimed he was because he was not sentenced to life without parole.

Second, the paragraph that tells what the Parole Board considers, suggests that he should have been released.

- It said that they consider the years served. He had been incarcerated for forty years.
- It said they consider whether a death resulted. Generally in a murder case a death does result.
- Was there any physical or psychological injury to the victim? She was killed. Generally death is considered physical injury.
- As to psychological injury, a witness said the victim had a look of terror on her face which he saw through the untinted window of the car the abductor was driving.
- Was the crime a sexual offense? There was no evidence of sexual assault. Billy Mansfield Jr. originally claimed Lee killed the victim while trying to sexually assault her, but he later admitted he lied about his claim. When the judge first sentenced Lee, he tried to imply a sexual motive, but there was no evidence to support the claim.
- What about prior convictions? Lee had no felonies on his record. There were only a few minor misdemeanors.
- What about Lee's age? He was 67.
- What about his physical and mental health? He was dying of cancer, he had diabetes, and he had a serious spinal problem,

which resulted in him being confined to a wheelchair. He was in nearly constant pain. His physical health alone should have been sufficient reason for him to be released.

- What about his institutional adjustment? He didn't need to adjust to the institution; he needed to be released.
- What about involvement in educational, vocational or therapy programs? He was dying. What point could there be to educational or vocational programs? The only therapy he needed was for his serious health problems.

What about the Parole Board's encouragement for him to participate and successfully complete self-help programs that would be beneficial to him? The man was dying. If the Board could suggest a self-help program that would benefit him, he certainly would have welcomed it.

In short, by the Parole Board's own criteria Lee should have been released.

In Lee's letter of July 1, 2019 he said, "Got turn down for a commutation by the Governor.

"Cancer has really been kicking my butt…The cancer went to my bones, and its eating up my bone marrow. I weight 161 lbs from 243 pounds…I look like the walking dead, only worst than they look on T.V.

"And thanks for mentioning me in your paper.

Your help is surmountimous

"As a guy that you know been in prison 40 yrs for a crime he did not commit. Your help is surmountimous, very important.

"No one else has even tried to consider us. The fact that you fight for us thru your paper is very important to us all. I wish and hope that there are others like you.

"So have you heard anything about the ex-Grand Rapids prosecutor William Forsyth and Judge Donald Johnston? How they doing? Keeping a innocent person in prison, when they know its wrong.

"I wonder how they justify this with their conscience? They are probably so use to it, because I know I'm not the only one they have done this too."

Lee wrote again in July, August and September.

September 14, 2019, I wrote a letter to Governor Whitmer. This is what I said,

"Dear Governor,

"I am an advocate for justice for the innocent, as well as a member of the press and an author.

"The reason I am writing to you is because on May 22 of this year you signed into law House Bills 4129 through 4132, which allow the Michigan Department of Corrections to parole seriously ill prisoners.

"There is a prisoner I would like to recommend for parole. His name is Albert Lee, who is incarcerated at the Macomb Correctional Facility. He should not be in prison at all because he is not guilty. I have studied his case for the last ten years and can find no evidence of guilt. The Michigan Supreme Court overturned his conviction because he had clearly been framed. Then they sent him back to the same people who framed him, which meant he was framed again.

"If he cannot be exonerated as he should be, he should at least be released for medical reasons since he is dying. He has had diabetes and prostate cancer for several years, and the cancer has now spread to his bone marrow. He is in constant pain and probably only has a few months to live. I cannot imagine the guards want the burden of caring for him. He cannot be a threat to anyone because he is confined to a wheelchair due to a serious back problem.

"If he could be released, I am willing to accept full responsibility for his care.

"If you would like to know the full story of the injustice that has been done to this man, I am willing to meet with you as I did with former Lieutenant Governor Brian Calley.

"Please give this matter your consideration.

"Sincerely,

"Gerald Kinsey"

I provided my contact information in the letter, and I did receive a phone call from one of the governor's assistants. He said Lee could not be paroled because he was serving a life sentence. However, as Lee pointed out a number of times, he was not serving life without parole, but life with the possibility of parole.

On December 27, 2019, Governor Whitmer sent a letter in response to my request for a medical parole for Mr. Lee. In the letter she thanked me for reaching out to her and said Lee was welcome to apply for a pardon or commutation. She provided a web address to obtain the forms to apply. She also said, "Additionally, health care staff at the Michigan Department of Corrections are responsible for determining whether or not a prisoner is medically frail. Should prison staff determine that Albert is medically frail and should be paroled, my office will act accordingly."

I responded to the governor's letter on January 1, 2020. This is what I said in my letter,

"Dear Governor,

"Thank you for your response to my letter of September 14, 2019. I asked you to consider parole for Albert Lee since he is dying. In your letter you directed me to a web site for a form to apply for pardon or commutation. I visited the site and copied the form. It seems to be intended for the prisoner or a family member. Mr. Lee has applied for commutation in the past and been denied. I am not a relative. I am an advocate for justice.

"One problem I noticed with the application is that the judge and prosecutor in the sentencing county are asked for their position on the matter. They are clearly biased against the prisoner. There should be input from both sides.

"A pardon or commutation in this case will soon be meaningless since Mr. Lee has little time left to live. What I requested was a parole for medical reasons. You said that the health care staff at the MDOC are responsible to determining if a prisoner is 'medically frail'. Anyone who takes one look at Mr. Lee can see he is very 'medically frail'. He is dying. I have written before to the warden regarding Mr. Lee's health and will do so again. Since it is an incontrovertible fact that Mr. Lee is extremely ill, I cannot imagine that the health staff could claim otherwise. Hopefully, they will do their job properly and your office will then be able to act accordingly.

"Thank you again for your consideration in this matter.

"Sincerely,

"Gerald Kinsey"

I had written to Lee about the new Conviction Integrity Unit that Attorney General Dana Nessel had started. Lee responded February 24, 2020. In his letter Lee said,

"I received your mail, concerning the Attorney General's Conviction Integrity Unit. But they are all the same. A lot of hope that leads one to despair.

"The University of Michigan did that 10 yrs ago…don't contact us, we will contact you claiming they were interested 10 yrs ago.

"The same with the Innocent Project, that was 6 yrs ago. Both of them had me send in answers to their questions, I never heard from them again, there were others, but it is useless. As far as I'am concerned, a waste of time.

"Just like Gov. Gretchen Whitmer's bill…if you read on the back of it…these frail medical prisoners if you really read it, they are not giving you a parole. They are sending to a facility that's another prison.

"Only the sick and dying are there. And eventually you will die a lot quicker cause it is hidden and since you are already considered terminal ill. They don't have to give an explanation when it is self-explained, that it was going to happen anyway, just a matter of time.

"That's how they plan to get rid of us. Through these types of program.

"I got a friend that was considered, never heard from him again, until I heard he passed form (?) no longer above ground.

"As for filling out those forms, I've done that, with those places I mentioned, I've done that. As for you being my representative… that I would do, except, I got a sister who is already doing that.

"But I wouldn't mind you doing that for me, cause my sister is 78 years old, in a wheelchair and is a horder…"

I wrote to the Attorney General about Lee's case. Lee received a reply, and I was sent a copy. It said,

"Dear Mr. Lee:

"I received a letter from Mr. Gerald Kinsey, indicating his belief in your innocence. The Conviction Integrity Unit (CIU) reviews claims of innocence based on new evidence that was not considered at trial or during post-conviction appeals. Additionally, we are reviewing cases for potential new DNA testing and unreliable forensic issues that could help prove innocence…"

The letter went on to say that they would contact Lee once they had reviewed his application. They said they could not tell how long their review would take.

I didn't hear from Lee again for a while. The COVID pandemic came along and caused a lot of trouble for everyone, especially for those in prison. Lee's health continued to decline. The next time I heard from him he was in the Duane Waters prison hospital in Jackson. In fact, he was there the rest of his life. On June 17, 2021 he wrote,

"Well, the same old crap for me. I'm in the hospital, in the bed, I can't walk. I broke my hip and I got rods in me.

"Got tubes in both kidney, they are bad and they hang out of back, plus I got to wear a cathter …the rest of my life…Still got bone cancer and prostate cancer.

"Other than that I'm hanging on to life. It's hard to write…"

Lee wrote again in July. He had drawn three rough sketches to show what he was dealing with everyday. The first showed the tubes that were sticking out of his body. The second showed that he was bedridden all day every day. The third showed that he had to use a wheelchair to go to the doctor or hospital. He said, "This is what my life has come to being. But its life. And that's better (than) not having life."

He also asked me to send the 2021-2022 football schedule. He said, "So, you can say no, I will understand. And our friendship will remain the same.

"The reason why I like it, it keeps my mind occupied. You know 365 days a year one gets bored, depress, etc."

A little later in his letter he told about a bird that had kept him company. He said, "The other day, I was laying wondering what happen to my lil friend…My lil friend has been with me ever since autumn. My lil friend is a lil red robin.

"She/He would come by every morning, knock on the window and start sing at first I thought it was annoying.

"Then I thought, maybe it was and angle pointing my window out because whenever it stops by there, there is no pain from the angry cancer and any other pain. I just feel fine, all over.

"But lately I haven't heard from it, which maybe it did time to clean up its good or bad deeds. But I surely miss the lil fella."

He then went on to say, "You mention, You might want to write my life story. I'll write it might make close to a million.

"You will always get to edit it. I think we could do it? Tell me what you think? We should have done it earlier, when we (were) younger."

He was quite right. Here is what he wrote:

"Friday, Feb. 9, 1979. My feance that morning, tells me what needs to be done. To renew the insurance, registration for car, to get a sticker for car driving license plate, down at license bureau.

"To get my stepson of on the sch. bus that stops right outside. So he can get to sch. on time.

"When I got started, first I went to Denny restaurant to get breakfast. Also the license bureau is in the mall on 28th Street.

"I live right across the street in these Apt. building. I don't have far to go. After breakfast I (go) to mall, the driving license bureau is in the mall so is the unemployment.

"They campers, trailers are on show. I walk around until 9'oclock when the license bureau open. I'm looking at campers, window shoping, just killing time.

"Once the license bureau opens, I went to counter where the lady tells me I have tarrift tickets needs paying, I need updated insurance before she sell me the tags for the car. So I leave heading for the tariff div. to pay for the fines at the police station.

"So I'm driving back& forth to the Hall of Justice to get fines paid. I having been successful getting the insurance.

"But I'll continue Monday, Feb. 12, 1979. So over the weakin my feance go visit her sister which is my sister-in-law.

"She was married to my brother. Her name is Mattie, my brother name is Eugene.

"Mattie & Eugene were teachers in Battle Creek, Mich. Mattie has remarried, her name now Mattie Fluellen.

"We go to visit them, do a cookout, go dancing at a night club. I visit my brother Eugene and James.

“James is the oldest of us three. Eugene is next then me Al (Albert).

“On Monday, it was just like Friday. Going to mall to pay off fines. So I started off at Denny restaurant for breakfast.

“Waiting on the mall to open up at 9’oclock still could not get my plates (Tag) so I went out got some no-fault insurance.

“The mall was still showcasing campers. Going to the Hall of Justice paying off fines, getting my insurance renewing my license and purchase a card call I.D also this shows I have sideburn, thick mustache.

“Whereas the assailant in this was clean shaving no side burn, no mustache. The police went to the driving license and mess up both license & I.D picture.

“And we full well know that the bureau does not take unclear picture.

“Now on this day a lil girl gets kidnap, her father where the city personel manager. Who hires and fires police officer.

“The lil girl was kidnap around 7’oclock or 7:30 A.M. It was reported that city personel manger had a beef with police officer.

“The lil girl was found at a embankment in a parking lot around 5:30 or 6’oclock

“Getting a lil head of myself. The claim the victim was strangle, but when examiner and his assistant claim when they turn the over hot air came from the victim’s mouth.”

Lee ended his account there. I wrote back and asked some questions. He responded July 24, 2021. Here is what he said:

“Got your letter and was elated to hear from you. It’s only by luck these letters reach their destination. With Covid-19, coronavirus, the pandemic etc.

“I did receive the N.F.L schedule and thanks a million time. I know it was time consuming and not easy to get. Once again thanks.

"As for the license plate, as much as I can remember we kept the same plate and just put a sticke (tab) on it.

"I don't know what plate the abductor had this is the first time I heard anything concerning bicentennial plates.

"As for the arrest it went like this…I had gotten my car back from the police saying no trace evidence was found from the victim in my car, they had it for a week.

"The car alignment was out of whack, brakes tune up everything was mess up.

"So I took my car to Goodyear off of Wealthy Street in G.R. My car was at Goodyear for week.

"On March 28, 1979 I went to Goodyear checking on my car. The proprietor told me the police was there searching my car and cut a piece of the car carpet fiber and took it went him, the officer name Larry Crace.

"The next day March 29, 1979 I went back to Goodyear to pick up my car.

"Officer Larry Crace met me there and told me that if I pass the polygraph test, they would stop harassing me. Just follow him and his partner to the station. I did.

"When we got to the Hall of Justice, I was led into this room and was hook up.

"I pass the test as the examiner told me, Lt. Steele of the task force ask the examiner if he could see him outside of the room for a minute.

"When they came back in the examiner said the test had a glich in it, would I take it again? Like a fool I did and he said I fail.

"This time Lt. Steele told me to stand and he cuff my hands behind my back said I was under a arrest for the murder of victim, Linda Vanderveen.

"And I have not been free since March 29, 1979. That's how the arrest went.

"I would like to say this, there two polygraph test… the first one pass, the second one they lied.

"There were two DNA test on the blond hair found in a snowbrush from my car, the first test said it was not her hair – the 2nd test the prosecutor said the blond hair found on car's snowbrush is 5% of G.R. blond hair population and the victim Linda Vanderveen falls in that category the jury accept that.

"There were a coroded chew up barette victim's mother said belong to her daughter, DNA said it did not belong to the victim, not the teeth marks or saliva (spit marks) belong to the victim, the prosecutor refuse to let the jury know this.

"He (Billy Mansfield Jr.) escape from Michigan went to Florida where he rape two females and bury them in his back yard.

"Florida did not want to give Mansfield to Mich. but Mich. said they would give him life. So Florida let him go.

"But Mich. made a deal with Mansfield if he lie on me. Mansfield accept the deal.

"When Mansfield left Michigan he went to Calif. And rape and kill to mothers and sit on death row in California.

"Doing the 2nd trial Mansfield was going to tell the truth about the deal with David Sawyer who had become a court of appeals justice.

"To make sure I get denied by the court of appeals. The prosecutor William Forsyth would not bring Mansfield back to testify. Some of the jury wanted him too.

"As you research this case, and read newspaper article or go to G. R. library and get things off of microfilm.

"You will see how I was railroaded. Also, the victim's father was the city personel manager who hired & fired police officer.

“It was rumor that a ex-police officer kill the victim Linda Vanderveen took the one thing he loved the most…why not the son? Ten years later they kill the father.

“While in prison I receive a letter saying the victim was not strangle…she died of hyperthermia it was so cold that.

“That’s why I had to have a alibi from 7’0clock to 2’oclock that day.

“The there were two illegal post hypnotic suggestion planted in the witnesses head.

“The first one said “When the police arrest this man, that will be the man committed this crime!”

“The second one done by a different police officer said…When you wake up you will remember not if you were hypnotize.

“I would like to say, when they found the victim a man’s footprint size 9 ½ was found.

“I at the time wore size 11 shoes. The Footprint was not mind.

“The car’s tireprint was not mind, fingerprint on the victim’s body were not mind. A hook use to pull the assailant’s blue Monte Carlo out of the snow was never hook up to my black Grand Prix. The hook was painted yellow.

“The victim supposedly had three hands. There was testimony that where the victim was kidnap…some books and glove was found belonging to her.

“Witnesses testified the victim was looking out the back window of the abductor’s car waving a glove hand. This glove suppose to had a pin hole and a lot of feathers fell out duck, chicken, turkey, feasant, feathers

“The third glove was found in a garbade dump by a trash man along with the victim’s instrument, books, tablet etc.

“Then there is Billy Mansfield who prosecutor David Sawyer got Mansfield to lie on me saying I told him I murder the victim.

"Mansfield, had raped two young girls that was babysitting for his wife and him.

"This is also in a newspaper of microfilm. But David Sawyer sitting as a court of appeals justice made sure my case was affirmed.

"I didn't get a reversal until the Mich. Supreme Court on hypnosis saying those witnesses could not testify again in the 2nd trial should there be one.

"The S. Ct. told the prosecutor to stop his innuendo of suggestion sexual assault? There was to be no I. D. of the defendant? The three questions could not be used? The deal with Mansfield was to be brought out to the jury?

"When I file my case again in the S. Ct. they denied me a review saying the questions were not answer. My appeal attorney left me, saying his state obligation was over file in federal court.

"Then I got sick real bad with cancer, and was in the hospital. I miss the time limit date to file in Fed. Ct.

"They said being sick was no excuse I could have hired an appeal atty or ask the court to grant me one. So they denied my application to appeal in federal court.

"I think the prosecutor William Forsyth & the circuit court judge Donald A. Johnston had something to do with the federal court denying me.

"They were telling the Fed. Ct. it was time to bring my appeal to an end they said two juries found me guilty, I had my chance to appeal and failed & a lot of other stuff. Because they knew the Fed. Ct. would have appealed my case – They spent money to block my appeal.

"As you investigate this case you will see how they were so involved in this case. And still is with the governors, I forget the Gov. before Engler, and Gov. G. Whitmer. Anyone with any intelligence can see I was railroaded and still is. Gov. Whitmer let out guys doing two life and lifer doing life with no parole if they have done 40 yrs & was 65 yrs. old or more.

"At the time I was a lifer with possibility of parole and had done 40 yrs. was 68 yrs. old.

"She turn me down and others, that's why her life was threaten. People did not like the way she was letting prosecutors tell her who to let go and who to deny.

"Anyway I know it will be hard for you to have a open mind. But try too.

"These facts I brought out will appear anyway. But do your best, sorry I interfere with your writing this book, blind justice.

"I can't wait to read it, how you saw the case or interpret it.

"It will be a best seller, because at the time it was a crime to be driving while being a young black man.

"They were pulling black men over on a traffic ticket and shooting them in back while running way… because the officer would say…your fast. Lets see how fast you are at running…then shoot you in the back.

"I wonder why they did not do this to me? They wanted to embarass me to the public, and say that's why we kill niggers, because they kill our children and date our women.

"They are no good, not even a human being, they were classified as 3/5th of a human being.

"Well, I end here my friend, I'll write again Take care.

"Sincerely

"A Friend Always

"Al"

After receiving Lee's letter I wrote back to him with some questions. He replied August 6, 2021.

In his letter he said, “You say where was the arrest occur? At the Hall of Justice, the minute after the polygraph test…I then taken to the city jail, where I was finger printed, mug shot taken, dress out, place in the drunk cell, later that night given a cell by myself, two or three days later taken to the county jail (sheriff).

“I was arrested March 29, 1979. It was not at my home. I was at Goodyear to pick my car up. After paying the bill, and I got my car.

“I was ask to follow them to the Hall of Justice to take the polygraph test. The officers was the complaining officer Larry Crace and his partner officer Freeman.

“Officer Larry Crace was the complaining witness, his name is on the arrest warrant. Like I got 3 legal blue foot lockers.

“I wish I could get my footlockers everything is in there. But I’m sort of paralize from waist down.

“And I don’t want the officers going in there they have already thrown away half of my legal work and trial transcripts from both trials, and DNA trial.

“So I don’t want to send them back in there. But a good way to try to get stuff as I said in the last letter.

“You can go to a library, research the microfilm & newspapers.”

Lee then wrote about how I might be able to get more information about his case. He then continued with his report.

“Getting back to your letter. The reason why I mention hypothermia. Was a letter I received while in prison at the beginning, but I had remember that the prosecutor spent a whole hour talking about how cold it was that day Feb. 12, 1979. This is the examiner testimony

“That the temperature out at the airport, it was below 10 degree. And if the victim was kidnap between 7 & 8’ oclock.

“Left outside in a snowbank, tied up freezing, that would be like a ice box, because the body wasn’t found until I think that night, that is a long time outside in the cold snowy weather.

"The examiner and his assistant said when they turn the body over hot air came out the victim's mouth, her tongue was not hanging.

"The examiner could not come up with a time of death for the victim, which would give a alibi as to where I was at, when the victim was killed.

"By the victim freezing to death, there is no time as to when death occurred. As for the necklace in court it look like a old 10 cent bubble gum necklace. It even broke while the prosecutor was showing it to the jury. It was a lil silver child necklace, it would have snap to pieces if you tried to choke someone with it.

"The prosecutor could never place the victim and I together, every time he tried my time was accounted for, buying insurance, paying traiff ticket at the Hall of Justice, being at the driving license bureau, or at the mall unemployment office, buying something in the mall, shopping etc.

"The reason why the prosecutor don't give any info out the fingerprints on the victim's neck, because they were not mine, the thumb print on the victim's chest, did not belong me.

"All of this proves my innocence, like I said those in the justice system does not respect a black person life in the U.S.A. Whenever it suit them, a black person life is not worth anything. That's in all 50 states.

"As for Billy Mansfield, yes he was put in the cell on purpose. David Sawyer went to Florida and extradicted Mansfield. Sawyer was the original prosecutor.

"He told Mansfield everything about the case, that they did not have a witness to say they saw the victim and I together.

"So he would make a deal with Mansfield if he say that I told him that I killed the lil girl. Mansfield agreed to lie on me & he told the jury that.

"The only interaction I had with Mansfield is when we played cards, when we got bored. You see it was a four man cell.

"It was a four man cell. Each had our own cell. Mansfield was in cell one and I was in cell 4 by the shower. There two more guys, both of them were black guys like me. They were offer the deal but refused that's why they got Mansfield. I was never along (sic) with Mansfield, whenever we got together to play cards, all four of us were together. We would lay on our blanket on the floor with our pillow The gallery was big, we use to walk up & down it to think.

"The crime lab scientist Edward Gundy get his testimony in the 1st& 2nd trial. The examiner Dr. Harvey Wilks trial testimony 1st& 2nd trial both would be interesting to read, call trial transcripts."

Lee added a long P.S. after writing his main letter. In it he said,

"You want to know about the arrest whether it was legal or illegal? It was illegal both times…the1st & 2nd time of the arrest.

"The 1st time… I was arrested after a polygraph test…which is illegal because a polygraph test can not be used in a court of law.

"I was not arrested at my home or on the street. Also I was never served a complaint, arrest warrant or information charging me with a crime.

"These document must be served on you before an arraignment is held. Why?

"First a district judge (known as a magistrate) must sign a arrest warrant based a complaining witness and a person who observed a crime happening.

"In this case none of that occurred. Because the complaining witness & the person who observed a crime is brought before the magistrate & placed under oath to give deposition (statements) the giving of the oath before the magistrate is illegal if a notary public is not present.

"Once this is done legal…the magistrate signs the three above copies for your arrest, using a habeas corpus (produce the body) which would be the suspect or assailant.

"None of this was done, the only paper I received was a copy of the habeas corpus in the county jail.

"Remember I was taken to the local city jail after the polygraph test. Where I was book, fingerprinted and dress out, place in jail clothes.

"Now those three documents, complaint, arrest warrant & information. Guess who is the person listed in all three document?

"As the person who is the complantant, arresting offer, etc.

"You guess it? Officer Larry Crace. He is the complaintant complaining witness, the one gave information a crime has occurred.

"He is also the officer who perform a illegal search & seizure of my car at Goodyear on Wealthy Street in Grand Rapids. He cut off a piece of my car's carpet fibers to place on the victims clothes.

"But yes, the arrest was illegal… both times the 1st and 2nd trial arrest…using a habeas corpus document each time.

"This is what I was going to file my civil suit about against. Now I did not know any of this at the time.

"I wasn't a criminal and knew nothing about the law. That's how they get black people Give them a public defender for a lawyer who really works for the system, that's why they say if you can not afford a attorney one will be appointed at the state expense.

"You see all those things would be brought forth in a arraignment you only have 11 days…next would be 12 days in a preliminary examination. If you violate the time limit of days you lose them."

I didn't hear from Lee again until November. We exchanged letters, but he didn't tell anything more about his case. After receiving my response to his letter he sent a message thanking me for writing. He said that if I wanted to visit now, it was allowed, but he said it might be at his bed side because the cancer had gotten worse. He said it would be very good to see me in person. Regrettably, I did not get to visit him again.

Lee wrote again January 18, 2022. His health was getting worse, and as he said in his letter, it was affecting his hand writing. Here is what he said:

"I finally get a chance to drop you a few lines. Reason why it took so long.

"I been in the hospital off and on. As soon as I get one thing taken care of another one happens.

"Stomach infection, the next kidney failure, diarrhea, irregular heart beat (beating to fast), ulcer, colon…you be surprise how many times I been at Henry Ford hospital or McClaren in Lansing, sometime Coldwater hospital, then back to Duane Waters health center.

"Right now I'm in DWH. As you can see my handwriting not to good.

"Thanks for the paper, it's the only thing that keeps me sane."

Lee wrote again in June, 2022. It was the last letter he wrote himself. His handwriting was not good because he was shaking. In the letter he said that after five days of testing the doctor said the bone cancer had spread to his brain. He was still mostly coherent, but he was having trouble remembering. He again asked for a football schedule, which I sent to him. He said, "I can sure use ways to keep me busy while laying on my back." Earlier in his letter he had pointed out that he could not stand, walk or sit in a wheelchair. He was still hoping for a medical discharge.

Chapter 17 – The Passing of Albert Lee

July 13, 2022 Lee wrote again, but the handwriting did not look like his. The letter was brief. He thanked me for the NFL schedule and said he was feeling bad. He said he would write more next time, but that was the last letter I received from him.

A couple days later I received a letter from another inmate who gave his name and said that he had been helping Lee with the things he couldn't do for himself. Among other things, he said he had helped Lee read our paper, and he had helped write the letter I had just received. He also said, "You would be surprised how much just talking to a guy can change his day. I'm just a man trying to shed light on someone who needs it."

I didn't hear any more for a while. Then the September 29, 2022 issue of our paper was returned to us. It said, "unable to forward." I checked online and found that Lee was listed as "discharged." I knew that normally would mean he had passed away. The discharge date was given as September 26, 2022. Checking some more I found that Ross Mortuary Inc had a brief obituary. It said, "Albert Lee III, 'Shorty' departed this life September 26, 2022. Graveside Services will be held Saturday October 22, 2022, at 1pm. Services will be held at Mohorn Baptist Church Cemetery, Opelousas, Louisiana. 70570"

Ross Mortuary is in Houston, Texas where Lee grew up. He still has family members who live in that area. Lee had told me that his family originally came from Louisiana, and he still had relatives there. That would explain why he might want to be buried there.

To get more information, I wrote to the inmate who had been helping Lee in his last days. He sent back a message saying that he had been trying to find a number to call to let me know that Lee had passed. He said, "He's in a better place. He was in bad shape. I don't wish that on anyone, especially how MDOC treats the patients."

I do believe he is in a better place.

Then a few days later I received another message from him. In it he said, "I'm not exactly sure what happened to Mr. Lee in the days leading up to this death. They suspended the program due to a covid outbreak so we didn't go to the hospital for a few weeks. During that time is when he passed. I do know he talked to his sister in Texas on the phone some days I was in the room with him. He also talked to some guy which I think is his son or a good friend. Not exactly sure. I remember Al getting some paperwork from the parole board saying they are going to look at his case and he was happy as all hell. He called that guy and he said he would fly him to where ever he needed to go if they decided to let him out. I never got into detail with him about it. Some things we keep to ourselves in this environment. The last time I was with Al he was out of it. Very demanding and not himself. From previous experiences I knew it wouldn't be long. So I just helped as much as possible and tried to comfort and be there the best I knew how. I'm pretty sure he appreciated it. I made him a fish sandwich one day and boy did he love that. He didn't eat much. Bone cancer is very bad. I've seen it first hand what it does to people who were very healthy and how fast it will knock someone down and not think twice about it. He kept a clean shaved head and face. Liked to show off his tattoo…A lot of people didn't like to go sit and help him but I took a liking to him. So I did what I could. I do believe he is in a better place. He was suffering a great deal. Each day was a struggle and you could see the hurt and pain in his eyes. I always read him the Kinsey Retort in the paper. He didn't care for nothing else but that column. I read the rest after I read that to him."

Chapter 18 – The Questions

Since Albert Lee is now deceased, does that mean that the Linda Vanderveen case should be considered closed? The answer is a definite *no*. There are still several questions that remain unanswered. The main question is, "who killed Linda Vanderveen?" Of course, the prosecutor and the police will insist that Lee was the killer. The prosecutor claims he proved Lee guilty, not once, but twice. As pointed out previously, for a man to be proven guilty twice, he has to be tried twice. To be tried twice his first conviction has to be overturned. A conviction will not be overturned unless there is a major problem with it. The general rule is to let the conviction stand. It was the Michigan Supreme Court that overturned Lee's first conviction. Since that court only looks at one case in a hundred, it is certain that there were major problems with that first conviction. It was plainly stated what the main problem was. The witnesses were hypnotized to get them to identify Lee after no one identified him before hypnosis even though given multiple opportunities to do so. Also, Lee did not look like the man the witnesses described.

Let us review the evidence for and against Lee's guilt. First, let us look at the evidence the prosecutor offered at the first trial.

Lee was identified (under hypnosis) by five witnesses as the man they had seen. As just stated, the Michigan Supreme Court threw out that evidence.

The prosecutor claimed Lee had confessed to the crime. That evidence did not need to be thrown out by the Michigan Supreme Court because by the time they heard the case, Billy Mansfield Jr., who was the only one who claimed to have heard the confession, had already admitted he lied about it. At the first trial it was stated that some jurors believed Mansfield and others did not.

Since the first conviction was overturned along with all the evidence, let us look at the evidence offered at the second trial.

The prosecutor said that the evidence for Lee's guilt was 1) Linda Vanderveen's barrette in Lee's car, 2) Linda Vanderveen's hair in Lee's car, 3) Carpet fibers from Lee's car on the clothes of the victim, 4) Lee's hair on the victim, and 5) A similar act committed by Lee a few days before the Vanderveen murder.

As pointed out earlier, the barrette could not have been the victim's barrette because it had a different type of clasp. The hair was proven not to be the victim's hair by DNA testing, which was totally ignored at the trial and the subsequent appeal. The carpet fibers presented as evidence were the same as those from thousands of other cars (thus inconclusive at best). The source of the hairs from the alleged assailant which were discovered on the victim could not be identified definitely as Lee's because they were the same as those from millions of other Black men. Finally, the similar act evidence was meaningless and a misnomer because it was not known that Lee was the man involved, and whoever the man was, he made no attempt to commit any crime.

It is quite apparent that Lee's guilt was not proven beyond a reasonable doubt. Why then was he convicted? There are at least two reasons that are apparent to an honest, objective investigator.

First, at the second trial the defense attorney was not allowed to present all his evidence. He stated that key to his defense was that there had been a police conspiracy to convict Lee. A significant piece of evidence supporting the assertion of conspiracy was the deal the prosecutor and police made with Billy Mansfield Jr., but the judge banned the defense attorney from mentioning Mansfield. Also, the jury was not allowed to know why the case was being retried. The reason was that the police had hypnotized the witnesses, which was further evidence in support of a police conspiracy.

Second, the jury was not unbiased. The defense attorney said that he would have dismissed at least four more jurors if he had been allowed to do so. He also complained that he had to use peremptory challenges to dismiss jurors who should have been dismissed for cause by the judge. When he was not able to get an acceptable jury, he requested a change of venue, which was denied. Later it was learned that at least two of the jurors should not have been on any jury because one was facing charges from the prosecutor and the other had a daughter who was facing charges. Also, it should be pointed out that, even though Lee was a Black man, the only Black person on the jury was the woman whose daughter was facing charges from the prosecutor.

Next, let us look at the evidence that Lee was not guilty. This should not even be necessary since a person accused of a crime is not required to prove his innocence. It is sufficient that the prosecutor cannot prove his guilt. However, it is always best to look at both sides of any issue.

First, it is apparent that Lee was not the person the witnesses saw because he didn't fit the description they gave. Anyone can go to the Grand Rapids library and check the microfilm of the March 2nd, 1979 issue of the Grand Rapids Press. There is a copy of the police sketch of the man the five witnesses described. Their descriptions were in close agreement, which suggests we have a very good idea what the man looked like. The most obvious difference between Lee and the man the witnesses saw was that Lee had a beard, and the perpetrator did not.

Second, it is obvious for several reasons that Lee's car was not the one the witnesses saw. Lee's car did not have wide whitewalls, which witnesses identified. It did, however, have tinted windows, which would have prevented the witnesses from seeing the victim in the back seat. Also, the tire tracks left by whoever dumped the body did not match the tread of Lee's car tires. The car used by the abductor was probably a Monte Carlo, rather than a Grand Prix, because two witnesses said they were sure it was a Monte Carlo, and one said he saw the words *Monte Carlo* on the car.

Third, we know Lee could not have been the one who dumped the body in the snowbank because it was placed there sometime after 2 p.m. and the police were watching Lee from noon on. Before that Lee was busy getting his license plates and driver's license. Also, the footprints in the snow near where the body was discovered were too small to be from Lee.

Fourth, the police said they would dismiss him as a suspect if he passed a lie detector test. That can only mean they had no proof of guilt. He passed the test. Then they gave him the test again and claimed he failed.

Fifth, there were fingerprints on the neck of the victim and on her notebook that were not from Lee. These fingerprints were almost certainly those of the killer.

Sixth, why would the prosecutor and the police need to lie and suppress evidence if they truly believed Lee was guilty? If the evidence showed that he was guilty, they would want the whole truth to be brought out.

Finally, no one can suggest a motive Lee could have had for the murder. He had no criminal record and no connection to the victim or her family. It would make no sense at all for him to take time out of his busy schedule that day to abduct and kill some little girl he knew nothing about.

In summary, there is no proof of guilt and extensive evidence Lee was not the one who committed this crime.

If he didn't do it, then the question remains as to who did. Several other questions also remain. Whose fingerprints were on Linda Vanderveen's neck and on her notebook? Who knew she would be at that corner at that time? Whose hairs were on her clothes? What car left tire tracks in the snow where the body was dumped? What was the true motive of the murder? Why did the police frame a man they knew was innocent? Why was the defense attorney not allowed to present his case? Why were people allowed on the jury when they were facing charges from the prosecutor? Why was Mansfield not brought back for the second trial? Why did the judge show a prejudice against the defense? All of these questions can be summarized with one question: "Who killed Linda Vanderveen?"

There is another question that should be asked. Since Albert Lee and all the Vanderveen family are now deceased, why should anyone still care about this case? That is a question we can answer. This case should be of interest to everyone because what happened to Lee could happen to any one of us. In many cases in which an innocent man is sent to prison, he did something to bring the problem on himself. He may have offended someone, and that person decided to lie to get him in trouble. However, in Lee's case he did nothing to cause his problems. He happened to be a Black man with a dark colored car, and the police and the prosecutor needed someone to frame.

Another related question that should be asked is how a man can be convicted twice for a crime when there was no evidence at all that he was the perpetrator? How does an innocent man get convicted? There are about seven tactics commonly used to do so. Every one was used in Lee's case.

The March, 2021 issue of the National Geographic had an article on people on death row who had been exonerated. As part of the article there was a section that stated reasons for exoneration. The six reasons given were: official misconduct (68%), perjury or false accusation (62%), misleading forensic evidence (29%), inadequate legal defense (25%), mistaken witness identification (19%) and false confession (13%). Another reason not stated in the article was jury tampering. It is not known how many are convicted for that reason, but it is probably a small percentage.

Let us look how each of these was used in Lee's case.

First, there was official misconduct. That is a euphemism. It means that corrupt people in our justice system deliberately pervert justice. That is certainly what happened in Lee's case. The prosecutor and the police lied, planted evidence, suppressed evidence and made a deal with a serial rapist and murderer to get Lee convicted. In addition the judges showed a clear prejudice against the defense. There was even jury tampering.

Second, there was perjury and false accusation. In this case, as in many others, the false accusation was from a jailhouse snitch who had a clear motive for lying. He was facing two life sentences which he clearly deserved, and his only hope was to make a deal with the prosecutor. It was so obvious that he had made such a deal that the defense attorney put the prosecutor on the witness stand and asked about the deal. The prosecutor lied under oath by saying there was no deal, but as soon as Lee was convicted the snitch was set free to rape and murder again and again. This takes us back to official misconduct. The prosecutor should not have let a dangerous criminal go free to convict an innocent man, and he should not have lied under oath about the deal he had made.

Third, there was misleading forensic evidence. This is sometimes called "junk science." Nearly every piece of physical evidence presented would fall into this category. One of the most glaring examples was the DNA evidence. The first tests on the hair found in Lee's car proved conclusively that the hair was not from the victim, but those tests were completely ignored, and the PCR test was the only one mentioned. As the appeal court pointed out, the PCR test cannot be used to identify a person; it can only be used to eliminate a person. However, the prosecutor tried to use the test to identify the victim as the one who supplied the hair. There are tens of millions of people who have the same genotype as the victim, but the prosecutor tried to imply that the hair must be from the victim because it had the same genotype.

Fourth, there was inadequate legal defense. This was probably less of a problem in Lee's case than in many others, but it likely was still a factor. Lee said that he was satisfied with his first attorney, but not with the attorney at his second trial. There is a question as to why the second attorney in each trial is only mentioned once. Since Lee had two attorneys in each trial, it would seem like there should be some mention of what the other attorney did. It is unclear why Mansfield was not brought back for the second trial since he was crucial to the defense claim of a police conspiracy. We know that the prosecutor didn't want Mansfield back, but the defense attorney should have been able to insist. We also find that in Lee's later appeal attempts his lawyers seemed unwilling to help.

Fifth, there was mistaken witness identification. In Lee's case this was deliberate since the police hypnotized the witnesses to get them to identify Lee when no one identified him before hypnosis.

Finally, there was a false confession. Of course, Lee never confessed, but Mansfield said he did. The National Geographic article says that false confessions are involved in 13 % of exonerations. We need to remember that this relates to cases of people on death row. When a person knows a confession is likely to lead to his death, he is less likely to confess. Since Michigan does not have the death penalty, that statistic may be less relevant to Lee's case. It should also be pointed out that confessions are more common in cases other than murder. About 95 percent of all cases are resolved with a plea bargain. In most of those cases the defendant pleads guilty, which means he is confessing to the crime. There are also many instances of the police and the prosecutor claiming a defendant has confessed when he has not. Coerced confessions are very common in our justice system. Also, when a person is convicted, there is intense pressure to get him to "accept responsibility for his actions." Of course, a person is not responsible for something he didn't do. It is interesting that in Lee's Michigan Supreme Court case Judge Boyle claimed that Lee had confessed when Mansfield had already admitted he lied about the confession.

As stated, everyone should be interested in this case because what happened to Albert Lee could happen to anyone. Not only should we all be afraid; we should also be angry. We should demand justice from our justice system.

Chapter 19 – The Solution

What is the solution to the problem? In actuality, it is quite simple. When someone is murdered, the way to resolve the case is to find the murderer. That is exactly what needs to be done. When the true murderer is found, it will automatically prove that Lee was not the killer.

Can we find the perpetrator? We should be able to. We know what he looks like. We know the kind of car he was using. We have his fingerprints. We have his hairs, which have mitochondrial DNA. We know (in the perception of a witness, anyway) he spoke with a Cuban accent. We know his probable motive. We know he had a criminal mentality, which suggests he may have a criminal record. Finally, there is a suspect who should be checked out.

How should we proceed? The first step would be to secure the evidence before any more of it mysteriously disappears. Next, run the prints. There are over 50 million fingerprints in the police database. It is possible (probable?) that someone has made sure the prints are not there, but it would only take a few minutes to do a search. When we match the prints, we have the perpetrator. It is nearly certain everything else will fall into place when we find the man who left the prints.

If it is confirmed that the fingerprints are not in the database, the next step would be to check out the one suspect. It is possible that he had nothing to do with the case, but whenever anyone suggests a suspect, he should be checked out. It should also be pointed out that he should be checked thoroughly since whoever was behind the murder may have altered some evidence to throw off a potential investigator. If the suspect is proven not to be the one who committed the crime, the next thing to do would be to find all the Black men in Michigan who had blue, green or black Monte Carlos. Since the police did this for Grands Prix, it should be possible to do it for Monte Carlos. Another way to proceed would be to check the hundreds of tips that people gave the police.

We need to remember that from the beginning the Grand Rapids police were suspected because they had made the death threats against Andrew Vanderveen. The defense attorney at the second trial said that there was a police conspiracy to convict Albert Lee. There was extensive evidence to support that claim. This suggests that the original suspicion may be correct.

Appendix I

01/10/90 PEOPLE STATE MICHIGAN v. ALBERT LEE III

[1] SUPREME COURT OF MICHIGAN

[2] Docket No. 78005

[3] 1990.MI.43 <http://www.versuslaw.com>, 450 N.W.2d 883, 434 Mich. 59

[4] January 10, 1990

[5] PEOPLE OF THE STATE OF MICHIGAN, PLAINTIFF-APPELLEE,v.

ALBERT LEE III, DEFENDANT-APPELLANT

[6] Frank J. Kelley, Attorney General, Louis J. Caruso, Solicitor General, William A. Forsyth, Prosecuting Attorney, and Timothy K. McMorrow, Chief, Appellate Division, for the people.

[7] State Appellate Defender (by Chari Grove and Charles J. Booker) for the defendant.

[8] Brickley, J. Levin, J., concurred with Brickley J. Cavanagh J. (in Agreement in part and Dissenting in part). Archer J., concurred with Cavanagh, J. Boyle, J. (minority OPINION(S)ing in part and Concurring in part). Riley, C.j., and Griffin, J., concurred with Boyle, J.

[9] The opinion of the court was delivered by: Brickley

[10] Defendant, Albert Lee, III, was convicted of first-degree felony murder *fn1 and sentenced to life imprisonment. We granted leave to appeal limited to:

[11] (1) Whether the testimony of witnesses who had been hypnotized was properly admitted; and

[12] (2) Whether similar acts evidence was properly admitted.

[13] We hold first that the rules of People v Gonzales *fn2 and People v Nixon *fn3 were violated and thus that it was error for the trial court to admit the identification testimony of the hypnotized witnesses. Second, the similarities between the charged crime and the similar acts testimony satisfies the standards of People v Golochowicz, 413 Mich 298; 319 NW2d 518 (1982).

[14] I

[15] Procedurally this case has a long history. Following his conviction, defendant moved for a new trial which was denied. Defendant appealed by right. The Court of Appeals held that the standards of People v Gonzales, supra, dealing with hypnotized witnesses were not satisfied. *fn4 However, the Court of Appeals held that because this case was decided before Gonzales its holding was inapplicable "but that reversal is nevertheless required in a pre- Gonzales case if defendant was prejudiced by admission of testimony as to recollections induced by hypnosis." Thereafter the Court found that the identification procedures were not "unnecessarily suggestive or conducive to irreparable misidentification," upholding the trial court's admission of the testimony of hypnotized witnesses.

[16] Judge Maher Dissented on the hypnosis issue. He concluded that on the basis of the factors pronounced by this Court in People v Hampton, 384 Mich 669; 187 NW2d 404 (1971), People v Gonzales, supra, should be applied retroactively. *fn5 Thus, he found that defendant was denied a fair trial because the eyewitness testimony was tainted by hypnosis.

Relative to the similar acts testimony, the Court of Appeals found that the facts were sufficiently substantial to justify admission to show identity. The Court held that the trial court did not abuse its discretion and that the evidence was not erroneously admitted.

A request for review was filed with this Court and it was held in abeyance pending release of another hypnosis case, People v Nixon, 421 Mich 79; 364 NW2d 593 (1984). Following the release of Nixon, the case was remanded to the Court of Appeals for reconsideration. On remand, the case was reaffirmed. *fn6 We granted leave to appeal. 429 Mich 885 (1987).

II

The undisputed facts of this case are that an eleven-year-old Grand Rapids girl was abducted from her school safety patrol post on the morning of February 12, 1979. Later that same day her body was found near the Regency Park Apartments. The cause of death was strangulation.

The extensive investigation by police produced four categories of evidence: (1) eyewitness identifications, (2) physical evidence, (3) similar acts evidence, and (4) testimony of defendant's former cellmate which is not at issue in this appeal. The propriety of the similar acts evidence is discussed below. We therefore turn to a Discussion of the eyewitness identification and the physical evidence.

A

There were seven key prosecution witnesses (Jack Hill, James Vos, Jack Vos, Greg Start, David Orr, Jr., Timothy Wilcome and Jim Bonnema), all of whom were hypnotized. Moreover, five of the witnesses were hypnotized on two separate occasions by different hypnotists. The first hypnotic session was conducted by Mr. Robert Mazur, a local hypnotist, who operates the Grand Rapids Hypnotic Clinic. Mr. Mazur is not a psychiatrist or a psychologist and did not testify at trial. Dr. Donald Rossi of the Michigan Department of State Police conducted the second hypnotic session. Most of the hypnotic sessions were audiotaped but not videotaped. According to the experts who listened to the tapes, the hypnosis sessions themselves were conducted without any deliberate "attempt to alter [witnesses'] memories."

Police were notified of the incident by Jack Hill who witnessed the last stages of the abduction. At the intersection of the abduction,

Jack Hill noticed a car parked on the wrong side of the road and stopped to offer assistance. He spoke to a black man standing outside the vehicle and noticed a young white girl in the back seat. As the black man drove off Mr. Hill attempted to follow the car. Mr. Hill described the car as a clean, shiny black two-door. He originally told the police that he thought the car might be a Chrysler; however, at trial he testified that the car was a black Grand Prix. The driver was described as a neatly dressed black man with a neat haircut. Mr. Hill did not notice any facial hair on the man. *fn7

James Vos was driving his son, Jack Vos, to school at the time of the abduction when he noticed a black car skidding fast around a corner towards his vehicle. Mr. Vos was stopped for traffic when Mr. Hill informed them that he needed assistance pursuing a vehicle because a young girl had been abducted. James Vos described the car as a clean black two-door hardtop Pontiac Grand Prix with fancy wheel hubs and white walls. Mr. Vos noticed a black man driving the car who was approximately twenty-five to thirty years old, clean in appearance, wearing a dark leather jacket, and having an afro haircut moderate in length. However, he was unable to clearly identify the man driving the car. He did not notice anyone in the car and, in fact, stated that his main concentration was on the car and not on the person driving the car. At trial he was confident about his testimony concerning the make and model of the car.

Like his father, Jack Vos observed the car as being a Grand Prix because of the insignia and the grill on the vehicle. He was confident about the description of the car. However, unlike his father, he did observe a small girl in the back seat. He testified that she was a white girl, with blond hair, wearing a blue hat and a green coat.

On the day of the incident, February 12, 1979, Jack Hill was taken to the police department where two composite drawings were made. The first composite drawing was made prior to Mr. Hill being hypnotized. A second composite was compiled during the hypnotic session with Mr. Mazur. Jack Hill, James Vos, and Jack Vos were also all hypnotized-on February 12 by Mr. Mazur.

Greg Start, a school crossing guard, gave testimony that he had seen a black car with red pinstriping and a red interior drive by his patrol corner twice. He noticed the car a second time because the driver had run a stop sign. Greg's testimony was more specific in that he identified the car as a Grand Prix because he saw the letters on the front fender of the car. Further, he described the driver as a young black man with a mustache and an afro hairstyle.

The victim's knapsack was recovered from a dumpster at the Georgetown Condominiums by the rubbish collector sometime on the afternoon of February 12, 1979. The Georgetown Condominiums are located within one mile of where the victim's body was found. On the morning of February 12, a black car driven by a black man was lodged in a snowbank at the condominium. Two grounds maintenance men, David Orr, Jr., and Timothy Wilcome testified that they helped the man free his vehicle. Specifically, Mr. Wilcome testified that a black man with neat hair (not an afro style), wearing a leather jacket walked up to the shed and asked for assistance to push his car out of a snowbank. Wilcome stated further that the black man smoked Kool cigarettes *fn8 and that the car looked like a black Monte Carlo. *fn9 Mr. Orr stated specifically that the car was a black Monte Carlo because of the emblem on the back of the car. *fn10 Also that the car had bicentennial license plates *fn11 and spoke-type wheels with curb feelers. Thereafter, Mr. Orr saw him get out of the car and throw something away in a nearby dumpster. Two days after the incident, February 14, 1979, Timothy Wilcome and David Orr, Jr., were hypnotized.

As the police continued to receive tips on the abductor, three mugbooks were compiled. Defendant's picture appeared in mugbooks one and two, however he was not pictured in the third mugbook. The first photo showing (mugbook one) occurred on February 15, 1979. Jack Hill, David Orr, Jr., James Vos, Jack Vos, and Timothy Wilcome participated, but no positive identification was made. In fact, each witness identified persons other than defendant as possessing features similar to the abductor.

Mr. Jim Bonnema notified the police about seeing the particular vehicle on the morning of February 12 after reading about the incident in the newspaper and seeing a story on television. He was hypnotized on February 16, 1979, *fn12 and while under hypnosis he gave a license plate number. However, he was unable to positively identify the driver of the vehicle.

On February 23, 1979, Jack Hill, Jack Vos, David Orr, Jr., and Timothy Wilcome were hypnotized for the second time by Dr. Donald Rossi. During the hypnotic session with Mr. Hill, a police artist was present who attempted to sketch a third composite drawing while Mr. Hill was under hypnosis. Following the hypnotic sessions each witness participated in a second photo showing (mugbook two). Mr. Orr identified the defendant, among others, from this mugbook. Otherwise there was no positive identification by any other witness.

On February 26, 1979, defendant went to the police department for a polygraph examination, *fn13 at which time he agreed to participate in a corporal lineup. The participating witnesses were Jack Hill, Jack Vos, James Vos, David Orr, Jr., and Timothy Wilcome. Of these witnesses, only Timothy Wilcome picked defendant from the lineup; however, he could not make a positive identification.

*fn14

On March 15, 1979, mugbook three was shown to Hill, Orr, Wilcome, James Vos, and Jack Vos. The witnesses did not positively identify any person (defendant was not pictured). Mr. Wilcome is the only witness who did not pick anyone from these photographs.

Defendant participated in a second lineup on March 29, 1979. At this lineup the defendant was identified by Mr. Hill, Jack Vos, and Mr. Wilcome. Mr. Orr picked someone other than defendant from this lineup as being the alleged perpetrator. James Vos also participated in the lineup but could not identify the perpetrator.

Two months later, on June 19, 1979, Greg Start was hypnotized by Dr. Rossi. *fn15 The next day he participated in a corporal lineup and picked defendant. *fn16

Prior to the second lineup, March 29, 1979, one day prior to defendant's arrest, most witnesses at one time or another had made false identifications or at least identifications of persons other than defendant. Mr. Wilcome was the only witness who picked defendant from both lineups. However, he did not make a positive identification at either.

All of the in-court identifications of defendant, except by Jack Hill, were tentative. Mr. Hill made two in-court identifications of the defendant, the first being at the preliminary examination and the second during trial. He was extremely confident about each in-court identification.

At trial, Jack Vos made an in-court identification of the defendant as the man he picked from the second lineup. However, he testified that, while defendant looked identical to the man, he could not identify defendant as the man he saw on February 12. Greg Start positively identified defendant as the man he picked from the lineup on June 20. However, this identification occurred after considerable publicity attendant to defendant's arrest, *fn17 and at trial he stated that he expected to see the suspect in the lineup.

Timothy Wilcome made an in-court identification of defendant as the person he selected from both lineups. At trial he testified that he was not confident in his identification of defendant but that he looked the closest to the person he saw on February 12. At the time of trial James Vos did not make an in-court identification. Rather, he testified that he could not state, one way or the other, whether defendant was the person driving the vehicle on the morning of February 12. Jim Bonnema was unable to positively identify the defendant at trial. However, he did state that there was nothing unusual about defendant to rule him out as the driver of the Grand Prix.

B

Our analysis on the issue of admissibility begins with two basic premises offered by the prosecution from the Rules of Evidence. First, all relevant evidence is admissible, absent prejudice, confusion, or waste of time. MRE 401, 402, 403. Second, all witnesses are presumed competent to testify. MRE 601, 602. The relevancy of eyewitness identification is not questioned. Therefore our only concern is the admissibility of a witness' testimony after being subjected to hypnosis.

The test to be applied is derived from our holdings in People v Gonzales, and People v Nixon, supra.

*fn18 In Gonzales, we held that hypnotically induced testimony is inadmissible, but left open the question whether a hypnotized witness could testify regarding facts recalled and related prior to hypnosis. We answered the question in People v Nixon, holding that a witness may testify regarding facts " demonstrably recalled prior to hypnosis.'" The burden is on the party offering the testimony of a hypnotized witness to "establish its reliability by clear and convincing evidence." Nixon, supra at

90. The clear and convincing standard adopted in Nixon does not, as the Dissent would suggest, extend to the question whether any posthypnotic testimony is reliable. *fn19 Rather, testimony of a hypnotized witness is reliable only when the clear and convincing evidence offered by the proponent of the testimony demonstrates that the witness is testifying only with regard to those facts which were recalled and related prior to hypnosis.

Further, in Nixon we reaffirmed our position, quoting with approval the following language from Gonzales :

"The process of hypnosis is not a reliable means of accurately restoring forgotten incidents or repressed memory, and to permit posthypnotic testimony would unfairly denigrate the defendant's right to cross-examination. Therefore, we hold that until hypnosis gains general acceptance in the fields of medicine and psychiatry as a method by which memories are accurately improved without undue danger of distortion, delusion or fantasy, and until the barriers which hypnosis raises to effective cross-examination are somehow overcome, the testimony of witnesses which has been tainted by hypnosis must be excluded in criminal cases." [People v Nixon, supra at 88, quoting People v Gonzales, supra at 626-627. Emphasis in original.]

The Dissent advances that this Court erred in Nixon by applying the Davis/Frye test to hypnosis.

*fn20 However, hypnosis is a scientific procedure which renders a subject susceptible to external influences which could distort the memory. *fn21 " understanding of the phenomenon and of the means to control the effects of hypnosis is still in its infancy." *fn22 " expert can determine whether memory retrieved by hypnosis, or any part of that memory, is truth, falsehood, or confabulation . . . .

Such results are not scientifically reliable as accurate." *fn23 Accordingly, we can find no justifiable reason for overturning clear precedent established in this state. *fn24

Defendant argues that the procedures established by this Court in People v Nixon, were not followed, so corrupting the identification process by the suggestive effect of hypnosis as to deny defendant his right to a fair trial. The prosecutor admits that the hypnotic sessions were not conducted in light of the safeguard procedures adopted by the Court in People v Nixon. *fn25 However, the prosecutor asserts that under a totality of the circumstances, the testimony of each eyewitness was not tainted by hypnosis and, in fact, was based on prehypnotic recollection. We disagree that such an approach is allowable under the precedent of Gonzales and Nixon.

The investigation in this case took place before Gonzales was decided. In Nixon, we ruled with regard to the application of Gonzales, holding that the principles set forth therein are not to be applied retroactively but are applicable to all cases tried after its release and to those pending on appeal where the hypnosis issue is preserved. Defendant's case was pending on appeal when Gonzales was released, and the hypnosis issue was properly preserved. Thus defendant is entitled to application of Gonzales.

Although the rules enumerated in Gonzales and Nixon are applicable, factually the two cases differ from this case because neither involved a posthypnotic lineup identification. The only case we dealt with involving posthypnotic lineup identification was People v Centers, 422 Mich 951 (1986). We addressed the issue of admissibility of a witness' testimony after submitting to hypnosis to resolve a conflict in the Court of Appeals. See People v Centers, 141 Mich App 364; 367 NW2d 397 (1985), and People v McIntosh, 142 Mich App 314; 370 NW2d 337 (1985). *fn26

Centers and McIntosh were tried together, and both were convicted of murder and armed robbery.

Following an evidentiary hearing, the trial court allowed testimony concerning the identification of the suspect made at a posthypnotic lineup. The lineup occurred eight months after the hypnotic session. Prior to hypnosis, the witness gave police a description of the suspect on two occasions.

During the hypnotic session, the witness gave basically an identical description of the suspect. The hypnotic session was tape recorded and transcribed, as well as reviewed by the court during the evidentiary hearing. *fn27. The trial court reached its decision to allow the testimony by comparing the descriptions made by the witness pre- and posthypnosis. On appeal, both defendants argued that t the trial court erred in admitting the testimony of an eyewitness who had been hypnotized during the police investigation.

The Court of Appeals in Centers ruled that identification of a suspect at a corporal lineup by a witness who had been hypnotized was error requiring reversal. The Court found significant the fact that identity was central to the issue at trial, so that the testimony of the witness regarding identification of the defendant was not a harmless error. The Court remanded the case to the circuit court holding that the circuit court shall not admit any posthypnotic testimony or testimony concerning posthypnotic statements unless it is demonstrated that the testimony is based solely on facts recalled and related by the witness or declarant prior to hypnosis and the party offering the testimony establishes its reliability by clear and convincing evidence. [Centers, supra at 371.]

Contrary to the holding in Centers, the McIntosh panel found that because of the similarity in the witness' descriptions of the suspect, both pre- and posthypnosis, the identification at the lineup was based on facts recalled and related prior to the hypnotic session.

In lieu of granting leave to appeal, we vacated the decision in People v Centers and affirmed the decision of People v McIntosh, 422 Mich 951 (1986). Justice Levin Dissented, stating that the prosecutor had failed to establish by clear and convincing evidence that the witness was recalling facts related prior to the hypnotic session.

In McIntosh and Centers, testimony from the eyewitness was admitted on the basis of a comparative analysis of the information given during hypnosis and the prehypnotic statements. Because the information was substantially the same, the Court found that the identification was based on information recalled and related prior to hypnosis. However, in this case, we cannot make such an analysis. We do not have prehypnotic statements from the witnesses, nor an identification of the defendant prior to the hypnotic sessions.

It is obvious in this case that the police department was in a most difficult investigative posture, knowing as they did that an eleven-year-old girl had been abducted and that she, and possibly other potential victims, were in serious jeopardy. Thus, they devoted their efforts to extract every conceivable bit of information from the witnesses as quickly, and as thoroughly, as possible. The dissent suggests that under the rule adopted in Michigan the state must "choose between use of hypnosis during the investigative stage and the potential loss of a witness' testimony at trial." (Post, p 107, Boyle, J., Dissenting.) However, the use of hypnosis as an investigatory tool is not foreclosed by today's decision. The error in this case resulted from the fact that the investigation was conducted with little or no thought to the preservation of evidence for testimonial purposes. It is admitted that there was virtually no attempt to establish a record of the prehypnotic state of mind of each witness.

Three witnesses were hypnotized on the day of the abduction, and three other witnesses were hypnotized two days after the incident. Furthermore, five of the seven key prosecution witnesses were hypnotized twice. This further complicates and accentuates the inherent difficulties that are present in even a single hypnotism of a witness and that have already led us to exclude hypnotically induced testimony. The administration of hypnosis to the witnesses was interspersed among the photographic and corporal lineups, making it nearly impossible to track the purported state of each witness' memory, even if such evidence were available.

The prosecution argues and the defense experts agree that the hypnotic sessions were conducted without any deliberate attempt to alter witnesses' memories. However, even if, as proposed by the Dissent, nonsuggestiveness eliminates the unreliability of posthypnotic testimony, the fact that the police originally did not have a suspect toward whom the interrogator could possibly nudge an uncertain witness, there undoubtedly was in this case, and understandably so, a strong desire to have an identification made. *fn28 While the Dissent suggests we "ignored" the lack of a suspect at the time of the "initial" hypnosis, the Dissent ignores the fact that Mr. Wilcome was the only witness to identify defendant from the first lineup. The identification of the defendant by Mr. Wilcome during the first lineup was not positive. Mr. Wilcome initially did not identify any individual, but rather as an afterthought picked the defendant as the man who looked the closest to the perpetrator. Further, the defendant was a primary suspect *fn29 at the time of the second hypnosis which occurred one month prior to the identification of the defendant at the second lineup. The second hypnotic session took place after police had an opportunity to verify defendant's alibi statement which resulted in discrepancies in times and places.

The prosecutor further argues that because there was a uniformity of reactions by all the witnesses at the lineups, the identifications were based on prehypnotic memory. We disagree; first, because even though each witness gave a general description of a black man prior to hypnosis, it was not until after the hypnotic sessions that the witnesses were given the opportunity to select or reject the defendant. Furthermore, each witness at one time or another identified persons other than defendant as the perpetrator. Lastly, there is no record of the prehypnotic descriptions of the perpetrator available upon which to make a comparison, as we did in Centers and McIntosh, to support the admission of identification testimony by the hypnotized witnesses.

Further, the plaintiff did not argue, nor can we conclude, that the prehypnosis composite drawing by witness Jack Hill can be considered a statement recalled and related under Nixon. The composite drawing represents the work of the artist and cannot substitute for oral testimony related and recorded.

The Dissent also claims that the uniformity among witnesses of the identification of the vehicle driven by the abductor supports the Conclusion that the identification was reliable. The record, however, paints a fuller picture. Jack Hill, the man who witnessed the last stages of the abduction, initially and while under hypnosis identified the vehicle as a shiny, black Chrysler. *fn30 Subsequent to both hypnotic sessions Mr. Hill saw defendant's vehicle in the police garage and thereafter testified at trial that the vehicle was not a Chrysler. *fn31 Further, David Orr and Timothy Wilcome, the grounds maintenance men who freed a black car from a snowbank near where the victim's body was found, both testified that the car was a black Monte Carlo. *fn32 The Dissent states that "Orr did identify the car as a black Monte Carlo" but discounts the inconsistency in its analysis by suggesting that the purpose of Orr's testimony was merely corroborative. The procedures employed in this case were totally lacking in safeguards too ensure the reliability of the testimony being offered. *fn33 The standards and analysis employed by the Dissent *fn34 suggest that reliability of posthypnotic memory can be tested on the basis of the other independent evidence offered in the case. However, this Court has never proposed that the proper test for admissibility of evidence should be based on the strength of the case against a defendant. If there is enough independent evidence to prove identity, there would be no need to introduce unreliable evidence of identification. Merely because the other evidence offered in the case corroborates defendant's guilt or innocence does not mean that it confirms the reliability of a hypnotized witness' identification of defendant. To establish the reliability of testimony offered by a hypnotized witness would require an evaluation of evidence that would suggest that the memory produced from hypnosis was actual memory and not merely evidence which would further corroborate defendant's guilt or innocence.

The Dissent relies on testimony from Dr. Orne to support its Conclusion that the testimony received from the hypnotized witness was reliable. *fn35 At trial, Dr. Orne was allowed to comment about the nature of the physical evidence presented and whether, in his opinion, it corroborated the hypnotized witness' testimony. We note first that such an evaluation is beyond the expertise of Dr. Orne and should not have been permitted. Further, the physical evidence served only to circumstantially support defendant's guilt and did not operate to afford a basis for distinguishing between what was the witness' actual memory and what was confabulation.

The Dissent has, in our view, mischaracterized the work of this Court in Gonzales. In that case, we unmistakably expressed the view that posthypnotic testimony was "inherently unreliable." Gonzales, supra, p 626. However, we recognize that hypnosis does not always produce unreliable information, and in some cases the technique may have no effect on memory. *fn36. But because the science of hypnosis itself cannot aid us in distinguishing which effect is being achieved in individual cases, we have and should continue to consider as unreliable all posthypnotic testimony that is not recalled and related prior to hypnosis.

The purpose of the Davis/Frye doctrine is to determine if the scientific technique as a general rule produces reliable evidence. We cannot agree with the Dissent that reliability can be determined in every case. The tenet that the trial Judge can make a determination in each individual case and place the stamp of reliability and credibility on a hypnotized witness' testimony is without merit. The Dissent today would scrap the Davis/Frye decision of Gonzales :

agree with the Conclusion that the process of hypnosis and its outcome is inherently unreliable. Hypnosis has not received sufficient general acceptance in the scientific community to give reasonable assurance that the results produced under even the best of circumstances will be sufficiently reliable to outweigh the risk of abuse or prejudice [Gonzales, supra, p 626 (emphasis supplied),]

and put the trial courts in the position of determining on an ad hoc basis when hypnotically induced testimony is reliable and, therefore, admissible. This Court has over the years not deviated from application of the Davis/Frye doctrine to new scientific discoveries. The best way to achieve reliability of the results of scientific principles is to only allow admissibility of the results when the technique has gained general acceptance within the recognized field.

In a further attempt to recast Nixon from a rule that posthypnotic testimony is inherently unreliable into a rule that the trial courts can determine whether or not hypnotically induced testimony is reliable, the Dissent states that " we did say in Nixon that a witness could testify on the basis of facts recalled and related prior to hypnosis, we did not say that this was the only way" that you could establish its reliability. (Post, p 105, Boyle, J., Dissenting.) First, the "recalled and related" rule did not make posthypnotic testimony reliable. Rather, because posthypnotic testimony is so unreliable, the rule ensures that a hypnotized witness only testifies with regard to prehypnotic memory if the facts from that prehypnotic memory were recalled and related prior to the hypnosis. If there is any doubt about what we said on that point in Nixon, it should be resolved by the very language of the Nixon opinion.

In order to ensure that the witness' trial testimony is based solely on facts recalled and related prior to hypnosis, we hold that the party offering the testimony must establish its reliability by clear and convincing evidence. [Nixon, supra, p 90. Emphasis supplied.]

Nixon did not, as the Dissent advocates, establish a "heightened reliability standard" for hypnotically affected testimony. (Post, p 108, Boyle, J., Dissenting.) To the contrary, it established a reliability and burden threshold for testimony supported by prehypnotic actions.

We adhere to the standards adopted by this Court in Gonzales and Nixon, and hold that testimony of the hypnotized witnesses is inadmissible absent proof by clear and convincing evidence that the testimony being offered was based on facts recalled and related prior to hypnosis.

[17] C

Where the reviewing court finds that evidence was improperly admitted it must also make a determination regarding whether the error was harmless. As defined by the court rules, " error in the admission . . . of evidence . . . is not ground for granting a new trial . . . unless refusal to take this action appears to the court inconsistent with substantial Justice." MCR 2.613(A). The prosecution asserts that the physical evidence corroborates the eyewitness identification and therefore that any error in the admission of testimony from the hypnotized witnesses was harmless.

[18] Justice Levin, writing for the Court, in People v Young (After Remand), 425 Mich 470, 505; 391 NW2d 270 (1986), defined the standards for determining if an error is harmless.

[19] As an appellate court, we do not independently evaluate this evidence. " is not the appellate court's function to determine guilt or innocence. . . . Those judgments are exclusively for the jury " Our responsibility is to determine how the error might have affected the jury's decision. The inquiry is "what effect the error had or reasonably may be taken to have had upon the jury's decision."

[20] If it were clear that the erroneous admission of the evidence did not prejudice [the defendant], the error would be harmless. Citing Kotteakos v United States, 328 U.S. 750, 763-764; 66 S Ct 1239; 90 L Ed 1557 (1946).

[21] The error in the instant case was prejudicial to defendant. Defendant was identified as the perpetrator of the crime only by witnesses who were hypnotized. The jury was apprised of the fact that the key witnesses for the prosecution were hypnotized, and we do not know what significance it had in their determination of defendant's guilt. Furthermore, absent the testimony of the hypnotized witnesses, the remaining evidence does not positively link defendant to this crime. Thus we cannot conclude that the evidence against defendant was overwhelming.

[22] The Dissent criticizes our Conclusion that the error in this case was not harmless for two reasons. The first is because of the "wholesale application of Nixon to all the witnesses who were hypnotized

. . . ." (Post, p 105, Boyle, J., Dissenting.) However, by accepting the rule as set forth in Nixon as clear precedent in this state, there is no need to separate and examine individually each witness' testimony. The Dissent's analysis and charge that we have " to engage in any meaningful separate analysis of the testimony of each witness" (post, p 104, Boyle, J., Dissenting) is the best fortification of our decisions in Gonzales and Nixon that all posthypnotic testimony which is not based on prehypnotic memory recalled and related is unreliable.

[23] The second is that we have " ignored . . . the fact that the defendant admitted to a cellmate that he accidentally killed the victim while attempting to sexually molest her." (Post, p 105, Boyle, J., Dissenting.) We note first that the cellmate stated on the record that the only reason he contacted police with any information concerning defendant's purported confession was because he found the crime "sickening." Yet, at the time of trial, the cellmate had pending against him two counts of criminal sexual conduct in the first degree. Further he testified that he received no promises from thestate in exchange for his testimony. One month after defendant's trial the cellmate entered into a plea bargain agreement where these charges were reduced to CSC IV, a misdemeanor. Additionally, defendant testified that he observed his cellmate reading documents pertaining to his case prior to testifying.

[24] The evidence that was particularly incriminating to the defendant was that he was one of three black men in Kent County who owned a 1976 or 1977 black Grand Prix with a red interior. *fn37 Evidence found on the victim's body at the time of the autopsy included a number of short black negroid hairs and reddish-orange carpet fibers, the source being unidentifiable. Additionally, a barrette was combed out of the victim's hair. When the police searched defendant's car, they found several long blond hairs and feathers that allegedly came from the victim's down mittens. Additionally, under the seat, police found a plastic barrette. The barrette found in defendant's car and the one combed from the victim's hair were manufactured by the same company, although the manufacturer could not state

specifically that the barrette came from the same package as the barrette found in the victim's hair.

[25] The prosecution brought in various expert witnesses to testify as to the similarities between the physical evidence found on the victim and in defendant's car. However, these experts could not positively state that the evidence comparatively matched that produced from defendant's car. As a result of the experts' testimony, the trial Judge stated:

[26] As I understand it, Mr. Murray [defendant's attorney] objects to Exhibits 139 through 144 *fn38 because they apparently have no probative value other than to show what the authorities have done in an attempt to investigate this matter, and I suppose to head off any defense argument that they didn't do enough.

[27] But, really, I have been surprised I haven't heard this argument a long time ago. I have been listening to this type of testimony for two days, now. It is really just a failure to link the Defendant with any of the evidence.

[28] The Dissent described the trial Judge who expressed these doubts as "a scrupulously fair Judge"(post, p 106, Boyle, J., Dissenting). We agree.

[29] Although the totality of the evidence makes for a stronger circumstantial case, the physical evidence was not overwhelming, even though circumstantially significant. It has a limited probative value, absent the eyewitness identification of defendant, and therefore we cannot conclude that all reasonable doubts would have been eliminated in the jurors' minds.

[30] III

[31] We now turn to the question whether the similar acts evidence offered by the prosecution was properly admitted.

[32] A

[33] The prosecution was allowed to admit the testimony of ten-year-old Judy Sanchez and nine-year-oldAmy Combs over objection. The trial court endorsed the witnesses pursuant to

MRE 403 and 404. They testified that on February 6, 1979, approximately one week prior to this incident, a black man in a black car approached them while they were walking to school. Defendant did not work on February 6, 1979. He called in sick and claimed to have been home all day.

[34] The testimony of the two girls varies somewhat, although they generally testified that the man stopped his car and put one foot outside the door. He asked them for the time and the location of Hall Street. The girls responded to the questions, and after doing so the man motioned to the girls to come closer to the car. Both girls testified that they were scared and that the man recognized their fear. Judy had apparently run from the car, but Amy had stayed longer. As Judy gradually came back, the girls testified that the man got into the car and left.

[35] The two girls identified defendant from a mugbook consisting of six photographs. *fn39 Both girls identified defendant in a corporal lineup on March 29, 1979. While participating in the corporal lineup on March 29, Judy Sanchez identified two persons, one being the defendant and a second individual whose voice she felt sounded closest to the person. At trial neither of the two girls were able to positively identify the defendant as the man who approached them on February 6, 1979. On cross-examination Judy Sanchez made the following statement concerning the in-court identification of defendant:

[36] Q. Judy, you are not saying that this man, here, Mr. Lee, Albert Lee, is the man you saw on that particular date, are you?

[37] A. No it looks the closest description to the guy.

[38] Amy Combs testified that she was "pretty sure, but not positive" that Mr. Albert Lee was the man who approached her and Judy.

[39] B

[40] The introduction of similar acts evidence is an exception to the general rule that evidence of other crimes is inadmissible. *fn40 In order to be admissible, the prosecution must show a high degree of similarity between the charged and uncharged acts. These standards are to be strictly applied and have been narrowly defined by this Court in an attempt to safeguard the defendant's right to a fair trial. The policy considerations underlying the safeguards are an attempt to avoid convicting the defendant because of prior misconduct rather than on the proofs of the charged offense. The standards governing the admissibility of similar acts testimony were set forth by this Court in Peoplev Golochowicz, 413 Mich 298, 309; 319 NW2d 518 (1982).

[41] evidence of defendant's other misconduct may be admitted: (1) there must be substantial evidence that the defendant actually perpetrated the bad acts sought to be introduced; (2) there must be some special quality or circumstance of the bad act tending to prove the defendant's identity or the motive, intent, absence of mistake or accident, scheme, plan or system in doing the act and, in light of the slightly different language of MRE 404(b) we add, opportunity, preparation and knowledge; (3) one or more of these factors must be material to the determination of the defendant's guilt of the charged offense; and (4) the probative value of the evidence sought to be introduced must not be substantially outweighed by the danger of unfair prejudice.

[42] The two girls testified that it was a black man in a black car that approached them on their way to school. That alone probably does not constitute substantial evidence to show that it was defendant who committed the bad act. However, there was testimony that defendant is one of three black men in Kent County who owns a black Pontiac Grand Prix, and, that defendant was absent from work on February 6, 1979, and could not verify his whereabouts.

[43] The facts which weigh against the substantiality of the evidence include defendant's own testimony that he was not the man, and, additionally, the tentativeness of the girls identifications. Further, one of the girls testified that the man did not have a mustache. Defendant had a mustache and noticeable sideburns a week later on February 12, 1979.

[44] Although the identification of defendant was tentative, the identification is bolstered because two witnesses identified defendant. This alone would not constitute substantial evidence. However, the identifications, coupled with the fact that the man had a black car and that defendant drives a black car, as well as the fact that defendant did not go to work on February 6, leads us to conclude that the prosecution has shown by substantial evidence that defendant was the perpetrator of the similar act. To test whether there is a special quality or circumstance sufficient to justify admission of the evidence on the issue of identity, this Court has made the following statements:

[45] It is the distinguishing characteristics which constitute the acts as similar within the meaning of . . . MRE 404(b), not the fact that all constitute the same crime or are violative of the same statute. The distinguishing, peculiar or special characteristics which are common to the acts and thus personalize them are said to be the defendant's "signature" which identifies him as the perpetrator [People v

Major, 407 Mich 394, 398-399; 285 NW2d 660 (1979).]

[46] Where . . . the only conceivable justification for admission of such similar-acts evidence is to prove the identity of the perpetrator, the link is forged with sufficient strength to justify admission of evidence of the separate offense only where the circumstances and manner in which the two crimes were committed are " nearly identical in method as to earmark [the charged offense] as the handiwork of the accused. Here much more is demanded than the mere

repeated commission of crimes of the same class The [commonality of circumstances] must be so unusual and distinctive as to be like a signature."

[47] It is because of the combined value of those two factors, the unique and uncommonly distinctive style employed by the defendant in committing the "substantially proved" uncharged similar offense, and the same distinctive modus operandi employed in the charged offense, that the jury is permitted to infer, if it believes the evidence, that both crimes were the handiwork of the same person, the defendant.

[48] It is the uniqueness and the distinctiveness with which both crimes were committed, combined with the proof that the defendant committed the "like act," that is the key. [People v Golochowicz, supra at 310-312. Citations omitted.]

[49] The similarity between the two incidents upon which the prosecutor bases its admission are that (1) both incidents involved a black man driving a black car, (2) each occurred in the early morning hours when children would be walking to school, (3) both incidents involved young girls, and (4) both occurred in the same general area. Generally, it could be argued that these factors are not peculiar or do not constitute the defendant's signature because they are common to many child molestation cases. However, the manner and circumstances of stalking and attracting victims can be and is, in this case, sufficiently distinctive and unique that it can pass the Golochowicz "signature" requirement. Child abduction cases, in the overall scheme of criminal activity, are rather rare and unique and relate to aberrant behavior, i.e., there is really no "run of the mill" child abduction, as in the case of a run of the mill robbery, or car theft. The coaxing of these two girls to the actor's car is in and of itself somewhat distinctive and, when coupled with the similarities in place and time, lend to the entire act a uniqueness and distinctiveness.

[50] The central issue in this case is identity. The evidence is material because identity is the only proposition at issue. Identity is a material issue, not because it is a factor of proof in generally all criminal cases, but because the defense has made it a genuinely controverted matter. Here, defendant does not offer any explanation for the killing, i.e., that it was unintentional or that he had some innocent purpose in inviting the victim into his car, rather he offers only an alibi defense that he could not have been the person to commit the act. Thus, the evidence, if admissible at all under MRE 404(b), could be used only to show identity.

[51] Defendant claims that he was prejudiced by the manner in which the prosecutor argued the similar acts incident. The trial Judge did not abuse his discretion in finding that the probative value of the evidence outweighs its prejudicial effect.

[52] In his closing argument, the prosecutor argued that Amy Combs and Judy Sanchez were in fact lucky to have gotten away from this man. He argued that what happened to the victim was intended by the defendant with regard to the two girls, however, it did not come about. Thus, in effect, the prosecution stressed the defendant's bad character and his propensity to commit such an act.

Although the prosecution agrees with the defense that the acts towards Judy Sanchez and Amy Combs did not constitute a crime, he argued that the acts in effect constituted an attempt, that the defendant intended to kidnap and kill the two girls. In his closing argument the prosecutor stated:

[53] addition to those three eyewitnesses, you heard some testimony, quite frankly, if you listened to it, the implications of what may have happened probably had to scare you a little bit, and that was Amy Combs and Judy Sanchez, and they described an incident that sounded

awfully familiar, except for the ending, as to what happened to [the victim].

[54] He said, "Come here." Why did he ask her to "come here"? Why did he ask her to do that? Not only did he do it once, he did it a couple of times. Mr. Murphy will say, "Well there is nothing wrong with what that person did, even assuming it was Mr. Lee, but we don't know what he wanted to do to her." Fortunately, Amy Combs ran away before he ever got a chance. But again, who did both of them identify? Just another coincidence. It was Albert Lee.

[55] The law says that I can bring these people in here to prove to you the identity of the person, the abductor and murderer of [the victim herein]. Again, compare all the similarities of what almost happened to those little girls to what did happen to [the victim], and it scares us.

[56] It is clear that the prosecutor's closing arguments were specifically designed to convey to the jury an improper purpose for the evidence. Indeed the trial Judge gave a cautionary instruction to the jury concerning the limited scope for which the evidence could be considered. In light of the fact that we have ordered a new trial on the basis of the hypnosis issue, we hold that in and of itself (i.e., absent the prosecutor's arguments) the similar acts evidence is more probative than prejudicial. While the prosecutor's use of the evidence was inappropriate in this trial, on this record the evidence was admissible. We are confident that on retrial the prosecution will confine its arguments within the permissible scope of MRE 404.

[57] Conclusion

[58] Defendant was prejudiced to the extent that reversal is required on the basis of the admission of identification testimony by hypnotized witnesses. Although the ruling of this Court in Gonzales was not available at the time of trial, defendant is entitled to the benefit of the Gonzales holding on the basis of the retroactivity analysis under Nixon. The

prosecution has failed to show by clear and convincing evidence that the hypnotic process and the resulting testimony was reliable and based on the facts recalled and related prior to the hypnotic sessions.

[59] On this record, the similar acts evidence offered by the prosecution in and of itself complies with the standards of Golochowicz.

[60] The decision of the Court of Appeals is reversed, and we remand the matter for a new trial.

[61] Cavanagh, J. (concurring in part and Dissenting in part).

[62] I join the result and reasoning of the other portions of the lead opinion, though I must write separately to express my Dissent from the lead opinion's analysis of the "similar acts" issue in partIII(B).

[63] I cannot join the reasoning of part III(B) since I would hold that it was an abuse of discretion for the trial court to have admitted the testimony of the similar acts witnesses at defendant's trial. The similar acts testimony simply does not support the inference that the defendant was about to entice the two young girls into his car, or that he was about to engage them in some other improper or criminal conduct. While this inference is necessary to support the admission of the evidence under MRE 404(b), it would be an abuse of discretion to infer that fact from this record.

[64] If I accepted the lead opinion's reading of the record, however, I might find that the similar acts evidence is admissible under MRE 404(b). See People v Golochowicz, 413 Mich 298, 309-312; 319 NW2d 518 (1982). For example, if the testimony did show that the actor had stalked his victims, or sought to attract the two little girls into his car by physically reaching out to them or verbally urging them into his car for no apparent proper purpose, then I might deem such acts to satisfy the requirements of MRE 404(b). On this record, however, the similar acts simply are

not so unusual and distinctive as to serve the purposes for which such evidence may be considered by the jury. *fn1

[65] I

[66] I accept the summary of the testimony of the similar acts witnesses contained in the lead opinion.(Ante, pp 90-91.) The lead opinion summarizes the testimony of Amy Combs and Judy Sanchez accurately. *fn2

[67] The lead opinion characterizes the similar acts testimony in a manner that the record does not support by describing the two witnesses' version of events according to what may have occurred when the black man stopped the two young girls, rather than what actually happened to them. The acts of the man who stopped Amy Combs and Judy Sanchez may have been a prelude to a child abduction, as the lead opinion suggests (ante, p 94), but the girls did not testify to that.

[68] Indeed, I am persuaded the record fails to support the lead opinion's interpretation of the testimony of the similar acts witnesses. *fn3 While the lead opinion states that the girls only testified that the defendant was coaxing them to come closer to the car, *fn4 it then draws unsupported Conclusions from this testimony that the man who committed the "similar act" was "stalking" the two young girls.

*fn5

[69] The similar acts evidence shows only that a man stopped the two young girls on February 6, 1979, to urge them to come closer to his car (i.e., as close as six feet), at which time he asked them the time of day and for directions. Any speculation by this Court about whether this man intended to carry out some improper (or criminal) intent is only speculation and has no record support. The circumstances of this incident do not indicate that the man intended to abduct the two young girls, though he may have secretly harbored such an unlawful intent. Moreover, the man's behavior

can as well be explained as motivated by a totally innocuous purpose.

[70] Perhaps, this Court could assume facts not in evidence because the "similar acts" incident bears such a close resemblance to the fears of all parents who have worried that their children will talk to a stranger while walking alone to school. I would reject that approach, however, for obvious reasons. This Court cannot simply take judicial notice of the fact that a black man who stops young white girls to ask them the time of day and for directions is engaged in acts that are a prelude to a child abduction. Since the lead opinion makes unsupportable assumptions about the quality of the similar act that are necessary to the finding that the similar act was so unique and distinctive when compared to the charged offense as to constitute a "signature," Golochowicz, supra at 310-311, I must Dissent.

[71] II

[72] The reasoning of the lead opinion does not address the question whether the similar acts evidence will be admissible on retrial. Rather, the lead opinion holds only that " the prosecutor's use of the evidence was inappropriate in this trial, on this record, the evidence was admissible." *fn6 Nevertheless, there remains the important issue whether the analysis of the lead opinion can be applied if the prosecutor seeks to introduce the same evidence on retrial. The similar acts evidence may well be inadmissible, under the reasoning of the lead opinion, if the prosecutor on retrial cannot prove with substantial evidence that a black man driving a black car committed the charged offense.

*fn7

[73] We simply do not know whether there will be any additional evidence to supplement this record in proving that the charged offense was committed by a black man driving a

black car. The evidence in this record contains proof of that fact only if the hypnotized witnesses' testimony is admissible. Yet, the evidence is necessary to show the uniqueness and distinctiveness of the "similar act" because it links the similar act to the charged offense in the manner required by MRE 404(b).

[74] Under the first prong of the Golochowicz four-part evidentiary safeguards, there must be "substantial evidence that the defendant actually perpetrated the bad act sought to be introduced," id. at 309. In analyzing this prong of the test, the lead opinion finds that there was substantial evidence to show that the defendant was the perpetrator of the similar act. The lead opinion reaches this Conclusion, despite the tentativeness of the witnesses' eyewitness identification of him, because of two additional, and crucial, facts:

[75] [1] the man had a black car and that defendant drives a black car,

[76] [2] that defendant did not go to work on February 6*fn8

[77] The fact that the defendant did not go to work proves very little, since it is the prosecutor's burden of production and persuasion to prove by substantial evidence that the defendant committed the similar act. *fn9

[78] The fact that the perpetrator of the charged offense was a black man and drove a black car plays an important role in the lead opinion's finding that this "similar acts" evidence was properly admitted for an additional reason. Under the second prong of the Golochowicz standard, when (as here) "the only conceivable justification for admission of such similar-acts evidence is to prove the identity of the perpetrator, . . . [commonality of circumstances] [between the act and the charged offense] must be so unusual and distinctive as to be like a signature,'" id. at 310-311 (citation omitted); *fn10 see ante, pp 93-94; see also People v Hall, 433 Mich 573, 586; 447 NW2d 580 (1989). *fn11 Indeed, if there is no substantial evidence linking the similar act to

the charged offense, then there is no basis for the admission of the similar acts evidence to prove identity under MRE 404(b).

[79] In analyzing the second prong of the Golochowicz standard, the lead opinion relies, in large part, on the fact that a black man driving a black car was seen both during the commission of the charged offense and during the similar act; indeed, this fact serves as the key factor which proves the similarity between the charged offense and the similar act that MRE 404(b) requires. *fn12

[80] Given today's holding that the testimony of the hypnotized witnesses who saw a black man in a black car at the scene of the charged offense "is inadmissible absent proof by clear and convincing evidence that the testimony being offered [to show that it] was based on facts recalled and related prior to hypnosis," (ante, p 94), the testimony of these witnesses may be inadmissible upon retrial.

*fn13

[81] Boyle, J. (dissenting in part and Concurring in part).

[82] We Dissent. The majority has applied the Frye/Davis test and reversed the defendant's conviction despite the fact that the defendant was identified by witnesses who were never subjected to suggestion. Further, the majority fails to engage in any meaningful separate analysis of the testimony of each witness. The overwhelming evidence in this case convinces us that the conviction of Albert Lee, III, did not constitute a miscarriage of Justice. We concur only in Justice Brickley's result that the prior act testimony, MRE 404(b), was properly admitted, although we do not endorse the reasoning.

[83] The point ignored by the majority in this case is that at the time of the initial hypnosis, the identity of the defendant was unknown to the police officers. Thus, on this record it is indisputable that there was no connection between that

hypnosis and the witnesses' later selection of the defendant from a lineup. Secondly, since the defendant's expert witness, Dr. Martin Orne, testified that hypnosis had no bearing on the identification of the car by the four witnesses who identified it before, during, and after hypnosis as a clean, black Grand Prix, it is indisputable on this record that identification of the vehicle was reliable. Thirdly, Dr. Orne testified that the defendant's ownership of the car was corroborative evidence of the reliability of the identification of the defendant. Finally, and most significantly, Dr. Orne also testified that the identification of the defendant by Jack Hill and Jack Vos was not the product of the hypnotic sessions. Despite these undisputed facts, the majority simply avoids any meaningful discrete analysis of the testimony and erroneously concludes that the conviction must be reversed because the identification was corrupted by the "suggestive effect of hypnosis," on the unfounded assumption that the hypnosis somehow induced the identification testimony.

[84] The assumption that hypnosis renders a witness incompetent to testify is a proposition we rejected in People v Nixon, 421 Mich 79; 364 NW2d 593 (1984). While we did say in Nixon that a witness could testify on the basis of facts recalled and related prior to hypnosis, we did not say that this was the only way that "the party offering the testimony" could establish its reliability. Nixon, supra, p 90.As this case illustrates, such a broad prophylactic rule is unwarranted.

[85] The majority opinion gives the state another opportunity to show reliability at the retrial it orders today. However, the fallacy in the majority's formulation is that it would appear that comparison of a witness's general description of a suspect with the defendant's actual appearance would rarely producea Conclusion that the taint is dissipated, except in the rare case of a defendant who has unique identifying

characteristics. On this record, the majority formulation in application thus all but obliterates the distinction drawn in Nixon.

[86] Even more disturbing, the majority's wholesale application of Nixon to all the witnesses who were hypnotized, obscures any meaningful examination of prejudicial error. MCL 769.26; MSA 28.1096. Inexplicably ignored is the fact that the defendant admitted to a cellmate that he "accidentally" killed the victim while attempting to sexually molest her. Consciousness of guilt was shown by a false exculpatory statement that the defendant was at the Secretary of State's office at the time of the abduction. On the morning of Linda Vanderveen's abduction, two men observed a black male, who smoked Kool cigarettes and drove a black car with bicentennial plates, throw something into a dumpster located within one mile of where the victim's body was found. Other evidence established that the defendant smoked Kools, had bicentennial plates, and drove a black car. Linda's knapsack was recovered from the dumpster. Only three black men in Kent County, one of whom was the defendant, owned a 1976 or 1977 Grand Prix with a red interior. A barrette, feathers that came from mittens similar to those of the victim, and long blond hairs were found in the defendant's car. A number of short black negroid type hairs were found on Linda's body, as were orange carpet fibers similar to those in the defendant's car. The testimony of Amy Combs and Judy Sanchez indicated that the defendant had approached two young girls for directions six days before Linda Vanderveen's abduction, one mile from where she was kidnapped. The defendant's admission to his cellmate, if believed by the jury, was itself sufficient to support the verdict. Absent the "tainted evidence," the remaining evidence of guilt was compelling. The case was magnificently tried by two able advocates before a scrupulously fair Judge. Upon a review of the entire

evidence, it cannot be said that AlbertLee, III, did not receive a fair trial. We would affirm the conviction below.

[87] I

[88] In People v Gonzales, 415 Mich 615; 329 NW2d 743 (1982), modified 417 Mich 968 (1983), we applied the Frye test to hypnosis and concluded that testimony which had been "tainted" by hypnosis should be excluded from criminal trials. Two years later, in People v Nixon, 421 Mich 79, 90; 364 NW2d 593 (1984), we declined to declare incompetent any witness who had been hypnotized, holding instead that a witness could testify subsequent to hypnosis when the party offering the testimony could show by clear and convincing evidence that the testimony was "based solely on facts recalled and related prior to hypnosis

" We are persuaded that Nixon's rejection of the rule of incompetence per se is correct. However, having there held that the testimony of a witness who has been hypnotized is admissible if shown to be reliable, it must follow that Frye v United States, 54 App DC 46, 47; 293 F 1013 (1923), should not be applied in these circumstances.1a As the majority's result demonstrates, it can be argued with expert support that every witness who has undergone hypnosis is somehow influenced by that experience. If Frye is applied to the testimony of any witness who has been hypnotized, it must follow logically that all such testimony is inadmissible unless and until hypnosis receives general acceptance in the scientific community, the very proposition we rejected in Nixon. In short, either we were wrong in Nixon and all such testimony is inadmissible per se, or there is a distinction between testimony recalled during hypnosis, as to which Frye/Davis may still be applicable, and testimony which has not been affected by hypnosis despite the fact that the witness was hypnotized, as to which Frye does not apply.

[89] This case vividly demonstrates that the application of Frye to identifying witnesses who have undergone hypnosis forces the state to choose between use of hypnosis during the investigative stage and the potential loss of the witness' testimony at trial, Nixon, supra, p 90. We do not agree with the majority's assertion that the loss of testimony in this case results only because the testimony of the witnesses was not preserved prior to hypnosis. Application of the Frye rule in this case and virtually all others will exclude subsequent identification if hypnosis is employed prior to actual identification of a defendant.

[90] However, while Frye should not be applied simply because of the fact of hypnosis, the basic reason for the Frye rule obtains, that is, concern whether the traditional means of assuring reliability of testimony are, in a given context, adequate to ensure prosecutorial fairness and just results. Hypnosis undoubtedly poses special problems which justify the application of the heightened reliability standard required in Nixon, that is, that reliability must be shown by clear and convincing evidence. Thus, while we would modify the Nixon formulation, we would not adopt the rule that the fact of hypnosis applies only to credibility and not admissibility. United States v Awkard, 597 F2d 667, 669 (CA 9, 1979), cert den 444 U.S. 885 (1979).2a

[91] Courts have taken three basic approaches to the admissibility of posthypnosis testimony: automatic admission, automatic exclusion, and admission conditioned on compliance with detailed procedural safeguards.

[92] Under the first approach, the testimony of a witness who has been hypnotized is viewed as present recollection refreshed by hypnosis. Awkard, supra, p 669. The fact and effect of hypnosis apply to weight and not admissibility, id.; State v Brown, 337 NW2d 138, 151 (ND, 1983); Chapman v State, 638 P2d 1280, 1282 (Wy, 1982).

[93] The second approach, inadmissibility per se, was adopted in People v Shirley, 31 Cal 3d 18; 181 Cal Rptr 243; 641 P2d 775 (1982). Courts taking this approach typically draw their Conclusions from application of the Frye rule of scientific acceptance. See State v Mena, 128 Ariz 226; 624 P2d 1274 (1981); State ex rel Collins v Superior Court, 132 Ariz 180; 644 P2d 1266 (1982); Polk v State, 48 Md App 382; 427 A2d 1041 (1981). Michigan is among those states that initially adopted a rule of inadmissibility per se but thereafter allowed a witness to testify regarding facts recalled prior to hypnosis, Nixon, supra ; see also Collins, supra. As already suggested, permitting a witness to testify as to identification of a defendant after he has been hypnotized is logically inconsistent with the Frye rule, since there is not general acceptance in the scientific community of the reliability of post-hypnotic testimony.

The third and preferable approach allows admission of posthypnosis testimony when, in the particular case, it is found to be reliable. See People v Romero, 745 P2d 1003 (Colo, 1987); State v Iwakiri, 106 Idaho 618; 682 P2d 571 (1984); State v Woodfin, 539 So 2d 645 (La App, 1989). The reliability centered approach is articulated in State v Hurd, 86 NJ 525, 538; 432 A2d 86 (1981), in which the New Jersey court held that the use of hypnosis could satisfy Frye in certain instances.3a Thus, in Hurd, hypnotically induced recall was held admissible if the proponent of the evidence could show that the use of hypnosis in the particular case was "a reasonably reliable means of restoring a person's memory." Id. The Hurd court adopted the procedural recommendations of Dr. Orne, the defense expert in this proceeding. Id., pp 545-546.

[94] Compliance with the Orne safeguards does not guarantee admissibility of the testimony; it merely provides a basis to assess its reliability. Id., p 546. Thus, even when the safeguards are followed, circumstances may suggest that the testimony of a witness who has undergone hypnosis is not

reliable. For instance, where the posthypnotic testimony is identification of a person known to be under suspicion by a witness who has been previously unable to identify the person, the danger of suggestion through hypnosis is evident. United States v Valdez, 722 F2d 1196, 1203 (CA 5, 1984). On the other hand, even where the conditions of hypnosis do not meet the Orne standards, an independent basis for posthypnosis identification may compensate for the deficiencies of the hypnotic session.4a

[95] Where posthypnosis identification is otherwise shown to be reliable, the rationale for Nixon is served and there is no purpose in limiting identification evidence to facts "related and recalled" prior to hypnosis. As the court noted in Harker v Maryland, 800 F2d 437, 442 (CA 4, 1986), suggestibility and memory hardening are concerns whenever a witness makes an identification. While exclusion would certainly remedy those problems, it would also sacrifice probative evidence which might be sufficiently reliable in a particular case to aid in the truth-finding process. In the context of posthypnosis identification particularly, the rule sweeps too broadly, eliminating reliable and unreliable evidence alike and insuring that, as a practical matter, "the police will seldom dare to use hypnosis as an investigatory tool because they will thereby risk making the witness incompetent . . .

." State ex rel Collins, supra, p 209.

[96] The more prudent balance should be struck by requiring a preliminary determination of admissibility on a case-by-case basis. Using a flexible test informed in particular by the Orne factors, the court should, pursuant to MRE 104, make a determination of the reliability of the evidence sought to be presented. If posthypnosis testimony is found sufficiently reliable for admission, the parties remain free to make the jury aware of the dangers of hypnosis with expert testimony

and to cross-examine the identifying witness as to the conditions of hypnosis and any independent basis for observation.

[97] II

[98] The identity of the defendant was not suggested to any witness during or after hypnosis. The initial hypnotic sessions were conducted by local hypnotist, Robert Mazur, on the day of the abduction and two days later on February 14, 1979. At this time, the police were acting on seven hundred to nine hundred tips, with as many suspects. Since Mr. Mazur himself could have known nothing about the defendant's identity, it is clear beyond question that he could not, even inadvertently, have suggested the identity of the defendant to the witnesses. The second hypnosis of the witnesses was conducted on February 23, 1979, still before defendant became the primary suspect. Commenting on the fact that witness Jack Hill could make no identification immediately before, during, or after his second hypnosis, Dr. Orne opined that the hypnotic sessions were carried out with some care, and that if the authorities knew who was believed to be responsible for the crime, it was not communicated to the hypnotized individual. While not all of the Orne safeguards were employed in the hypnotic sessions of February 12, 14 and 23, 1979, it is evident on the record that there was no suggestion of the defendant's identity.

[99] As the majority notes, there were seven prosecution witnesses in this case who were hypnotized. (Jack Hill, James Vos, Jack Vos, Greg Start, David Orr, Jr., Timothy Wilcome, and Jim Bonnema). Ante, p 65. Proper analysis requires an examination of the circumstances surrounding testimony of each of these witnesses' identification.

[100] Jim Bonnema testified only that he saw a clean, black, 1976 or 1977 Grand Prix automobile speeding though the vicinity of the abduction at 8:15 a.m. Bonnema saw a young

black man driving the car but could not identify the defendant as the driver. There was additional evidence that the defendant was one of three black men in Kent County who owned a 1976 or 1977 black Grand Prix with a red interior. Nevertheless, Bonnema was unable to give either the color of the interior of the vehicle he saw, nor was he able to give the license number of the car.

[101] Similarly, James Vos was only able to identify the vehicle as a black Grand Prix. Vos was unsure of the year of the vehicle and gave no testimony as to the color of the interior. James Vos gave only a general description of the driver, a twenty- to thirty-year-old black male with a medium afro hair style and a dark leather jacket. He was unable to identify the defendant as the driver of the vehicle.

[102] Dr. Orne testified that hypnosis had no bearing on the testimony of these witnesses as to identification of the car involved in the abduction:

[103] Q. [Assistant Prosecutor]: Now, again, you have no difficulty, given the sequence of the identification of the car in this case, that these witnesses who have identified a black Grand Prix actually saw -- at least they think they actually saw a black Grand Prix?

[104] A. [Dr. Orne]: I have no reason to doubt that particularly. I have no reason to agree with it. I take that . . .

[105] Q. In other words, in your opinion the hypnosis had no effect on that identification of the car.

[106] A. Given the facts the people identified it before in the same way as they identified it after. If it had been identified as a '76 before, then became a '77 afterwards, then I would worry about the hypnosis having an effect.

[107] Q. But the mere fact we are talking, now, about the Grand Prix, itself, it was before, it was during, and it was after, and it is your opinion that hypnosis had no effect on that identification?

[108] A. I'd say reasonably. This is for everyone except Mr. Hill.

[109] Therefore, the trial Judge did not err in admitting the testimony of Jim Bonnema and James Vos.

[110] Turning next to the question whether Jack Hill's testimony was shown to be reliable by clear and convincing evidence, we find ample support for the trial court's Rule 104 determination. There was clear and convincing evidence that Hill's identification was the product of independent recollection.

Jack Hill witnessed the last stages of the abduction and identified Mr. Lee at the second lineup and at the trial. The abduction occurred at 8:00 a.m. in "good" light. There was very little snowfall at the time. Hill observed the defendant from about four feet away. He spoke briefly with the defendant and noticed a lack of accent or slang. While Hill failed to identify the defendant upon viewing two mug books and one corporeal lineup, at the first lineup, all of the participants put their hair in "cornrows." There was nothing in the record to suggest that Hill was suffering from fatigue, nervous exhaustion, or alcohol or drug use, and Hill ultimately picked the defendant out of a corporeal lineup some six weeks after the abduction.

[111] Most significantly, the majority simply fails to acknowledge that Judge Boucher based his ruling onthe effect of the hypnosis on Jack Hill on the testimony by the defense expert Orne. Dr. Orne not only testified that there was no deliberate attempt to alter the memory of Mr. Hill though hypnosis, but also concluded that the hypnosis was not the source of Mr. Hill's memory.5a

[112] It is clear from this testimony that, while Dr. Orne did not believe that Hill's identification was actually based upon memory, Dr. Orne was convinced that the identification was not the product of hypnosis, but of some "third events."

[113] Additionally, Dr. Orne acknowledged at trial that corroborating facts were significant to the determination of whether the testimony was based on actual memory, and he

admitted that he had been unaware of the corroborative physical evidence of blond hairs, carpet fiber, barrette, or feathers prior to his testimony.6a

[114] Curiously, the majority asserts that Dr. Orne's comment regarding corroborative evidence was outside the area of his expertise. In fact, Dr. Orne testified that reference to corroborative facts is a means by which experts determine that a posthypnosis memory is a true memory. However, whether Dr. Orne concluded that Hill's identification of the defendant was the result of "third events" or his "alternative hypothesis," i.e., Hill's actual memory, is irrelevant. The fact that identification was not the product of the hypnosis stands uncontroverted on this record. Thus, the issue of the reliability of Hill's identification of the defendant was an issue properly submitted to, and resolved by, the factfinder. The trial court's preliminary ruling admitting the testimony of Jack Hill was not erroneous.

[115] Although Jack Vos, the seventeen-year-old son of James Vos, had considerably less time in which to view the defendant than Jack Hill, as with Jack Hill, the testimony by the defense expert, Dr. Orne, is dispositive of admissibility. Dr. Orne's testimony that Jack Hill's identification of the defendant was not the product of hypnosis applied equally to Jack Vos. Moreover, Dr. Orne's testimony as to the significance of the corroborating evidence also applies to Jack Vos. Whatever differences might exist in the initial observation by Jack Vos, there was no error in the admission of his testimony.

[116] Timothy Wilcome was employed as a maintenance man at the Georgetown Apartments on the morning of February 12, 1979. He was cleaning snow at approximately 10:00 a.m. when a black male approached him on foot. The man asked Wilcome for a push, explaining that his car was stuck in the snow. Wilcome agreed to help him, and the two walked to his car. After an unsuccessful attempt to push the car out by

hand, Wilcome suggested that they ask his coworker, David Orr, to pull the car out with his truck.

[117] While Orr hooked up the car, Wilcome spoke to the individual. Wilcome asked for a cigarette and was given a Kool cigarette. Wilcome then pushed the car while Orr pulled the car with the truck. Wilcome testified that the car was a black Monte Carlo in good condition. He did not notice any particular details about the car or any writing on it but identified it by the body size and shape. Linda Vanderveen's knapsack was uncovered from a nearby dumpster later that day.

[118] Wilcome was interviewed by the investigating officers two days later on February 14, 1979. He was hypnotized by Mr. Mazur and later shown a mugbook containing the defendant's photograph. Wilcome failed to identify the defendant from the photograph and in fact selected another photograph as "close."7a The following day, Wilcome was shown a second mugbook without the defendant's photograph. He selected no one.

[119] About ten days later, Wilcome attended the first corporeal lineup in which all of the participants appeared with hair styled in cornrows. He was hypnotized prior to the lineup by Dr. Rossi of the Michigan State Police. Wilcome was unable to pick out the defendant "confidently," but did select the defendant as closest to the man he had seen on February 12. At the March 15 lineup, when the participants appeared in afro-styled hair, Wilcome was again unable to "confidently" pick out the defendant. Again, however, he picked out the defendant as closest in resemblance to the man he had seen on February 12. Wilcome also identified the defendant at trial but was similarly unable to give a "confident" identification.

[120] The evidence of record establishes that Timothy Wilcome had an excellent opportunity to observe the defendant for some time, including speaking with him. The lighting

was good, there was proximity, and there was nothing startling in the encounter. Wilcome failed to identify the defendantat the first photographic viewing, but he did pick out the defendant in the "cornrow" lineup about ten days later.

[121] David Orr also worked in maintenance at the Georgetown Apartments on February 12, 1979. However, Orr had no direct conversation or contact with the defendant and never identified the defendant as the driver of the car. Orr did identify the car as a black Monte Carlo. It appears that Orr's testimony was offered for two purposes: first, to provide a general corroboration of Wilcome's testimony, and, second, to establish that the driver of the car, identified by Wilcome as the defendant, threw something into the dumpster in which Linda Vanderveen's knapsack was found. Orr also testified that the defendant left the scene "in a hurry" after he was towed out of the snowbank.

[122] Here again Dr. Orne's testimony must be examined. Dr. Orne gave no specific opinion either at the pretrial hearing or at trial regarding the effect of the hypnosis on the testimony of Timothy Wilcome. However, the circumstances and quality of Wilcome's initial observation supported the trial court's determination that Wilcome's testimony was based on factors unrelated to the hypnosis. 8a Further, Dr. Orne, did not believe that the descriptions of the vehicle were affected by hypnosis. Assuming arguendo that Orr's description was unreliable, any error in the admission of this testimony must be deemed harmless. Orr's consistent description of the vehicle as a Monte Carlo was, in fact, exculpatory. Orr was never able to give a description of the defendant and never identified him. Thus, the only potential prejudice to the defendant that would flow from the testimony of David Orr is the general corroboration of Wilcome's account of pulling someone out of a snowbank and Orr's testimony that he saw the driver

afterward throw something into a dumpster. The admission of this evidence presents no basis for a reversal of the defendant's conviction.

[123] Finally, turning to the testimony of witness Greg Start, Dr. Orne expressed particular concern as to the possibility of hypnotic suggestion in Start's identification. He believed that Start was particularly vulnerable to suggestibility and was concerned about the use of a posthypnotic suggestion by Dr. Rossi to the effect that Start would be able to identify the person he saw on the day of the incident. 9a Start, a twelve-year-old safety boy, arrived at his post a few blocks from the scene of the abduction at about 8:00 a.m. on February 12, 1979. He testified that a little while after he arrived at his post, he saw a black Grand Prix with a red interior speed through the intersection. He further testified that the driver of the Grand Prix was a young black man, about twenty-five years old, with a mustache and a three-inch afro. The car went through the intersection "medium" fast. According to Start, the driver looked in his rear view mirror after he went through the intersection. Start saw the same car a few blocks away six or seven minutes later.

[124] Start did not see the car again, but he did see Jack and Jim Vos. They pulled over moments later and asked Start if he had seen a black Grand Prix. Start replied that he had not, but remembered a few minutes later that he had seen a black Grand Prix.

[125] In March or April of 1979, Start saw an article in the Grand Rapids Press about the defendant's arrest. A picture of the defendant ran with the article.

[126] Start was finally contacted by the investigating officers on May 2, 1979. The record is unclear as to whether he was shown mug-books with the defendant's picture. However, it is clear that Start had seen a picture of a person identified as the suspect prior to being hypnotized by Dr. Rossi on June 19,1979, and viewing a lineup on June 20, 1979. Start

picked out the defendant in the lineup and later identified the defendant at trial.

[127] Unlike the other witnesses whose hypnosis was conducted before defendant became the primary suspect, Start was hypnotized subsequent to defendant's March 29 arrest. The danger of suggestibility as to Start was heightened by the fact that prior to hypnosis, Start had seen defendant's picture in the newspaper and had been given a posthypnotic suggestion. In short, unlike the other witnesses, there is a basis in this record to find both that Start was subject to suggestion as to the identity of the suspect, and that the prosecution has failed to show by clear and convincing evidence the reliability of his testimony.

[128] Two final observations regarding the hypnotized witnesses are in order. Except as to Greg Start, Dr.Orne found no indication of cuing or suggestion in the hypnotic sessions. 10a Thus, except as to Start, the potential danger of suggestibility was negated on this record. Second, the evidence in this case includes three mugbooks containing a total of 316 pictures. Additionally, there are photographs of three lineups, two containing eight persons and one containing six. As the experienced and scrupulous trial Judge observed, the "utterly bewildering array" of mug shots shown the witnesses, together with the care with which the photographic and lineup sessions were conducted, actually increased the reliability of the identification testimony.11a

[129] Conclusion

[130] For the reasons explained, we would hold that the Frye test should not be applied to exclude the testimony of a witness simply because he has been hypnotized. The dangers of hypnosis do, however, require application of a Hurd -type test in which the reliability of the testimony must be established by clear and convincing evidence. The test to be employed is flexible; the primary considerations in the

reliability determination are whether the appropriate safeguards were employed at the hypnotic session, and whether the testimony offered has a basis independent of hypnosis. So analyzed, we conclude that error occurred in this case only in regard to the admission of Gregg Start's testimony, but that error does not compel reversal.

[131] The Code of Criminal Procedure provides:

[132] No judgment or verdict shall be set aside or reversed or a new trial be granted by any court of this state in any criminal case, on the ground of misdirection of the jury, or the improper admission or rejection of evidence, or for error as to any matter of pleading or procedure, unless in the opinion of the court, after an examination of the entire cause, it shall affirmatively appear that the error complained of has resulted in a miscarriage of Justice. [MCL 769.26; MSA 28.1096.]

[133] The prosecution built an impressive direct and circumstantial case involving over fifty witnesses and six days of trial. The prosecution established that only three cars matching the defendant's car were owned by black males in Kent County. A barrette, matching a second one worn by the victim was found in the back seat of the defendant's car. Feathers, such as those in the victim's gloves, and long blond hairs were also found in the back seat of the defendant's car. Carpet fibers matching those of the defendant's car and negroid type hairs were found on the victim's clothing, and a cellmate of the defendant's testified that the defendant had admitted that he accidentally killed the victim while attempting to sexually molest her. The defendant's alibi was effectively rebutted by testimony that placed him at the Secretary of State's office several hours after the abduction, rather than at the time of the abduction as the defendant testified.

[134] The erroneous admission of Greg Start's testimony did not result in a miscarriage of Justice. The defendant's conviction should be affirmed.

Opinion Footnotes

[135] *fn1 MCL 750.316; MSA 28.548, kidnapping being the underlying felony.

[193] *fn2 415 Mich 615; 329 NW2d 743 (1982), modified 417 Mich 968; 336 NW2d 751 (1983).

[194] *fn3 421 Mich 79; 364 NW2d 593 (1984).

[195] *fn4 People v Lee, unpublished opinion per curiam of the Court of Appeals, decided May 9, 1983 (Docket No. 51044).

[196] *fn5 The law on hypnosis has been changed considerably since then and the basis on which Judge Maher Dissented is no longer applicable.

[197] *fn6 People v Lee (On Remand), unpublished opinion per curiam of the Court of Appeals, decided November 21, 1985 (Docket No. 85840).

[198] *fn7 A police officer testified that he stopped the defendant on February 12, 1979, and described defendant as having a mustache and noticeable sideburns. The defense attempted to emphasize at trial that none of the eyewitnesses remembered the perpetrator as having facial hair or sideburns thus suggesting that defendant could not have been the abductor. Additionally, the girls who testified about the similar act do not recall the man having a mustache or sideburns.

[199] *fn8 A police officer testified that during an investigatory interview with defendant, he smoked Kool cigarettes.

[200] *fn9 During the investigation stage of this case, Mr. Wilcome told defendant's attorney that the vehicle he saw on the morning of February 12 could not have been a Pontiac Grand Prix.

[201] *fn10 To free the car from the snow he had to attach a tow rope to the back of the vehicle.

[202] *fn11 Defendant apparently got new license plates sometime during business hours on February 12, 1979. Testimony suggests that it was sometime before noon. However, we would note that this was not a spontaneous attempt on the part of defendant to "cover his tracks." In the week preceding the slaying, defendant had attempted to transfer title on the vehicle and obtain new license plates but was unable to complete the transaction.

[203] *fn12 The tape of Mr. Bonnema's hypnotic session was not available to defendant. It was apparently lost or erased during the investigation. However, defendant did receive a copy of the synopsis made after the session.

[204] *fn13 Polygraph testing and the results were not introduced at trial. However, according to testimony given during the pretrial motions, defendant apparently failed the polygraph testing.

[205] *fn14 Eight men participated in the lineup. All the men had their hair in cornrows, and thus defendant fixed his hair in a similar fashion. However, on the day of the incident, the perpetrator was described as having a neat, small to medium afro. As a result the participating witnesses claimed that identification was impossible because defendant was disguised.

[206] *fn15 Greg Start is one of the few witnesses who admits at trial that he does think he was hypnotized. The audiotape of his hypnotic session with Dr. Rossi was played to the jury; however, it was not transcribed in the record. At trial, defendant's attorney cross-examined Greg Start as to various statements he made to Dr. Rossi during the hypnotic session. Relevant to the issue of identification, Greg Start made the following statements: "No, I didn't get a good look at him either time"; in response to Dr. Rossi's question "Did you see his face a little bit?" he answered, "A

little bit"; in response to a question concerning whether or not Greg saw the car, he answered "Not too good, not at all"; he also stated, "I didn't pay much attention to him."

[207] *fn16 This occurred after the arrest of defendant (March 30, 1979) and after pictures of the defendant appeared in the newspapers and on television.

[208] *fn17 Defendant filed two motions relative to the publicity surrounding the incident. First, defendant sought to have the proceedings closed on the basis of a balancing of the substantial amount of publicity and defendant's ability to obtain a fair trial. The trial court denied defendant's motion. The court found that the First Amendment rights of the press were a substantial interest in this case and that defendant could still receive a fair trial with an open courtroom. Second, defendant moved for a change of venue, consideration of which was reserved until the jury was selected. Defendant raised two grounds for his motion, (1) damaging media coverage, and (2) the emotional effect of the crime on potential jurors and the community. The court denied the motion, stating that an impartial jury had been empaneled.

[209] *fn18 In People v Nixon, we rejected the defendant's arguments that a witness was totally incompetent because of being placed under hypnosis relying on the holding of the Arizona SupremeCourt in State ex rel Collins v Superior Court, 132 Ariz 180; 644 P2d 1266 (1982), and the New York decision of People v Hughes, 59 NY2d 523; 453 NE2d 484 (1983). For a summary of the development of the law on hypnosis in other jurisdictions, see People v Gonzales and People v Nixon.

[210] *fn19 The Dissent justified our holding in Nixon concerning the admissibility of posthypnotic testimony by labeling it as a "heightened reliability standard" which would require "that reliability must be shown by clear and convincing evidence." (Post, p 108, Boyle, J., Dissenting.)

[211] *fn20 We note that the parties in this case did not raise or argue on appeal the applicability of the Davis/Frye doctrine to the hypnotic process. People v Davis, 343 Mich 348; 72 NW2d 269 (1955); Frye v United States, 54 App DC 46; 293 F 1013 (1923).

[212] *fn21 See, generally, Scholder, The argument against use of hypnosis to improve or enhance the memory of courtroom witnesses, 7 Law & Psychology R 71 (1982); Curato, Plifka & Schroeder, Recent decision: Evidence: Hypnotically enhanced testimony -- A question of admissibility or credibility for criminal courts? 58 Notre Dame L R 101 (1982); comment, Hypnosis -- Should the courts snap out of it? -- A closer look at the critical issues, 44 Ohio State L J 1053 (1983).

[213] *fn22 Rock v Arkansas, 483 U.S. 44, 61; 107 S Ct 2704; 97 L Ed 2d 37 (1987).

[214] *fn23 State v Mack, 292 NW2d 764, 768 (Minn, 1980).

[215] *fn24 Defendant's expert, Dr. Martin T. Orne, whose testimony the Dissent relied upon in its finding of reliability and admissibility of posthypnotic testimony stated that hypnosis, although a valid investigatory tool, should not be used as a means by which to get an accurate eyewitness account of an event for testimonial purposes. He cautions against such use because it is virtually impossible to separate an actual memory from that created while in a hypnotic state. Dr. Orne is a renowned expert in the area of hypnosis and hypnotically refreshed memory.

[216] *fn25 We note that the safeguards announced by Dr. Orne and adopted by the Dissent in formulating a new test were not adhered to in this case. (See post, pp 109-110, Boyle, J., Dissenting). First, the initial hypnotic sessions of six of the seven hypnotized witnesses were conducted by Mr. Robert Mazur, a local hypnotist. Mr. Mazur is not a psychiatrist or psychologist. Second, Dr. Donald Rossi, who conducted the

second hypnotic sessions, although a psychologist, is not independent of the state. Third, neither hypnotist extracted from the subjects a prehypnosis description of the events. Fourth, all contacts between the hypnotist and the subject were not preserved for review by a recording. Finally, outside third parties were present during the hypnotic sessions.

[217] *fn26 In a footnote, the McIntosh panel recognized that a conflict existed between its holding and the holding in People v Centers.

[218] We recognize that the panel in People v Centers, supra, concluded that admission of evidence in Faulkner's identification of suspects at the posthypnotic lineup was reversible error because the actual identification was not something recalled and related prior to hypnosis. We are unable to agree with this Conclusion because we understand Nixon to permit trial testimony which is based on facts recalled and related prior to hypnosis even if the statement (including identification) was obtained after hypnosis. We base this analysis on the Nixon Court's statement in footnote 3 that " obtained after hypnosis are inadmissible per se under Gonzales, except as otherwise stated in this opinion and in accordance with applicable evidentiary rules." 421 Mich 91. In this case, we find, as did the trial court, that Faulkner's tentative identification of defendant at the posthypnotic lineup was based solely on facts recalled and related by her prior to hypnosis. Her in-court testimony about this identification was, therefore, solely based on facts recalled and related prior to hypnosis. [142 Mich App at

321-322, n 5. Emphasis in original.]

[219] *fn27 In a footnote, the Nixon Court ruled as to the admissibility of tape recordings of the hypnotic sessions. The Court stated:

[220] The trial court correctly ruled that statements made during hypnosis are inadmissible to prove the truth of the matters asserted therein Given the inherent problems of investigative hypnosis, we also hold that statements obtained from a witness during hypnosis cannot be used to bolster or impeach the witness' credibility. [Nixon, supra at 91, n 3. Citations omitted.]

[221] *fn28 The hypnotic state is a condition of altered consciousness marked by heightened suggestibility. A subject in a hypnotic state may not have accurate recall. A hypnotized subject is highly susceptible to suggestion, even that which is subtle and unintended. Such suggestion may be transmitted either during the hypnotic session or before it The person under hypnosis experiences a compelling desire to please either the hypnotist or others who have asked the person hypnotized to remember or who have urged that it is important that he or she remember certain events. The subject may produce the particular responses he believes are expected of him. In this state of hypersuggestibility and hypercompliance the subject will unconsciously create answers to the questions which the hypnotist asks if he cannot recount the details being sought. This process of filling the gaps of memory with fantasy is called confabulation. Neither the person hypnotized nor the expert observer can distinguish between confabulation and accurate recall in any particular instance. [Gonzales, supra, pp 623-624.]

[222] *fn29 The Grand Rapids Police Department received two tips concerning defendant. Defendant was first contacted by police on February 16, 1979. Defendant was again contacted one week later to clarify discrepancies in the statements he gave to police concerning his whereabouts on the day of the incident. This is the same day that the second hypnotic sessions were conducted. It was at this time that arrangements were made for polygraph testing. Only six to

eight other individual suspects were contacted on more than one occasion by police and only one other suspect took a polygraph exam. Defendant was the focus of the police investigation on February 23, 1979.

[223] *fn30 On cross-examination Mr. Hill gave the following testimony:

[224] Q. As you approached the car, did you see the front of the car, the grill, any name brand markings?

[225] A. No, sir.

[226] Q. In fact, Mr. Hill, wasn't it your belief on February 12 that the car was a Chrysler?

[227] A. I -- I assume I thought it was. I wasn't sure.

[228] Q. Do you remember telling Mr. Mazur on February 12 that it was a shiny, black Chrysler?

[229] A. Yes.

[230] Q. Do you remember telling Mr. Mazur on February 12, the night of this incident, "I'm damn sure it was a Chrysler"?

[231] A. I assumed it was, yes.

[232] Q. Do you remember telling the police, the first statement on February 15, that it was a black Chrysler?

[233] A. I thought it was.

[234] Q. My question is: Do you remember telling them that?

[235] A. Yes.

[236] Q. Do you remember telling them, also, that it was black and you were sure it was a Chrysler?

[237] A. Yes, sir.

[238] Q. Do you remember telling Dr. Rossi on February 23 that you remember seeing on the chrome on the top of the grill, "I'm sure it said Chrysler there. Letters staggered. I didn't see all of Chrysler -- Chrysler, but spelled something similar to Chrysler."

[239] A. I think I did.

[240] Q. But, now, you don't think you did?

[241] A. Yes, I believe I told him that.

[242] Q. What about now?

[243] A. I know it's not.
[244] Q. Why do you know it's not?
[245] A. I just know it wasn't a Chrysler.
[246] Q. You know it is not because Mr. Lee does not have a Chrysler, is that true?
[247] A. No, sir. I just assumed it was. I told them I wasn't positive. It was a black, shiny car.
[248] Q. But you weren't positive . . .
[249] A. That it was a Chrysler, no. Never was.
[250] Q. Your statement "damn sure it was a Chrysler," to you is not being positive?
[251] A. (No response)
[252] Q. Pardon?
[253] A. At times I thought it was a Chrysler. I admit that.
[254] *fn31 Memory hardening and confabulation as a result of suggestion from external sources are dangers inherent in the hypnotic process.
[255] *fn32 Mr. Wilcome testified:
[256] Q. And the car you saw in your view was a Monte Carlo?
[257] A. Yes.
[258] Q. Do you remember telling me [defendant's attorney] at that time the car you saw could not have been a Grand Prix?
[259] A. Yes.
[260] Q. Is that your view today?
[261] A. Yes.
[262] Mr. Orr testified:
[263] Q. Now, the car that you helped tow on February 12, did you touch that car with your hands?
[264] A. Yes.
[265] Q. The car you saw was a Monte Carlo?
[266] A. Yes.
[267] Q. You remember seeing the emblem on the back saying that it was a Monte Carlo?
[268] A. Yes.

[269] *fn33 We recognize that the standards adopted by this Court in Gonzales and Nixon, as to the admissibility of testimony from a hypnotized witness, were not available at the time of this investigation. However, the issue had been addressed by the Court of Appeals in People v Hangsleben, 86 Mich App 718; 273 NW2d 539 (1978). In Hangsleben, the Court did not allow the testimony of a psychiatrist who was willing to testify that defendant claimed innocence while under hypnosis. The Court held that defendant had failed to demonstrate the general theory that hypnotically induced memory had achieved general scientific acceptance.

[270] *fn34 The Dissent finds "preferable" and has incorporated into its rule the safeguards of the "reliability centered approach . . . articulated in State v Hurd, 86 NJ 525, 538; 432 A2d 86 (1981) . . .." (Post, p 109, Boyle, J., Dissenting.) However, in Gonzales, supra, pp 624-625, this Court specifically considered and rejected the Hurd standards as insufficient to guard against the dangers inherent in the hypnotic process. (See n 24.)

[271] *fn35 See n 24.

[272] *fn36 See, generally, Rock, n 22 (supra) at 59-61.

[273] *fn37 The witnesses' identification of the vehicle varied regarding whether it was a 1976 or 1977 Grand Prix or Monte Carlo. The police received a list from General Motors of the vehicle identification numbers of all 1976 and 1977 black Pontiac Grand Prixs with "firethorne red carpet."

Over five thousand vehicles were manufactured during the two-year period. Three hundred thirty-four vehicles were titled in Michigan, of which twelve were in Kent County. Of the twelve titled in Kent County, three were owned by a black person, one of whom was the defendant. The police did not obtain statistics on Monte Carlos manufactured during 1976 and 1977.

[274] *fn38 Exhibits 139 through 144 consisted of hair fragments described as being of Negroid origin that were found on the victim's body and clothing. Additionally Exhibit 142 also contained several orange fibers found on the gag.

[275] *fn39 Amy Combs on her first viewing of the book identified someone other than Albert Lee. However, she was asked by the police officers to go through the book a second time more carefully and thoroughly. Following her second viewing of this picture book she did identify defendant as the man who had approached them on February 6. At trial she stated that on the first viewing she did not pick defendant because of the mustache he had in the picture.

[276] *fn40 Prior to the introduction of the similar acts testimony the trial Judge gave the following instruction:

[277] You are the sole Judges of whether to believe any such testimony. However, should you believe such evidence, you are cautioned that it is before you for a limited purpose. That is, for the purpose of determining if it tends to show the identity of the assailant of [the victim] on February 12, 1979.

[278] This evidence must not be considered by you for any other purpose. You must not, for instance, regard this evidence as showing that the Defendant is a person of bad character or that he has the Disposition to commit crimes. You must not convict the Defendant because you believe he is guilty of some other improper conduct.

[279] 1 I need not address whether or not there was substantial evidence to show that the defendant was the man who committed the similar acts (on February 6, 1979), Golochowicz, supra at 309, given that the testimony of the similar acts witnesses cannot suffice to meet the requirements of the second prong of the Golochowicz test, id. at 309, 310-312.

[280] 2 The testimony of the two girls varies somewhat, although they generally testified that the man stopped his car and put

one foot outside the door. He asked them for the time and the location of Hall Street. The girls responded to the questions, and after doing so the man motioned to the girls to come closer to the car. Both girls testified that they were scared and that the man recognized their fear. Judy had apparently run from the car, but Amy had stayed longer. As Judy gradually came back, the girls testified that the man got into the car and left. [Ante, p 90.]

[281] 3 The lead opinion interprets the similar acts testimony as follows:

[282] manner and circumstances of stalking and attracting victims can be and is, in this case, sufficiently distinctive and unique that it can pass the Golochowicz "signature" requirement. Child abduction cases, in the overall scheme of criminal activity, is rather rare and unique. The coaxing of these two girls to the actor's car is in and of itself somewhat distinctive and, when coupled with the similarities in place and time, lend to the entire act a uniqueness and distinctiveness. [Ante, pp94-95.]

[283] 4 Ante, p 94.

[284] 5 The lead opinion suggests that the actions of the man who stopped these two young girls is analogous to "child abduction." (Ante, p 94.) Yet, on this record, with only the testimony of the two girls to describe what happened on February 6, 1979, the trial court could not have legitimately drawn the inference that the similar acts testimony was evidence of an attempted abduction. On appeal, the prosecutor conceded that the man's behavior does not even amount to an inchoate crime of any sort.

[285] 6 Ante, p 96.

[286] 7 See Discussion below.

[287] 8 Ante, p 93.

[288] 9 The defendant is not required to give proof of an alibi in his own defense in order to justify the exclusion of evidence of extrinsic acts if the prosecutor cannot prove with

substantial evidence that, given the qualities of the charged offense and the similar act, he was the perpetrator of both acts.

[289] 10 The finding of similarity between the similar act and the charged offense cannot be dispensed with since it, "assures thereby that evidence of the separate offense is probative of some fact other than the defendant's bad character . . . [namely, that] the circumstances and manner in which the two were committed are nearly identical in method as to earmark [the charged offense] as the handiwork of the accused ''' Id. at 310, citing McCormick, Evidence (2d ed), § 190, p 449.

[290] 11 In Hall, the plurality stated that " be sure, where the prosecution uses similar acts to prove the identity of a perpetrator, the commonality of circumstances must be unique and distinctive." While this language is dicta from a plurality opinion by Justice Boyle (joined only by Justice Griffin and the Chief Justice), that sentence is nevertheless an accurate statement of the law.

[291] 12 The lead opinion reasoned that the similar act is sufficiently unusual and distinctive when compared to the charged offense because both acts share four factors in common:

[292] The similarity between the two incidents upon which the prosecutor bases its admission are that (1) both incidents involved a black man driving a black car, (2) each occurred in the early morning hours when children would be walking to school, (3) both incidents involved young girls, and (4) both occurred in the same general area. [Ante, p 86.]

[293] 13 The fact that the charged offense was committed by a black man in a black car was established at the first trial by the testimony of the hypnotized witnesses. In fact, these witnesses were the only ones who identified the racial background of the perpetrator of the charged offense and the

color of the car he drove at the scene of the abduction on February 12, 1979.

[294] The trial court considered the testimony of the hypnotized witnesses in making a preliminary ruling on the admissibility of the "similar acts" evidence under MRE 404(b).

[295] The lead opinion states:

[296] [The testimony of the two girls] alone probably does not constitute substantial evidence to show that it was defendant who committed the bad act. [Ante, p 92.]

[297] 1a The Frye test is concerned with the admission of expert testimony deduced from the results of a scientific technique. The issue in these cases is not the admissibility of the testimony of a hypnotist regarding observations or statements made during hypnosis but, rather, the admissibility of testimony by lay witnesses in their normal state.

[298] 2a I would not alter the well established rule that statements made under hypnosis are inadmissible, McCormick, Evidence (3d ed), § 206, p 632.

[299] 3a The Hurd court's use of Frye on a case-by-case basis seems somewhat anomalous since the Frye inquiry concerns the "general acceptance" of a scientific principle or method. Frye, p 47.

[300] 4a Factors which might be relevant in making this determination would be analogous to those set forth in People v Kachar, 400 Mich 78, 95-96; 252 NW2d 807 (1977). These factors are:

[301] 1. Prior relationship with or knowledge of the defendant.

[302] 2. The opportunity to observe the offense. This includes such factors as length of time of the observation, lighting, noise or other factor affecting sensory perception and proximity to the alleged criminal act.

[303] 3. Length of time between the offense and the disputed identification. See [People v] Anderson, 389Mich [155,

214; 205 NW2d 461 (1973)], for analysis of the curve of forgetting.

[304] 4. Accuracy or discrepancies in the pre-lineup or showup description and defendant's actual description.

[305] 5. Any previous proper identification or failure to identify the defendant.

[306] 6. Any identification prior to lineup or showup of another person as defendant.

> 7. Still another consideration, not mentioned in [United States v] Wade [388 U.S. 218; 87 S Ct 1926; 18 L Ed 2d 1149 (1967)], but essential to a determination of judging the reliability of the witness's perceptions is the nature of the alleged offense and the physical and psychological state of the victim. "In critical situations perception will become distorted and any strong emotion (as opposed to mildly emotional experiences) will affect not only what and how much we perceive, but also will affect our memory of what occurred." 389 Mich at 211. (Emphasis in original.)

[307] Factors such as "fatigue, nervous exhaustion, alcohol and drugs," 389 Mich 213 (emphasis in original), and age and intelligence of the witness are obviously relevant. Levine and Tapp, The Psychology of Criminal Identification: The Gap from Wade to Kirby [v Illinois, 406 U.S. 682; 92 SCt 1877; 32 L Ed 2d 411 (1972)], 121 U Pa L Rev 1079, 1102-1103 (1973).

[308] 8. Any idiosyncratic or special features of defendant.

[309] Additional factors would be the existence and amount of corroboration.

[310] 5a Dr. Orne gave the following testimony at the pretrial motion to suppress:

> It is very unlikely, in my view, that the identification which took place was based upon an actual memory of the original events -- a personal memory of the original events of either

Mr. Hill or Mr. Vos. The reason for that is that if the memory trace was there, the recall was possible, then it should have been elicited either originally before hypnosis or by hypnosis with Mr. Mazur, or by hypnosis with Dr. Rossi. You will recall that the unreliability of hypnosis stems from the fact that you cannot distinguish between actual recall of what you saw and the importation of additional materials, additional details which are confabulated. Nobody questions the fact that hypnosis will facilitate getting recall of what there is in the memory system. So since you didn't get it at those points, the likelihood of what you are getting much later being an actual memory is extremely small.

[311] [Defense Counsel]: Why is that?

[312] [Dr. Orne]: Because if it were a memory, it should have come forth earlier and in our view, it is very unlikely that if you have got two people who have repeatedly failed to identify someone and failed to identify him under two hypnotic sessions, failed to bring forth the memory trace, if you will, so that there is recall, then a month and a half later about the same time they both suddenly are able to identify someone, that this new basis for identification comes from their individual memories, their original memories, it is more likely to come from third events which the two of them somehow shared, and for that reason it strikes me as extremely unlikely that we are talking about a memory. I don't know whether what they identified is right or wrong. I have no way of judging that. I can only say it didn't appear to come from memory. [Emphasis added.]

[313] 6a Q. Would you consider it corroboration, Doctor, again, of the identification of both the car and the person -- that the little girl in this case, when she left home that morning, had two barrettes in her hair, and that when she was found, there was only one barrette left on her body, and a barrette of the same kind was found in Mr. Lee's car?

[314] A. What is a barrette?

[315] Q. A barrette is to tie your hair back, to hold your hair back, a clip, or whatever you want to call it.

[316] A. Okay, yeah.

[317] Q. Would you consider that corroboration?

[318] A. I would consider that, certainly, a kind of corroboration, right.

[319] Q. Did Mr. Murphy provide you that information?

[320] A. No.

[321] Q. Did he provide you the information about the number of cars in town?

[322] A. No, he did not.

[323] Q. Would you consider the fact there were 16 blond hairs found in the back seat of Mr. Lee's car, which are identical in all respects that could be tested for, to the victim's hair? Would you consider that corroboration, again, of the identification of the car and the identification of Jack Hill and JackVos?

[324] A. I think you are really asking me to kind of get outside of what my area of which I am competent in. I would say yes, that is very convincing from one point of view. But in a sense, the real question is where did the identification come from?

[325] Q. Again, if the carpet fibers in Mr. Lee's car were identical to fibers found on the girl's clothes, that is, again, another type of corroboration we are talking about?

[326] A. Again, assuming that the carpet fibers are rare or specific to that car, certainly.

[327] Q. And the same thing, if feathers found on the girl's clothes were like the feathers found in Mr.Lee's car, would you consider that corroboration?

[328] A. I consider that kind of evidence certainly germane.

[329] Q. Mr. Murphy [defense counsel] didn't provide you with that information?

[330] A. No.

[331] Q. Now, again, if the testimony shows that after this first line-up at which nobody identified Mr. Lee, from that point until they did identify him at the second line-up, none of those witnesses, that is, Jack Hill and Jack Vos, saw any more pictures of the Defendant, nor saw the Defendant, nor were told or given any information about Mr. Lee by any police officers, nor did they talk to one another. Do you have any idea or opinion as to why they identified him?

[332] A. As I have indicated before, I don't know. There is an alternative hypothesis. It could be that is the person that they actually saw. [Emphasis added.]

[333] 7a My review of the mugbook indicates that number 217, the picture selected by Wilcome, clearly does resemble the defendant. David Orr also selected number 217 out of this mugbook.

[334] 8a Although not all of the Orne controls were used during hypnosis, the circumstances in the hypnotic sessions were the same as those of Jack Hill and Jack Vos, and Orne testified that those sessions were not the source of either witness' testimony.

[335] 9a In contrast, it may be fairly inferred from the trial testimony of Dr. Orne that the other witnesses were not given this suggestion.

[336] 10a In the interest of time, defense counsel did not provide Dr. Orne with tapes of the hypnosis of David Orr and Timothy Wilcome at the motion hearing. However, counsel instructed Dr. Orne to assume the procedures for these sessions were the same as for the others. Dr. Orne also was not provided with tapes of Jim Bonnema's hypnosis, again presumably in the interest of economy. I note that no question was raised at the motion hearing or at trial about the availability of the tapes.

[337] 11a In ruling on the defendant's motion to suppress pretrial and in-court identifications, the trial Judge stated:

[338] is amazing here is not any set of circumstances which would force witnesses into identification of this Defendant, but the fact that witnesses purport to make an identification after exposure not to the Defendant repeatedly but to an utterly bewildering array of young, black males whose characteristics in many instances differ in only very subtle respects. It seems to me that an equally convincing argument can be made for the assembly of showdowns here, that the reliability of identification has been enhanced, as that it has been made unreliable. Not only were the photographic and line-up sessions not tainted, but they were carried out, in the view of this Court, with scrupulous care given to fairness by personnel of both the Grand Rapids Police Department and the Kent County Sheriff's Department.

19900110

Appendix II PEOPLE v. LEE

Docket No. 140902.

---

212 Mich. App. 228 (1995)

537 N.W.2d 233

PEOPLE v. LEE

Michigan Court of Appeals.

Submitted April 13, 1995, at Grand Rapids.

Decided July 21, 1995, at 9:10 A.M.

Attorney(s) appearing for the Case

Frank J. Kelley, Attorney General, Thomas L. Casey, Solicitor General, William A. Forsyth, Prosecuting Attorney, and Timothy K. McMorrow, for the people.

State Appellate Defender (by Charles J. Booker) and Albert Lee, III, in propria persona, for the defendant on appeal.

Before: GRIBBS, P.J., and MARKMAN and D.E. SHELTON, JJ.

MARKMAN, J.

This case has had a long procedural history. Defendant was first tried and convicted of first-degree felony murder, MCL 750.316; MSA 28.548, in 1979. In 1983, this Court affirmed defendant's conviction (summary opinion, Lee I), but the Michigan Supreme Court remanded the case to this Court for reconsideration in 1985, People v Lee, 422 Mich. 928 (1985) (Lee II). Defendant's conviction was again affirmed on remand (summary opinion, Lee III). The Michigan Supreme Court subsequently granted leave to appeal. In January 1990, the Court by a 4-3 vote reversed defendant's conviction and remanded this matter for a new trial. People v Lee, 434 Mich. 59; 450 N.W.2d 883 (1990), cert den 498 U.S. 879 (1990) (Lee IV).

This matter was retried in February 1991. On March 1, 1991, defendant was again convicted of first-degree felony murder. He was sentenced to mandatory life imprisonment without the possibility of parole. Defendant appeals as of right. We affirm.

This case involved the kidnapping and murder of Linda Vanderveen in Grand Rapids in February 1979. Linda was eleven years old and worked as a school safety at the corner of Orville and Rosewood Streets.

On the morning of February 12, 1979, Linda left for her post at approximately 8:00 A.M. Witnesses observed her abduction and reported it to the police. Tragically, Linda's body was found later in the afternoon on the same day, over a snow embankment near the Regency Park Apartments.

Linda's hands had been bound behind her back and a sock was used to gag her mouth. The cause of death was strangulation with a necklace. She was killed at a location other than where her body was found and there was evidence that she had been sexually assaulted. The time of death could only be roughly estimated at between 9:00 A.M. and 1:00 P.M. on February 12.

Defendant was initially investigated in this matter on February 23 because he owned a car — a black Pontiac Grand Prix — similar to that observed by witnesses who saw the abduction.

Jack Hill was driving near Orville and Rosewood Streets on February 12 at about 8:05 A.M. when he noticed a black, shiny, two-door car parked on the wrong side of the road. He thought the car was a Chrysler model by its shape. Because he thought the car was stuck, Hill offered to assist the driver. He saw a well-dressed black male between twenty-five and thirty years old. The man was about five feet, eleven inches tall with neatly trimmed hair.

When Hill asked the man what he was doing, the man replied that it was none of Hill's business and that everything was all right. Hill looked in the back of the man's car and saw a young, white girl with blonde hair in the back seat, waving her arms at Hill. The girl looked frightened. Hill realized that something was wrong. Before he could do anything, the man in the car drove off and knocked Hill down with the car. Hill was able to follow the man to an intersection. The man drove through the intersection ignoring a stop sign, but Hill stopped at the intersection.

At about the same time, James Vos was driving his children to school and observed a black male driving a black Grand Prix at an excessive rate of speed fail to stop at a stop sign. Vos described the man as having a short Afro hairstyle and being about twenty-five years old. As the driver of the Grand Prix turned a corner, he nearly struck Vos' car. Vos got out of his car. Hill approached Vos and informed him that the driver of the car had kidnapped a young girl down the street.

Vos and Hill tried to follow the car, but had to ask some boys, working as safeties, which way the car had gone. Greg Start first told the men that he did not see a black Grand Prix go by. Douglas Bowman told the men that he did see a black car. Vos and Hill did not see the car or driver again. Both men immediately reported the incident to the police.

Start later realized that he had, in fact, seen the black Grand Prix earlier that day and had incorrectly told Vos and Hill that he had not seen the car. He described the driver as a black male with a short Afro hair style and about twenty-five to thirty years old.

Vos' son, Jack Vos, saw a young girl with blonde hair in the back seat of the car as it sped by. He thought she was about eight to ten years old and had her mouth open as if she was screaming. The girl was also waving her hands. Jack recalled that the girl looked terrified. He later saw a picture of Linda Vanderveen and believed that the girl in the car was her. He also described the car as a black Grand Prix.

Jim Bonnema was driving his son to school on February 12 when, at approximately 8:17 A.M., he saw a black Grand Prix accelerating toward his car not far from Linda's post. He observed that the car was unusually clean for the weather conditions.

Residents of the Regency Park Apartments saw a black male drive a black, shiny, clean car into the parking lot of the apartments at a fast rate of speed at about 8:24 A.M.

Shortly after the kidnapping was reported, a police officer found a wood-handled kitchen knife in the snow at the intersection where Linda had been kidnapped.

Tim Wilcome and David Orr helped a black male who had his car stuck in the snow at the Georgetown Condominiums on a dead-end road at about 10:00 or 10:30 A.M. on February 12. Orr saw the man place something in a nearby dumpster before he left. Linda's knapsack was subsequently recovered from a dumpster at the Georgetown Condominiums on Wednesday, February 14. It was determined to have been placed there sometime between 8:00 A.M. on February 12 and noon on February 14.

The medical examiner found hair-like fibers on Linda's skin underneath her clothing. Some of the fibers, which were possibly hair, were black. Other fibers, which were pink or red, were found on both Linda's skin and clothing.

A sample of defendant's hair, when analyzed, showed that his hair was dyed black at the time of the kidnapping. Hairs that were found inside the victim's sock (which was used to gag her) and on her sweater were consistent with defendant's hair, including both the dye and that it was Negroidtype hair. Defendant was a likely source of the hair found in both the sock and the sweater.

The pink or red fibers found on the victim were identical to the fibers from the carpet in defendant's car. Fibers found inside the sock also matched the carpet in defendant's car.

A hair barrette was found in defendant's car, under the back seat, which matched the type that Linda wore in her hair to school the day she was killed. Feathers found in defendant's car also matched the type that were in Linda's mittens.

In a snow brush located in defendant's back seat, two long, blonde hairs were found intertwined in the bristles. Fourteen long, blonde hairs were also found in defendant's back seat. A visual inspection indicated that the hair was consistent with the victim's hair.

An expert in DNA1 testing, Dr. Edward Blake of Forensic Science Associates (FSA), tested DNA found in one of the hairs on the snow brush in defendant's car. The DQ alpha genotype of the hair was the same as Linda Vanderveen's genotype. Dr. Blake therefore was of the opinion that the hair found in the snow brush could have come from the victim. Statistically, the victim's genotype was the same as about five percent of the Caucasian population. Dr. Blake therefore could not positively identify the hair as the victim's.

The jury also heard expert testimony from Dr. Bonnie Blomberg, a molecular geneticist and immunologist at the University of Miami School of Medicine. She also believed, on the basis of DNA testing, that the hair from the snow brush could have come from the victim.

I

Following defendant's initial conviction after a jury trial, the Supreme Court reversed and remanded this matter for a new trial because several of the eyewitnesses had been hypnotized in order to assist them in recalling facts about their observations. The Supreme Court held that "testimony of the hypnotized witnesses is inadmissible absent proof by clear and convincing evidence that the testimony being offered was based on facts recalled and related prior to hypnosis." Lee IV, supra at 86. The Court did not specify the testimony that was affected by its holding, but, in the course of its discussion, focused on the testimony concerning the identification of the defendant. Id. at 75-86.

At the time of the second trial, the court was faced with the difficult task of how to implement the Supreme Court's ruling. 2 Because a long time had passed, witnesses could not recall what they had originally related to police and others about this crime. Furthermore, police officers who took statements from the witnesses had no independent recollection of what the witnesses originally stated.3

The approach taken by the trial court was to allow witnesses to testify consistent with the substance of the statements they gave to the police before undergoing hypnosis. For this reason, the trial court did not think it was necessary to conduct extensive pretrial hearings. However, the court did choose to hear certain testimony before determining its admissibility. The defendant was afforded some leeway in this area, for instance for any exculpatory evidence that witnesses had not previously recalled and related.

Defendant disputes the admissibility of various testimony throughout the trial. Defendant apparently only objected below to two of the areas of inquiry that he raises on appeal. We recognize the inherent difficulty confronted by the trial court, as well as this Court, in analyzing testimony from witnesses who have been hypnotized. Both the prosecutor and defendant set forth reasonable arguments with respect to the source of the testimony, because one can hardly be certain regarding whether a variance in testimony, however minor, has resulted from faded memory, recollection of detail, nervousness, or any other reason found in trials not involving hypnosis, or from the effect of the hypnosis itself. The trial court was faced with the daunting task of determining whether the prosecutor had presented clear and convincing evidence that the testimony was based on facts recalled and related before hypnosis. We review the trial court's decision to admit this evidence for an abuse of discretion. See People v Nixon, 421 Mich. 79, 91; 364 N.W.2d 593 (1984).

We believe the trial court generally applied the correct standards in attempting to determine the admissibility of the testimony of the hypnotized witnesses. While strict adherence to the police statements was not required by the Supreme Court, the police statements became vitally instructive in this case with respect to whether testimony was based on facts recalled and related before hypnosis. Trial testimony of a hypnotized witness is admissible where it is "based on facts recalled and related prior to hypnosis" even if the statement itself was obtained after hypnosis. See People v McIntosh, 142 Mich.App. 314, 321-322, n 5; 370 N.W.2d 337 (1985), aff'd in part, app den in part, 422 Mich. 951 (1985).

Defendant objected at trial to the admission of testimony by hypnotized witnesses that there was nothing about the physical appearance of the defendant that could lead them to believe that he was not the person they saw. The prosecutor agreed that witnesses who were hypnotized would not be allowed to point to the defendant and identify him as the person they saw. However, the prosecutor sought to make it clear that the witnesses could not exclude the defendant and, in fact, could not identify him one way or the other. Thus, the prosecutor sought a ruling allowing him to ask a sequence of questions based on the witnesses' general description of the perpetrator.4 The trial court allowed such questioning.

We do not believe the trial court abused its discretion in allowing this. Defendant does not contest the admissibility of the general descriptions of the perpetrator. Furthermore, the Supreme Court in Lee IV, supra at 80, found that the witnesses had given descriptions of the man they saw before hypnosis. We do not believe that the testimony in response to the prosecutor's questions was inadmissible. This testimony generally constitutes logical answers to legitimate follow-up questions, all of which are based on facts recalled and related before hypnosis.

Defendant in particular points to the prosecutor's question to Jack Hill regarding whether there was "anything about the man here in the courtroom [defendant] that's different than the man you saw that morning?" We acknowledge that this question is different from the one originally proposed by the prosecutor. However, we further note the witness' answer, "There's not, no. I can't identify him." From there, as the prosecutor had proposed, he asked, "In other words, what you're telling me is this happened quickly, and you can't tell me, one way or the other, whether that's him or not?" Hill answered, "Yes, sir." We do not believe that this testimony constituted an improper identification of the defendant. Furthermore, we believe for the reasons stated above that this testimony is based on facts recalled and related before hypnosis. The point is that these witnesses could not say one way or the other whether the defendant was the perpetrator.

Defendant also objected below to Hill's description of the girl waving her arms. The police report indicated that Hill observed a black male force a young white female into the back seat as she resisted. Defendant argued that Hill never told the police that he saw the girl waving her arms at Hill. The trial court was convinced that the differences between Hill's statement and his testimony were not significant because defendant denied committing the crime. The trial court further noted that cross-examination was available to defendant. Thus, the trial court did not find this testimony to be prejudicial to defendant. We find Hill's statement to be similar to and fully within the scope of the relatively thorough description he gave to the police. Moreover, we agree with the trial court that this statement is not prejudicial to the defendant. We therefore do not believe error requiring reversal has been shown.

Defendant further points to a number of variances and contradictions to which he apparently did not object below. This Court may consider such issues, brought for the first time on appeal, if the errors could have been decisive of the outcome. People v Grant, 445 Mich. 535, 553; 520 N.W.2d 123 (1994). ("[A] plain, unpreserved error may not be considered by an appellate court for the first time on appeal unless the error could have been decisive of the outcome or unless it falls under the category of cases, yet to be clearly defined, where prejudice is presumed or reversal is automatic.")5

Defendant argues that, when Hill testified, he gave additional details with respect to his description of the man and the car the man was driving. Defendant claims that Hill testified that the man was well dressed and had an Afro, estimated the man's weight and testified regarding the position of the vehicle and that it knocked him down. On the basis of Hill's descriptive report to police of the man and the incident, including where the cars (both his and the man's) were located and the direction they went, we believe that this testimony was based on facts recalled and related before hypnosis.

Defendant further argues that the testimony of Greg Start, Jim Bonnema, and James and Jack Vos comparing the defendant's car in a photograph with the car they saw that morning (or the identification of the defendant's car) was not based on facts recalled and related before hypnosis.6 However, these witnesses testified at trial regarding the car they saw. With the slight exception noted below, defendant does not contest these descriptions as being outside the purview of facts recalled and related before hypnosis. In fact, as the dissent observed in Lee IV, supra at 104, the defendant's expert testified in the first trial that the description of the car by James and Jack Vos, Start, and Bonnema was not influenced by hypnosis. In this case, a comparison (or identification) of the car was based on facts recalled and related before hypnosis; it was not necessary that the witnesses had made the actual identification before hypnosis. McIntosh, supra. Defendant contests that portion of Bonnema's description of the car at trial as a 1976 or 1977 Grand Prix as it varied from his description to police of a "newer Grand Prix." Although not identical to his description to the police, we nevertheless find that this testimony was based on facts recalled and related before hypnosis.

Defendant also contests the description of the car by Timothy Wilcome and David Orr. Defendant states that both witnesses had told the police that the car driven by the man was a Monte Carlo. Defendant claims, however, that Wilcome's testimony that the "body shape" of the man's car was similar to that of defendant's was not based on facts recalled and related before hypnosis. However, Wilcome's description of the car as a Monte Carlo before hypnosis would provide the basis for his comparison of a car's "body shape." Thus, we believe that Wilcome's statement was based on facts related and recalled before hypnosis, namely, his description of the car to the police.

Defendant further claims that David Orr testified during the first trial and before hypnosis that the car was a Monte Carlo yet testified during the second trial that the car could have been a Grand Prix or a Monte Carlo. Defendant argues that Orr's equivocal testimony at trial supported the prosecutor's theory that Wilcome and Orr were simply mistaken in their identification of the car. As defendant points out, however, Orr's statements before hypnosis and at the first trial, after hypnosis, were consistent. It was not until the second trial, approximately eleven to twelve years after the first trial, that the discrepancy in his testimony appeared. We believe that the lapse in time, rather than the hypnosis, was the cause of the discrepancy. In fact, Orr explained that by the time of the second trial he could not remember what the car looked like although he admitted that he testified at the first trial that it looked like a Monte Carlo. Defendant was fully able to explore any inconsistencies in Orr's testimony through cross-examination. Admission of the testimony was not error.

The mere presence of inconsistencies and variances do not automatically render testimony inadmissible as not being based on facts recalled and related before hypnosis. We further stress the importance of cross-examination in dealing with inconsistencies, especially where a substantial lapse of time may be the real cause of the inconsistency. As previously stated, the testimony at trial need not be identical to the police statements to be admissible under Lee IV; it must, and we believe it was in this case, based on facts recalled and related before hypnosis. Any inconsistencies or variances that may have occurred in testimony before and after hypnosis in this case would have been viewed as entirely unremarkable had they occurred in the context of varying statements made in a case not involving hypnosis. This is especially true where varying statements have been made twelve years apart. Moreover, questioning by the prosecutor involving comparisons of the man driving the car and the car constituted logical follow-up questioning in light of the testimony given. Nevertheless, even if the admission of these variances and inconsistencies was error, they by no means constitute error requiring reversal. The slightness of the variances and inconsistencies, coupled with the safeguards of cross-examination, rendered any errors harmless.

In Lee IV, supra at 86-90, the Supreme Court cited and followed the standards defined in People v Young (After Remand), 425 Mich. 470, 505; 391 N.W.2d 270 (1986), in its harmless-error analysis.

As an appellate court, we do not independently evaluate this evidence. "[I]t is not the appellate court's function to determine guilt or innocence.... Those judgments are exclusively for the jury ...." Our responsibility is to determine how the error might have affected the jury's decision. The inquiry is "what effect the error had or reasonably may be taken to have had upon the jury's decision."If it were clear that the erroneous admission of the ... evidence did not prejudice [the defendant] the error would be harmless. [Citing Kotteakos v United States, 328 U.S. 750, 763-764; 66 S.Ct. 1239; 90 L Ed 1557 (1946).] [Lee IV, supra at 86-87.]

Any error or combination of errors in this case was not prejudicial to defendant. The errors would merely concern the incremental or marginal testimony itself, not the complete testimony of the particular witness on the subject matter in controversy. Testimony of witnesses' regarding descriptions of the car, driver, and the incident itself, including the observations of the young girl, absent the relatively minor variations, would still have been heard by the jury. There was also significant physical evidence in this case, including the barrette and feathers found in defendant's car, the dyed hairs found inside the victim's sock and on her sweater, the carpet fibers found on the victim and inside her sock, and the long blonde hairs found in defendant's car. One of these hairs was further subjected to DNA tests that determined that the hair could have come from the victim. Given this and other evidence presented at trial, we believe that the exclusion of the variances in the testimony would not have affected the jurors' decision. When evaluated in the full context of the evidence presented in this sixteen-day trial, we further believe that any error or combination of errors was not decisive of the outcome.

II

Defendant next argues that misconduct by the prosecutor occurred when the prosecutor, during closing arguments, improperly referred to a prior incident involving defendant. Defendant did not object below to the argument. This Court's review is therefore precluded absent a miscarriage of justice or unless a cautionary instruction could not have cured the prejudicial effect. People v Stanaway, 446 Mich. 643, 687; 521 N.W.2d 557 (1994).

The trial court admitted evidence under MRE 404(b) to show defendant's pattern or plan for committing child abductions and that defendant committed this crime. The jury heard evidence that, as two young girls were walking to school only six days before Linda Vanderveen was kidnapped, defendant stopped his car and asked the girls for the time and directions. The girls ran after defendant motioned for one of the girls to come over to his car and asked if she was scared of him.

The prior bad acts evidence was admitted for the limited purpose of showing that defendant committed the crime at issue in this case. During closing arguments, the prosecutor argued that the evidence could explain why defendant might have used a knife as part of his plan to abduct Linda Vanderveen. He made further arguments that, in this Court's judgment, were relevant to show defendant's "manner and circumstances of stalking and attracting victims." Lee IV, supra at 94-95. Unlike the first trial, the evidence was not used to show that defendant earlier had attempted to commit a crime and that, in the instant case, he was acting consistent with that propensity. The prosecutor did not, for example, suggest that either of the girls had nearly been killed or that defendant had attempted to assault the girls, as may have been suggested in the first trial. The prosecutor also did not inordinately emphasize or focus undue attention upon the fact that defendant earlier may have attempted to abduct the two girls. We do not agree with defendant that the prosecutor's use of the evidence exceeded the limited purpose allowed under MRE 404(b).

The trial court instructed the jury on more than one occasion with regard to the limited use of the prior bad acts evidence. Any error here could have been cured by a further cautionary instruction had defendant objected to the statement. Stanaway, supra.

Even if the prosecution's argument was erroneous, it added little, if anything, to the jury's consideration of the evidence. The jury heard other evidence that a knife had been found near the area where Linda Vanderveen was kidnapped. The jury could have inferred from that evidence alone that a knife was used to accomplish the kidnapping. The jury did not need to determine why defendant would use a knife to commit this crime since it had sufficient information available to it that defendant, in fact, had used such a weapon.

Defendant further argues that the prosecutor deliberately injected an improper argument concerning the prior encounter with the two girls. He argues that the Supreme Court previously held that the prosecutor had improperly used prior bad acts evidence at the first trial. Defendant therefore contends that the prosecutor deliberately ignored the Court's decision when he again employed the same evidence in an overly broad manner.

A prosecutor may not intentionally inject inflammatory arguments with no apparent justification except to arouse prejudice. People v Bahoda, 448 Mich. 261, 266; 531 N.W.2d 659 (1995). We find defendant's assignment of error to be without merit.

First, as already noted, the purpose behind the prosecutor's use of the "bad acts" evidence in the case at bar was different in kind from his use of the evidence in the earlier trial. Lee IV, supra at 95-96. Second, the Supreme Court granted leave only to address whether the similar acts evidence was properly admitted. Id. at 63. Justice BRICKLEY, in his opinion, discussed the prosecution's closing argument only in relation to his analysis of the admissibility of the similar acts evidence. Id. at 95-97. A majority of the justices did not express agreement with Justice BRICKLEY'S discussion of the propriety of the prosecutor's remarks. Id. at 97, 104.7 Thus, the propriety of the prosecutor's closing argument during the first trial was not an issue decided by a majority of the justices. Accordingly, we would not infer an intent to deliberately disregard the Supreme Court's decision on these facts, even if the prosecutor's arguments were improper, which we do not find them to be.

III

Defendant next argues that the trial court denied him his right to a fair trial by (1) forcing him to use peremptory challenges to excuse jurors that should have been dismissed for cause, (2) refusing to grant defendant's request for additional peremptory challenges, and (3) refusing to change venue because an impartial jury had not been seated.

There was substantial concern over publicity in this case, even though it was retried twelve years after the crime was committed. Many members of the venire recalled facts from 1979 when the crime was committed, as well as facts from the first trial. The trial court conducted the voir dire on publicity and recollection of the first trial outside the venire's presence, by taking the jurors individually into the jury room. The court complied with the guidelines subsequently set forth in People v Tyburski, 445 Mich. 606, 621-624; 518 N.W.2d 441 (1994) (opinion of MALLETT, J.), by asking the jurors what they had heard about the instant case and about any attitudes the jurors may have developed. The court then independently decided if the jurors could be impartial.

On appeal, defendant challenges the trial court's decision not to remove three jurors for legal cause: Juror N, Juror O, and Juror F.8

A four-part test is used to determine whether an error in refusing a challenge for cause merits reversal. There must be a clear and independent showing on the record that (1) the court improperly denied a challenge for cause, (2) the aggrieved party exhausted all peremptory challenges, (3) the party demonstrated the desire to excuse another subsequently summoned juror, and (4) the juror whom the party wished later to excuse was objectionable. People v Legrone, 205 Mich.App. 77, 81; 517 N.W.2d 270 (1994). Defendant failed to expressly challenge any of the three jurors for cause. However, we will briefly review the trial court's decisions to determine if it properly found that the jurors could be impartial, because in at least one instance defendant alleges that he did not have the opportunity to object before the court ruled.

Juror N was not influenced by the publicity over this case because she was too young (age fourteen or fifteen) to recall much about the case and had not read or heard any of the more recent publicity. However, Juror N did express some concern about her ability to keep in mind that defendant was presumed innocent. Despite some concerns that it might be difficult for her to do so, Juror N assured the court that she could be fair, would follow the court's instructions, and would decide the case exclusively on the basis of the evidence.

We find no error with the trial court's decision not to excuse Juror N for cause. Juror N did not indicate that she had a state of mind that would prevent her from rendering a just verdict. MCR 2.511(D)(4). Nor did she possess opinions that would have improperly influenced the verdict. MCR 2.511(D)(5). Rather, she stated — apparently credibly to the trial court — that she would decide the case consistent with the requirements of the law. The court therefore was not required to dismiss her for cause. Legrone, supra at 81-82; People v Lamar, 153 Mich.App. 127, 135; 395 N.W.2d 262 (1986).

Juror O had followed the first trial, although not particularly closely, and recalled that defendant was convicted. She followed the trial because she had two small children and was concerned about the kidnapping. While Juror O denied forming an opinion concerning defendant's guilt or innocence, she thought that "as a mother back then I felt relief." She explained that it was a scary time in the community for those with young children. However, she could not remember details about the case.

Juror O assured the court that she could decide the case with an open mind on the basis of the evidence and the instructions. She further stated that she would not let an earlier jury decision sway her. The trial court did not err in not removing her for cause due to her cognizance of the first trial. Legrone, supra; People v Passeno, 195 Mich.App. 91, 98-99; 489 N.W.2d 152 (1992).

Juror O was also married to a Grand Rapids police officer and apparently knew or knew of some of the police witnesses. There is no indication on the record of the nature of this familiarity. Defendant, despite his burden to show a basis for the juror's disqualification, does not raise anything beyond the fact that Juror O was married to a policeman and responded that she knew or knew of some of the witnesses. Juror O assured the court that, despite the fact that she "knew of" these witnesses, she could make an independent decision. Her responses during voir dire did not require her removal for cause. Cf. People v Walker, 162 Mich.App. 60, 64-65; 412 N.W.2d 244 (1987) (fact that juror is a police officer himself is not sufficient to warrant an inference of bias, but nature of his relationships with prosecutors and police witnesses may give rise to such an inference).

Juror F also followed the first trial closely. She thought that defendant was guilty at the time and recalled that he was convicted, but did not remember many details. At the time of this trial, Juror F did not have any definite opinions about defendant's guilt or innocence. She thought that the retrial was occurring possibly because "there was another man involved that said that he admitted he was guilty." She assured the court that she could put out of her mind what she knew about the first trial.

The record does not support defendant's argument that Juror F should have been dismissed for cause. MCR 2.511(D)(4). Juror F had not formed a definite opinion about defendant's guilt at the time of trial and promised to keep an open mind. Although she previously believed that defendant was guilty at the time of the first trial, she did not recall details of the case. It therefore would not have been difficult for Juror F to set aside her previous opinion. The trial court was also in the best position to judge, on the basis of their credibility and demeanor, whether Juror F and the other members of the venire could render a fair and impartial verdict. Legal cause for Juror F's dismissal was not shown. People v Roupe, 150 Mich.App. 469, 474; 389 N.W.2d 449 (1986).9

On the basis of the foregoing, and the absence of objection by the defendant, he has not met the first prong of the test for reversal for failure to strike a juror for legal cause. Legrone, supra at 81. Error requiring reversal therefore has not been shown.

We also do not believe that defendant was improperly denied additional peremptory challenges under MCR 6.412(E)(2). The defendant's "request" for such additional challenges was made at the same time as the motion for a change of venue. At that time, defense counsel stated as follows:

If I would have had additional challenges, I would have removed a lot of the jury members that are now seated in this jury, and we would ask the Court to change the venue of this trial. I feel it is not a fair and impartial jury to Mr. Lee.

The motion, and thus defendant's request for additional challenges, was not raised until after the jury had been selected and sworn. Not only was it too late at that juncture to make such a request, but there was no showing of just cause for additional challenges. The trial court pointed out that it excused for cause those prospective jurors who "had any hesitancy of remembering too much about the case or those who indicated any real knowledge of the case...." In fact, the trial court excused for cause twenty prospective jurors. Of the twenty, fourteen were excused because of prior knowledge of the case or because of general bias or prejudice and six were excused for other reasons. The trial court did not abuse its discretion by refusing to grant additional peremptory challenges under MCR 6.412(E)(2).

Defendant has also not shown that the trial court abused its discretion by denying the motion for a change of venue because of the amount of publicity. The denial of a motion for a change of venue is reviewed to determine whether there has been an abuse of discretion. Passeno, supra at 98. The existence of pretrial publicity, standing alone, does not necessitate a change of venue. Id.

Defendant has not shown the existence of a strong community feeling against him or publicity so extensive and inflammatory that jurors generally could not remain impartial. Passeno, supra; People v DeLisle, 202 Mich.App. 658; 509 N.W.2d 885 (1993). Defendant has further failed to show that the impaneled jury was actually prejudiced or that there was an atmosphere that created a probability of prejudice. Id. The trial court examined each prospective juror separately to determine whether each had any prior knowledge of the case. As previously discussed, several potential jurors were in fact dismissed for cause because of prior knowledge, prejudice, or bias. We believe that an impartial jury was selected. The trial court reasoned in part, "I think that at least as it comes to pretrial publicity, the fifteen people we have are as untainted as you're going to find anyplace in the state." Given this determination, the trial court did not abuse its discretion in denying the motion for a change of venue.

IV

Defendant filed a motion with this Court to be allowed to submit a supplemental brief. We granted the motion and discuss in this section the issues raised in the supplemental brief filed by defendant in propria persona. Defendant first argues that he was denied a fair trial because of alleged misconduct by the prosecutor. Because there was no objection below to the alleged misconduct, this Court's review is precluded absent a miscarriage of justice or if a cautionary instruction could not have cured the prejudicial effect. Stanaway, supra at 687.

Defendant contends that misconduct by the prosecutor occurred during closing arguments when the prosecutor effectively told the jury that reasonable doubt constituted a doubt for which they could give a reason. Defendant cites People v Foster, 175 Mich.App. 311; 437 N.W.2d 395 (1989), in which this Court reversed the defendant's convictions on the basis of a series of acts of misconduct by the prosecutor. In Foster, one of the remarks made by the prosecutor during closing arguments was that the prosecutor did not have to prove defendant's guilt "beyond a reasonable doubt, not even beyond a shadow of a doubt." The prosecutor then stated that "you have to have a reason for the doubt before you can call it a reasonable doubt." This Court found that these instructions had the effect of improperly shifting the burden of proof. Id. at 319.

Defendant does not contend that, as was the case in Foster, the prosecutor ever stated that he did not have the burden to prove the case beyond a reasonable doubt. Further unlike in Foster, there was no series of acts of misconduct by the prosecutor. Instead, the defendant claims that the burden was effectively shifted by the isolated definition of "reasonable doubt" posed by the prosecutor. We do not believe that the prosecutor's statements, in context, in this case misstated the jury's obligations. In any event, the jury was properly instructed by the court regarding what constitutes a reasonable doubt.

Defendant next argues that the prosecutor argued facts not in evidence when the prosecutor suggested various theories to explain the testimony of Orr and Wilcome, which, defendant states, placed the assailant not far from where the body was found at about the time the prosecution claimed defendant was purchasing license plates. A prosecutor may not argue facts not entered into evidence. Stanaway, supra at 686. However, the prosecutor is "free to argue the evidence and all reasonable inferences from the evidence as it relates to [the prosecutor's] theory of the case." Bahoda, supra at 282.

The prosecutor argued several possibilities with respect to Orr and Wilcome, including that perhaps the man whom Orr and Wilcome assisted in the snow was not the assailant or that perhaps Orr was mistaken about the car he saw. These possibilities constituted part of the prosecutor's theory based on the evidence. The prosecutor may relate the facts to his theory of the case. The prosecutor further argued that Orr and Wilcome "didn't know at the time what time this was." The prosecutor apparently drew this inference on the basis of his further statements that "[t]hey're busy, they're cleaning, they're plowing some guy's truck, they pull him out, and away they go. They're frankly not paying much attention to it."

The defendant further argues that the prosecutor argued facts not in evidence when he suggested that the blonde hair probably came from a female.10 However, this argument did not constitute a statement of facts not in evidence. Instead, the prosecutor made this argument on the basis of the testimony of witness Edward Gundy, a crime laboratory scientist, who opined that because of its length, the hair probably came from a female.

Defendant next argues that the prosecutor vouched for the defendant's guilt and for the integrity of the case against defendant when the prosecutor told the jury that the defendant was there because he was guilty and that the prosecutor was trying to get at "what the truth is." We disagree. The prosecutor in his remarks to the jury said nothing more than that, on the basis of the facts as the prosecutor understood them, defendant was guilty of the crime charged. There was nothing inappropriate about these statements.

Defendant also argues that the trial judge denied him his right to present a defense when he told the jury that "you cannot acquit or convict based upon what the attorneys say." Defendant contends that the trial court effectively instructed the jury that they could not acquit defendant if they believed defense counsel's interpretation of the evidence. Defendant claims that, in light of the fact that defendant presented almost no evidence of his own, the only defense the jury could consider was contained in the defense attorney's closing argument.

We disagree with defendant's argument. Before closing arguments, the court, among other things, told the jury that "what the attorneys say is not evidence, and you cannot acquit or convict based upon what the attorneys say." The court further told the jurors that if they remembered something different than the attorney had remembered, they should rely on their own memory and not that of the attorney. The court continued:

So listen carefully to what they [attorneys] have to say to you, but bear in mind that ultimately the decision becomes yours, the twelve of you who are left, and that decision has to be based upon what you heard from the witness stand, what you glean from the various exhibits which have been admitted, and from other things which I tell you [that you] can or should consider as evidence.

The court's instruction in this regard is standard and accurately states the law. It did not deny defendant's attorney any right of argument, but merely instructed the jurors that their own recollection of the factual evidence was controlling, not those of the attorneys.

The defendant next argues that he was denied his rights of confrontation and due process when witnesses from the first trial were not able to testify in the second trial. We disagree. The defendant has a constitutional right to be confronted with the witnesses against him. However, defendant does not claim that he was denied the right to confront witnesses whose testimony in some form was considered by the jury. Instead, defendant claims that various individuals should have been called to testify in the second trial. Defendant does not explain why he was unable to call these individuals on his own. People v Cross, 202 Mich.App. 138; 508 N.W.2d 144 (1993). Thus, there has been no violation of defendant's right to confrontation11 or due process. While the prosecutor has certain obligations with respect to witnesses, it is not the prosecutor's responsibility to call any witness whom the defendant believes may support his defense in some way.12

Defendant further argues that the prosecutor failed to prove all elements of felony murder.13 Felony murder consists of

"(1) [t]he killing of a human being (2) with the intent to kill, to do great bodily harm, or to create a high risk of death or great bodily harm with knowledge that death or great bodily harm was the probable result (3) while committing, attempting to commit, or assisting in the commission of any of the felonies specifically enumerated in MCL 750.316; MSA 28.548." [People v Thew, 201 Mich.App. 78, 85; 506 N.W.2d 547 (1993), quoting People v Bush, 187 Mich.App. 316, 327; 466 N.W.2d 736 (1991).][14]

The underlying felony involved in this case is kidnapping, a felony enumerated in MCL 750.316; MSA 28.548. Defendant appears to argue that there was insufficient evidence to support his conviction. In reviewing the sufficiency of the evidence, this Court must view the evidence in the light most favorable to the prosecutor and determine whether a rational trier of fact could find that the essential elements of the crime were proven beyond a reasonable doubt. People v Wolfe, 440 Mich. 508, 515; 489 N.W.2d 748 (1992), modified on other grounds 441 Mich. 1201 (1992).

On the basis of the evidence presented, we conclude that a rational trier of fact could have found that the essential elements of felony murder were proven in this case. As we discussed earlier, substantial testimonial and physical evidence was presented at trial in support of the defendant's conviction. A reasonable trier of fact could have found that defendant kidnapped Linda Vanderveen and that, while committing this offense and with the requisite intent, he killed her.

Defendant's final argument deals with the propriety of testimony by witnesses who had been hypnotized. Defendant focuses on testimony regarding identification of his car through the use of photographs, as well as identification of the defendant himself as the assailant. We addressed these issues earlier in section I.15 However, defendant further appears to argue that the identifications and comparisons made by witnesses were inconsistent with their "first statements" or descriptions (before hypnosis). For instance, defendant claims that while witnesses testified that there was no difference between the car they saw and the defendant's car in the photograph, a comparison of witnesses' "first statement" and defendant's car reveals substantial differences. Defendant contends that "these witnesses' first statements" were of a black 1976 Grand Prix with black interior and no red pinstripe on the side. Defendant then points to the difference between that description and the actual description of his car as a black 1977 Grand Prix with red interior and red pinstriping. Defendant does not identify "these witnesses," nor does he provide citation to the record. He seems to suggest that all the witnesses testified in this manner. However, this is untrue. For instance, witness Greg Start testified that there was "no difference" in the car he saw and the car in the photograph. This was based on facts recalled and related before hypnosis, namely, a description of the car given by Start to the police before hypnosis. At that time, he described the car as a black Grand Prix with a red pinstripe and red interior. He further described the car as new and clean. Thus, defendant's general statement about the witnesses is not true. Defendant has failed to point to any identification or comparison that was not based on facts recalled and related before hypnosis.

Defendant further contends that witnesses who had described the assailant as "clean shaven, no facial hairs" nevertheless identified defendant who "has a thick mustache and sideburns." Defendant has not shown by whom or when these descriptions were given, nor has he pointed to any such identification at trial. As we discussed, the prosecutor conceded that witnesses who had been hypnotized could not identify the defendant. Although, as discussed in section I, the prosecutor asked questions to establish that witnesses could not say one way or the other whether the defendant was the perpetrator, defendant has not shown how the answers to those questions were not based on facts recalled and related before hypnosis. Defendant also contends that hypnosis tainted the "line-ups and photo books." However, defendant has not pointed to any particular testimony that he believes was inadmissible as a result, nor has he shown why such testimony would in fact be inadmissible.

V

Defendant's final issue on appeal concerns the trial court's decision to admit the DNA evidence linking the hair found in defendant's car to the victim. While this Court held that DNA evidence is admissible in People v Adams, 195 Mich.App. 267; 489 N.W.2d 192 (1992), modified in part on other grounds 441 Mich. 916 (1993), under the Davis-Frye rule,16 this case involves a significantly different method of DNA testing than was addressed in Adams. In Adams, this Court determined that results from the restriction fragment length polymorphisms (RFLP) method were admissible. This case, however, involves the polymerase chain reaction (PCR) method. Because of the significantly different methods of DNA testing, this panel is not bound to follow Adams on this issue pursuant to Administrative Order No. 1994-4. Rather, the PCR method must be subjected to separate scrutiny under Davis-Frye in order to determine whether there is "general acceptance" in the scientific community for this particular method of DNA analysis. People v Young (After Remand), 425 Mich. 470, 473, 479-480; 391 N.W.2d 270 (1986).

A

Because the PCR method had not yet been the subject of an appellate decision in this state, the trial court conducted a Davis-Frye hearing in September and October 1990. Under the Davis-Frye rule,17 novel scientific evidence must be shown to have gained general acceptance in the scientific community in order to be admissible at trial. Young, supra at 473, 479-480. The party offering the evidence has the burden of demonstrating its acceptance in the scientific community. People v Davis, 199 Mich.App. 502, 512; 503 N.W.2d 457 (1993).

In order to be admissible, the novel scientific evidence must have achieved general scientific acceptance for reliability, as supported by disinterested and impartial experts. Young, supra at 473, 479. The experts' livelihood must not be intimately connected with the new scientific technique. Id. at 483. Courts will not require that scientific tests be infallible to be admissible. Only reasonable certainty must follow from the tests. Adams, supra at 276.

At the Davis-Frye hearing, the prosecution presented four independent expert witnesses: Dr. David Ginsburg, Dr. Paul Coussens, Dr. Bonnie Blomberg and Dr. Julian Adams.18 The prosecution also called Dr. Edward Blake of FSA, a forensic serologist, who performed the DNA testing in this matter. Defendant presented one expert witness, Dr. Ashok Bhagwat.

As background information on how DNA testing is performed, the following description of DNA structure from Adams, supra at 270, is helpful.

Before reviewing the laboratory procedures, an understanding of the structure of the DNA molecule is necessary. The molecule is a double helix, shaped like a twisted ladder. Phosphate and deoxyribose sugar form the rails of the ladder. Four chemical bases — Adenine (A), Cytosine (C), Guanine (G), and Thymine (T) — lie next to each other on the sugar links along the sides of the ladder. Each A always bonds with a T on the other side of the ladder, and each C always bonds with a G on the other side of the ladder, so that the possible base pairs on the ladder are A-T, T-A, C-G, and G-C. The base pairs are connected by a hydrogen bond, such that the bonds form the rungs of the ladder. There are approximately three billion base pairs in one DNA molecule. Although no two human beings have the same sequence of base pairs (except for identical twins), we share many sequences that create common characteristics such as arms, legs, fingers, and toes. The sequences of variation from person to person are known as polymorphisms. They contain different alleles, which are alternate forms of a gene capable of occupying a single location on a chromosome. Polymorphisms are the key to DNA identification because they create the individual characteristics of everyone and are detectable in laboratory testing.

For a more detailed explanation of DNA testing, see anno: Admissibility of DNA identification evidence, 84 ALR4th 313.

The specific legal inquiry centered on whether the DNA evidence was reliable enough for forensic use. It was uncontroverted that the method was accepted as reliable for medical and biological research in the general scientific community. At the time of this hearing, only one laboratory, FSA, was regularly performing the PCR test for forensic use. As a result, there was obviously little evidence offered on the forensic use of the PCR method by those who actually used the method for forensic testing.

In the trial court, the challenge to the admission of this evidence centered on two specific areas. First, it was argued that the test results for the PCR method were not reliable because of errors caused by one of the enzymes used in the process, Taq polymerase. Second, it was argued that potential contamination at the crime scene or in the laboratory made the test unreliable for forensic use. We will address these arguments separately after discussing the scientific reliability of the PCR method in general.

The PCR method was first devised in 1985 and achieved widespread acceptance within one or two years. By 1990, it was one of the most widely used techniques in medical and biological research, ranging from screening for cystic fibrosis and sickle cell anemia to environmental monitoring.

The laboratory in this matter, FSA, uses the PCR method to look at one particular gene, the DQ alpha gene; it is a protein present on lymphocytes and other white blood cells and is part of the immune system. The DQ alpha gene represents only one gene out of thousands contained in the chromosomes of DNA.

The DQ alpha gene is genetically polymorphic, which means that it is both genetically inherited and appears in alternative forms in different people. The alternative forms of the gene are called alleles or traits.

There are six readily detectable alleles or traits in the DQ alpha system. These different alleles have been given numbers to identify them. These are 1.1, 1.2, 1.3, 2, 3, and 4. Every individual has two alleles, one inherited from each parent. These two alleles may either be both the same (homozygous, e.g., 1, 1) or different (heterozygous, e.g., 1, 4). The six combinations result in twenty-one possible "genotypes," each of which appears in varying proportions within the population. Each person is classified into one of the twenty-one possible genotypes. PCR analysis looks for matches for these combinations.

Testing of Linda Vanderveen's blood indicated that her DQ alpha genotype was 1.3, 4. Testing of the hair root found on the snow brush indicated also 1.3, 4. It therefore could have come from the victim. It could not have been defendant's hair because his DQ alpha genotype was 3, 4.

Using previously conducted studies, scientists are able to determine how often each of the different genotypes appears in different populations, generally defined by race. Dr. Blake explained that the statistics on how frequently each of the genotypes occurs in a population are compiled by the company that distributes the test used in this matter, Cetus Corporation, and that some scientists keep their own statistics. Dr. Blake kept his own statistics over several years from his laboratory work. On the basis of his research, Dr. Blake believed that the 1.3, 4 allele type appears in the Caucasian population at a rate of about 4.3 percent. The 1.3, 4 allele type appears in about 8 percent of the Black population.

B

The PCR method is, simply put, a procedure to replicate repeatedly part of the DNA of a cell so that millions of copies of a particular gene are eventually produced in order to analyze the DNA.

The steps used in the PCR process involve some of the same steps used in the RFLP method. First, the DNA must be purified. This means that the cell containing the DNA must be broken with an enzyme and a soap. It is simply a way to isolate the DNA from foreign elements.

The second step is for the isolated DNA to be amplified; this is where the PCR method is distinctive. No more than fifty percent of the specimen being tested is added to a special mixture containing the chemicals that amplify the isolated DNA. This includes an enzyme found in hot springs (Taq polymerase), buffer salts, and primers, which are small pieces of DNA that recognize the four bases, A, T, G and C. It is Taq polymerase specifically that copies the targeted gene.

The DNA in the PCR mixture is then denatured. This is done by heating and cooling a tube containing the mixture in cycles with a device called a thermal cycler. This process is automated with the use of a heating block. The cycle is typically repeated thirty or thirty-two times, but FSA repeated it thirty-five times in this case. The greater the number of cycles performed, the larger the amount of DNA is produced. Each cycle doubles the amount of DNA being tested.

During a cycle, the primer targets the specific gene and will only bind to the genetically complementary portion of the DNA. At a different temperature, the enzyme works to build-up or copy the targeted gene. At the end of the thirty-five cycles, there are approximately sixteen billion copies of the strand of DNA that incorporates the targeted gene.

The third step is for the DNA to be placed onto a nitrocellulose filter to view what has been amplified. The allele-specific DNA being searched for is already on the filter. Only the DNA from the sample that is compatible with the gene being searched for will adhere to the filter. By washing the DNA strip with an enzyme, the filter should turn blue if the DNA has bound to it. A blue dot is a match; a blank is a non-match. The amplified DNA may then be typed for the various DQ alpha genotypes. This process is referred to as the reverse-dot blot procedure or the blue-dot procedure.

C

The company that holds the patent on the PCR method, Cetus Corporation, has developed and marketed commercial kits with procedural manuals for use in forensic laboratories. The reverse dot-blot method, used by FSA to type the alleles, is generally accepted in the scientific community as reliable, according to the prosecution's experts. This was not contested by the defendant's expert witness.

Because of the advantages of the PCR method over other DNA testing methods, its impact has been enormous on a wide range of scientific disciplines. The great advantage of the PCR method compared to the RFLP method is that it is much quicker and may be used on much smaller samples of DNA, such as hair samples. It can be used on nearly microscopic specks of tissue containing as few as twenty to one hundred white blood cells rather than the five thousand to fifty thousand cells normally required by RFLP analysis. It also may be used more easily on samples of DNA that have degraded as a result of high temperatures or humidity. The results of PCR testing are also easier to interpret than the results of RFLP analysis.

A disadvantage of the PCR method, when compared to the RFLP method, is that only one probe or locus is analyzed. In contrast, there generally are at least four probes or loci that are viewed with the RFLP method. The possibility of distinguishing individuals is much lower with the PCR method than with the RFLP method. PCR analysis detects variations in actual genes that tend to vary much less from one person to the next than the DNA strands that are the subject of analysis in the RFLP method. As a result, each profile tends to be less unique as produced by the PCR than by the RFLP method. For example, in RFLP results, the typical statistical probabilities of a DNA match may range from one in two million to one in sixty-one million. In contrast, in the case at bar, the victim's DQ alpha genotype was consistent with about five percent of the Caucasian population or one in twenty people. In other cases, however, the genotype might be considerably more rare and thus more conclusive of a match. While the PCR method is conclusive in excluding persons or suspects, its use in an analogous manner to the RFLP method in affirmatively identifying suspects must proceed with considerable caution, with the factfinder being carefully apprised of its inherent limitations.

According to Dr. Ginsburg, an associate professor of internal medicine and human genetics at the University of Michigan School of Medicine, the PCR method is generally accepted in the scientific community as reliable. Dr. Ginsburg testified that he used it in his work and that all modern molecular biology laboratories use the method routinely. In fact, Dr. Ginsburg believed that the PCR method is so reliable that it is routinely used in making life and death medical decisions.

Dr. Coussens, an assistant professor of microbiology, public health, and animal science at Michigan State University, also believed that the PCR method is generally accepted in the scientific community as reliable on the basis of the scientific literature and his personal experience. Dr. Coussens has participated in workshops with the Michigan State Police and has worked with evidentiary samples using the PCR method.

Dr. Blake, the forensic serologist, had used the PCR method for four years. According to Dr. Blake, the PCR method has evolved significantly, even since 1988. In his judgment, the possibility of human error has been virtually eliminated. Dr. Blake observed, however, that the only perfect check on the PCR method is for another analyst to be able to reproduce the results. For this reason, Dr. Blake only uses one-half of the sample for testing.

Dr. Blomberg is an associate professor of immunology and genetics at the University of Miami School of Medicine. Dr. Blomberg also had not performed any forensic analysis herself. However, she testified that the PCR method was appropriate for forensic use.

None of the prosecution's independent witnesses had used the PCR method for forensic testing. Dr. Ginsburg was not aware of any literature, other than from employees or former employees of commercial laboratories, regarding the use of the PCR method in the forensic setting.

Because Dr. Coussens worked in the area of DNA testing with animals, many of the samples he worked with were not in pristine condition, similar to forensic samples. The samples he tested often came from slaughterhouses. However, in his judgment, contaminants rarely caused a problem once the DNA was reextracted and repurified.

The fact that the prosecution's experts did not have forensic experience in the use of the PCR method does not mean that the standard for the acceptance of the scientific technique was not met. Rather it speaks more to the fact that the PCR method of DNA analysis is a relatively new procedure. The prosecution's experts were in agreement that the PCR method is accepted as reliable in the scientific community, including for forensic use.

In Young, supra at 485, the Supreme Court did not require that only forensic scientists may establish the reliability of a novel scientific procedure where the community of forensic scientists was relatively small and a consensus of such community could not be reached in any meaningful sense. Instead, the experts should only be required to possess sufficient theoretical understanding and practical experience to be able to evaluate the evidence. Id. The experts, however, need to explain the gaps in their own knowledge and experience, and also reach general agreement about the reliability of the information they are using to fill these gaps, in order to testify as experts. Id.

The prosecution's experts had more than adequate knowledge and experience to determine if the PCR method could be employed in the forensic setting. Their major concerns were laboratory protocol and preventing contamination. These were thoroughly addressed by the prosecution's experts, as will be discussed below. They were able to address these problems on the basis of their own experience and knowledge. Consequently, the lack of forensic experience did not undermine their testimony.

Defendant's expert, Dr. Bhagwat, was an assistant professor in molecular biology at Wayne State University. Dr. Bhagwat also had no prior experience with the forensic use of PCR testing. While Dr. Bhagwat admitted that there was no real dispute that PCR testing was acceptable for academic work or laboratory research, he believed that there were problems with PCR testing for forensic purposes. First, there was possible on-scene contamination or contamination in the laboratory. Second, according to Dr. Bhagwat, there was a controversy in the scientific community over PCR testing in the forensic setting largely due to the errors caused by the enzyme Taq polymerase.

D

Few jurisdictions have addressed the reliability of the PCR method under the Frye test. In State v Russell, 125 Wn.2d 24, 54; 882 P.2d 747 (1994), the Washington Supreme Court addressed the admissibility of the results of the PCR method under the Frye rule. Dr. Blake also performed the test in Russell. More recently, the same court followed Russell in State v Gentry, 125 Wn.2d 570, 586-587; 888 P.2d 1105 (1995). The court in Gentry held that Dr. Blake's actual procedures in performing the test are relevant to the weight of the evidence, not to its admissibility. Gentry, supra at 588-589.

The Superior Court of New Jersey in State v Williams, 252 N.J.Super. 369; 599 A.2d 960 (1991), also held that PCR results were admissible under a version of the Frye test. Again, Dr. Blake performed the test at issue in that case. Other states have admitted PCR test results, but under tests other than the Frye test.19

The consensus among the other jurisdictions is that PCR test results are admissible because the method is a reliable one. The potential problems of contamination and errors caused by Taq polymerase have not been judged serious enough to undermine the reliability of the PCR method.

A new controversy that has developed over the reliability of the PCR method is predicated upon a report prepared by the National Research Council (NRC) of the National Academy of Sciences in 1992: DNA Technology in Forensic Science. The report did not exist at the time of the hearings in this case.

Although the report was not admitted in the trial court, we have reviewed it for the first time on appeal as have courts in other jurisdictions. In State v Bible, 175 Ariz. 549, 586, n 33; 858 P.2d 1152 (1993), cert den ___ US ___; 114 S.Ct. 1578; 128 L Ed 2d 221 (1994), the Arizona Supreme Court held that it would consider scientific literature published in between the time of the trial and appellate review. The court reasoned that technology is constantly evolving and there was no valid reason for the court to limit its decision to what was known at the time of trial. We also believe that it is appropriate to take notice of new scientific literature under the same rationale: in order to ensure that our decisions are fashioned on the basis of the most up-to-date scientific and technical information available, as well as to promote judicial economy. See also State v Anderson, 118 N.M. 284; 881 P.2d 29 (1994). We do not believe that the NRC's report alters the result in this case.

The NRC report endorsed the forensic use of DNA analysis while also concluding that potential problems existed with the procedure, which problems required a series of safeguards. But "as a general matter, so long as the safeguards we discuss in this report are followed, admissibility of DNA typing should be encouraged. There is no substantial dispute about the underlying scientific principles." DNA Technology, supra at 145.

In Russell, supra at 44-49, the Washington court addressed the effect of the NRC report on the admissibility of PCR testing under the Frye standard. In an analysis of both the report and decisions from other courts that had reviewed the report, the court concluded that the NRC's report primarily called for PCR quality assurance standards in both the laboratory procedures used and the persons who may perform the test. Id. at 46-49. The report called for accreditation and governmental regulation of laboratories. Id. at 49. Because there was no precedent for the regulation of forensic testing, the court concluded that, while regulation and accreditation might be desirable, the absence of either or both of them should not bar the admissibility of PCR-produced DNA evidence. Id.

The criticisms set forth in the NRC's report have limited relevance to the immediate case. Many of the concerns that were raised were the result of early DNA cases in which contaminants were allowed into the samples because of poor laboratory procedures. See, e.g., People v Castro, 144 Misc.2d 956; 545 N.Y.S.2d 985 (1989). As discussed before, other jurisdictions have recognized that DNA testing, including PCR testing, can be reliable for forensic use if the proper procedures and other safeguards are followed. In every significant respect, the procedures adopted by FSA in the instant case appear to have been in compliance with the precautionary recommendations of the NRC report. We do not find the presence or absence of a formal regulatory body to be significant one way or the other in terms of assessing the integrity of the actual safeguards adopted by the testing laboratory in this case.

E

The principal criticism of the forensic use of the PCR method raised by defendant's expert, Dr. Bhagwat, is that the enzyme, Taq polymerase, may create copying errors during the chain reaction and thereby cause false results.20 Dr. Bhagwat testified that the test was not appropriate for forensic use because of the error rate caused by the enzyme.

Taq polymerase is used because it is a heat-insensitive bacterium. For this reason, Taq polymerase made practical the PCR method. It allowed for automation of the cycling process whereas scientists previously had to add the enzyme manually at each cycle, thereby increasing substantially the risk of human error.

Both Dr. Ginsburg and Dr. Blomberg acknowledged that Taq polymerase is somewhat prone to causing errors. They estimated the error rate at about one in 10,000. The potential error is that the enzyme may copy a base incorrectly, i.e., read an A as a G. Dr. Ginsburg considered any such error to be insignificant in light of the amplification process. Because there are so many other molecules, the error would have to reoccur in order for there to be any effect and it is highly unlikely that the same error would be repeated. Statistically, the error would only occur once in the course of a test.

With such a low error rate, the actual chance of an error in the ultimate DNA analysis is not a problem, according to Dr. Blomberg. It is highly unlikely that any mutation caused by the Taq polymerase would affect the result in this type of a case, according to both Dr. Ginsburg and Dr. Blomberg. Nor did Dr. Blomberg have problems with the error rate in her own work. In this type of testing, the error rate was not viewed as a fundamental problem.

Dr. Blake also did not believe that the error rate for Taq polymerase was significant because of the number of copies made. In order for an error to be significant, it would have to occur during the first cycle or occur at a certain place within the 242-base pair sequence. Dr. Blake found it hard to conceive of a situation where a false positive result would obtain because of an error caused by Taq polymerase.

Dr. Bhagwat believed the error rate was actually higher on the basis of studies that had been conducted and because the number of molecules was multiplied. However, he admitted that in order for the results to be affected, the error would have to occur at a certain point in a cycle and the odds were one in 2,410,000 of this occurring. Nonetheless, Dr. Bhagwat maintained that the error rate was significant because there were unknown "hot spots" that could cause mutation and errors would accumulate because of the number of cycles performed.

Dr. Bhagwat thought that multiple tests should be performed to ensure reliability and accuracy. Because the PCR method is used principally when there are very small amounts of material to test, there often is insufficient material available to run multiple tests. Nonetheless, as explained previously, Dr. Blake's procedure was to use only one-half the sample for testing so there was some leftover material for additional testing.

In fact, the parties agreed in this case to run a second PCR test after the Davis-Frye hearing. The agreement was that if the same result came up in the second test, the second result would not be admitted at trial. However, if the test results were different, then defendant could present that evidence. Another company, Serological Research Institute, performed the second test. Dr. Blake and Brian Wraxall, who performed the second test, were instructed not to communicate the results of their tests with one another.

Wraxall also found that the victim's genotype was 1.3, 4, the same as Dr. Blake found. Defendant's genotype was also 3, 4, again the same as Dr. Blake found. The hair found on the snow brush also was the same, 1.3, 4. There also was no DNA found on the hair shaft in the second test, which indicated that the hair sample was not contaminated with another person's DNA.

Contrary to the original agreement, the jury was instructed, pursuant to a later agreement, that a second PCR test had been run and that the results were the same as the first test.

In Russell, supra at 52, 54, the Washington court addressed the error rate of Taq polymerase and it found it was not a reason for refusing to admit the evidence. The evidence in Russell, supra at 52, showed that errors are rarely caused by Taq polymerase and are generally detectable.

The evidence in this case also demonstrated that the error rate for Taq polymerase is not significant. It is highly unlikely that an error will affect the results in a given case. Although the error rate is low, performing a second test is one way of checking to make sure that an error has not occurred because of the enzyme. That was performed in this case although we do not believe that such a test is required in order for PCR evidence to be admissible under the Davis-Frye standard. The absence of a second test would merely be relevant to the weight to be given to the evidence. Consequently, we do not believe that the error rate associated with Taq polymerase undermines the reliability of the PCR analysis as a forensic method.

F

Dr. Bhagwat also opined that the possibility of contamination of the DNA sample, either at the crime scene or in the laboratory, established that the PCR method was not appropriate for forensic use.

The PCR method's great advantage can also be a shortcoming. Because of its power to amplify a single cell, if a cell from another individual migrates into the specimen (such as from a laboratory employee or someone collecting the sample), the result could be affected. Environmental factors, even if they cause the DNA to degrade, do not cause false results. Nor does DNA from animals cause false results.

This potential contamination problem could produce a false positive result when there should have been no result at all. This occurs where a sample lacks DNA but is contaminated with another's DNA such as from hair or skin cells. Carry-over contamination can also occur from the DNA created during the PCR process. The odds remain extremely high, however, that a defendant would be falsely excluded rather than falsely included if this occurred. Laboratories must be concerned with controlling or preventing carry-over contamination because human contamination would not be readily apparent where the original sample had no DNA. Laboratories therefore routinely follow rigorous procedures to avoid this risk.

Forensic laboratories, such as FSA, actually are more careful in their protocol to prevent contamination than research laboratories. A typical safeguard is to perform the work in two separate laboratories to prevent the contamination between samples and the amplified DNA. Further, control samples are used and processed at the same time, such as using a known DNA sample and a sample with no DNA in it.

In the case at bar, FSA used extensive controls in the work area to prevent contamination. The area where the PCR product was worked on was isolated from the rest of the laboratory. The different samples, including the reference and evidentiary samples, were prepared at different times to prevent cross-DNA contamination. Negative controls or blanks were also used to try to detect errors in the process.

Dr. Blake explained that FSA has numerous additional safeguards for the handling of specimens at each stage of the process. The following procedures, for instance, are routinely used by FSA in its laboratory:

(1) plastic gloves are used and changed frequently;

(2) tools and solutions are sterile;

(3) there is a substantial amount of room to work so that the work area is not congested or confusing;(4) the preparation of the DNA is done with a laminar flow hood;(5) reagents used are "pre-aliquoted" or exactly divided;(6) the DNA preparation area is physically isolated from the PCR amplification and work area;(7) hair shafts are used as a control when testing hair samples;(8) blank mixtures (without DNA) are run through the testing procedure, including keeping those mixtures open while the targeted DNA is added to other specimens in the work area;(9) known DNA samples are used in the testing process so that some test results are known and predictable; and(10) control probes are used on the DQ alpha allele typing strips.

Dr. Ginsburg believed that FSA adequately addressed the problem of contamination on the basis of all available information. The possibility of contamination has been well recognized in the scientific community. For this reason, scientific literature has addressed at length what precautions need to be taken to avoid problems.

Dr. Coussens also believed that FSA followed appropriate procedures to guard against carryover contamination. If any contamination occurred in the laboratory setting, it would be apparent to a competent analyst. Dr. Blomberg testified as well that FSA'S protocol and method of operation were acceptable and that it had taken reasonable steps to prevent contamination.

On the facts of this case, the shaft of the hair sample also served as a control. The root of hair contains DNA. In contrast, the hair's shaft contains no DNA. Contamination of hair samples can be detected if there is DNA on a hair shaft. If there is DNA present on the shaft, it means that the sample came into contact with some other cell. For this reason, when testing hair samples the hair shaft is used as a control to check for contamination. Dr. Bhagwat acknowledged that a hair shaft may serve as a control because of the lack of DNA in the shaft. No DNA was found on the hair shaft of the sample in this case.

The issue of contamination was also addressed in Russell, supra at 53-54. There, the Washington court held that strict adherence to sterile techniques and procedures specifically addressed to contamination were essential to assessing the reliability of the PCR test results and, therefore, the admissibility of the results. Whether proper techniques and procedures were followed in a given case was a separate inquiry from the general acceptance of the PCR method. In each case, the party offering the evidence must be prepared to establish that reasonable laboratory procedures and protocols were followed. Id. The court in Russell, supra at 50-52, held that Dr. Blake's actual procedures in performing the test were relevant to the weight of this evidence, not to its admissibility.

In State v Moore, 268 Mont. 20, 47-48; 885 P.2d 457 (1994), the Montana Supreme Court also held that the possibility of contamination did not affect the admissibility of PCR test results. There were appropriate steps that could be taken to avoid and detect potential on-scene and human contamination of the specimen. Id. The court concluded that the potential for contamination can occur with virtually any physical evidence collected at crime scenes and, therefore, that this problem did not undermine the admissibility of the evidence. Instead, this area is ripe for cross-examination and is properly a matter of weight for the jury to determine. Id. at 48. See also State v Lyons, 124 Or.App. 598, 607-608; 863 P.2d 1303 (1993), review gtd 319 Or. 406; 879 P.2d 1284 (1994).

The evidence at the Davis-Frye hearing in the case at bar established that there are adequate controls and procedures to guard against contamination in the PCR process, which, if followed, will produce reliable and accurate test results. Accordingly, as long as adequate safeguards are undertaken to prevent contamination in the laboratory, results from PCR testing are reliable. Potential problems are generally identifiable and subject to prevention through the proper procedures. It is a separate inquiry whether the proper procedures were followed in a given case. Gentry, supra at 588-589.

Defendant has not shown that the potential for contamination makes the PCR method unreliable. Again, if proper laboratory procedures are followed to prevent contamination, then the PCR method appears to produce accurate results. Whether the proper procedures and safeguards are followed in a particular case is a matter for the jury to consider in determining how much weight it should give the results. However, where there are serious errors in a particular laboratory's work, a court may rule the test results themselves to be inadmissible. Russell, supra at 54.

G

Defendant also argues that the PCR method has not been subjected to validation through independently conducted studies. Validation through the publication of independently conducted studies is only required when members of the relevant scientific community disagree on the reliability of a novel scientific technique. People v Stoughton, 185 Mich.App. 219, 229; 460 N.W.2d 591 (1990).

The existence of validation studies for the PCR method was not established in the trial court. This may be due to the fact that in 1990 there still was not a great amount of published information about the forensic use of the PCR method.

Since the time of the hearing in this case, it appears that many more reports and studies have been produced concerning the validity of the PCR method. As stated earlier, it is appropriate in the context of scientific and technical evidence to take notice of the most up-to-date research available, including research which may have been undertaken after the time of a trial. In Russell, supra at 49-50, the court determined that there had been extensive validation studies performed concerning PCR testing, citing in particular Comey & Budowle, Validation Studies on the Analysis of the HLA DQ Alpha Locus Using the Polymerase Chain Reaction, 36 J Forensic Sci 1633 (1991). The Russell court also noted that Cetus Corporation had produced a bibliography listing over one thousand articles on PCR analysis. Russell, supra at 49. Defendant has not argued that any current research has called into question the reliability of the PCR method other than by citing the NRC's report. Because we believe that the Davis-Frye hearings in this case established that there was agreement in the scientific community concerning the acceptance of the PCR method for forensic use, the lack of validation studies at the time does not justify reversing the trial court's decision. We are aware of no more recent independent validation studies that have called into question the reliability of the PCR method.

The prosecution met its burden under the Davis-Frye test in establishing that the PCR method is generally accepted as reliable in the scientific community. The trial court's findings regarding this issue were not clearly erroneous. Adams, supra at 269. Therefore, we hold that trial courts in Michigan may take judicial notice of the reliability of DNA testing using the PCR method.21 However, before a court admits the test results into evidence in a given case, the prosecutor must still show that generally accepted laboratory procedures were followed. Adams, supra at 277. The testimony of experts may then be considered by the jury in determining the weight that it should give to the evidence. FSA'S procedures in this case were consistent with generally accepted procedures for PCR testing and were reasonably designed to minimize any risk of error in the procedures.

If there are concerns regarding the weight that juries will give PCR test results, those concerns are overstated. As long as it is made clear to juries that this type of testing contains inherent limitations and care is taken to avoid confusing the PCR and RFLP methods, the evidence should not be misinterpreted. Where the prosecution attempts to use PCR evidence along the same lines as RFLP evidence — to identify rather than to exclude an individual — then greater care must be undertaken to explain to the jury its probative limitations.

Linda Vanderveen was kidnapped and murdered on February 12, 1979. The defendant came under suspicion on February 23, was arrested on March 30, and was convicted on November 9. This was sixteen years ago. It is long overdue that this case be brought to a conclusion and that justice be obtained for the victim, her family and friends, her community, and the defendant.

Affirmed.

FootNotes

* Circuit judge, sitting on the Court of Appeals by assignment.

1. Deoxyribonucleic acid.

2. The prosecutor conceded that witnesses who identified defendant at the first trial (witnesses Start, Hill, and Vos) would not be able to identify him at the second trial under the strictures set forth by the Supreme Court.

3. In addition to the passage of time, it appears that substantial preservation of prehypnotic statements is lacking. *Lee IV, supra* at 78. We note, however, that the investigation in this case took place before *People v Gonzales,* 415 Mich. 615; 329 N.W.2d 743 (1982), modified 417 Mich. 968 (1983), and *People v Nixon,* 421 Mich. 79; 364 N.W.2d 593 (1984), in which the Michigan Supreme Court addressed the admissibility of testimony of hypnotized witnesses, were decided.

4. The prosecutor requested that he be allowed to generally ask the following questions (with expected answers):(1) "[C]an you tell me whether he was the person you saw driving the car that morning?" "No, I cannot."(2) "Is there anything about him, as he sits here in court today, that would lead you to believe he is not the person you saw that morning?" "No there's not."(3) In other words, "You can't say one way or the other?" "That's correct."

The prosecutor explained that these were questions that had been asked in the first trial of witnesses who did not and could not identify the defendant.

5. The Supreme Court's decision in *Lee* rested upon the unreliability of posthypnotic testimony under the Michigan Rules of Evidence, not upon any constitutional defect. *Lee IV, supra* at 72-86.

6. With respect to the testimony of Jack Vos, defendant actually points to testimony defendant himself elicited on cross-examination.

7. Defendant contends that Justices CAVANAGH's and ARCHER's votes constitute the third and fourth votes on this issue, in addition to the votes of Justice BRICKLEY and Justice LEVIN. We disagree. Neither Justice CAVANAGH nor Justice ARCHER expressed an opinion on the propriety of the prosecution's closing argument. Justice CAVANAGH, joined by Justice ARCHER, dissented with regard to the portion of Justice BRICKLEY's opinion where the closing argument was discussed. 434 Mich. 97. As long as it would not be illogical for Justices CAVANAGH and ARCHER to reject the admissibility of the MRE 404(b) evidence yet concede the propriety of the prosecutor's closing argument if such evidence were admissible, we decline to read the minds of these justices.

8. The jurors' initials are used here to protect their privacy. Juror O and Juror F were peremptorily excused by defendant. Juror N was not.

9. Although it is unclear whether defendant also contends that another juror, M, should have been stricken for legal cause, he is alluded to in defendant's brief on appeal. Juror M did not have any clear recollections about the first trial (indeed, he was unaware of the verdict) and communicated an open mind in considering the evidence at the second trial. The fact that his wife had spoken to him briefly about an article appearing in the newspaper about the case before jury duty does not, in our judgment, constitute legal cause for his removal. Juror M was later stricken by peremptory challenge.

10. Defendant actually claims that the prosecutor stated that the hair found in defendant's car "must have come from a female, and that for this reason, his own expert's statistics based upon the DNA evidence, were wrong." However, it appears that the prosecutor stated that it probably came from a female on the basis of its length and the opinion of a witness. The prosecutor then proceeded to continue his argument with the assumption that it was a hair from a female.

11. In *People v Frazier (After Remand),* 446 Mich. 539, 543-544; 521 N.W.2d 291 (1994), a plurality opinion, Justice BRICKLEY, quoting *California v Green,* 399 U.S. 149, 156; 90 S.Ct. 1930; 26 L Ed 2d 489 (1970), noted the origins of the Confrontation Clause:"[T]he particular vice that gave impetus to the confrontation claim was the practice of trying defendants on `evidence' which consisted solely of ex parte affidavits or depositions secured by the examining magistrates, thus denying the defendant the opportunity to challenge his accuser in a face-to-face encounter in front of the trier of fact."

12. Defendant stresses the absence of testimony from Billy Mansfield, Jr., and the effect on the juror who defendant claims remembered his testimony from the first trial. Ironically, Mansfield testified that, while he and defendant were temporarily cellmates, defendant had confessed to him that he had committed the crime. In the course of defendant's argument, he further points to the recollection of Juror F. Juror F thought that the retrial was occurring possibly because "there was another man involved that said that he admitted he was guilty." However, it is unclear whether Juror F was referring to defendant's alleged confession to Mansfield or whether Juror F incorrectly recollected that a mistrial may have occurred because another individual admitted his own responsibility for the crime. In any event, Juror F assured the court that she could put out of her mind what she knew about the first trial and committed to keep an open mind.

13. Defendant incorrectly states the elements of felony murder as "who, what, whom, when, why and how." Defendant further claims that the jurors "chose" not to consider these "elements." The jury should have, and presumably did, consider the elements as instructed by the trial court.

14. MCL 750.316; MSA 28.548 was amended slightly by 1980 PA 28, presumably after the offense was committed in this case. However, that amendment does not appear to affect this case in any way.

15. Defendant does not specify any particular witness, but instead argues the inadmissibility of all such identifications or comparisons. As we discussed in section I, the prosecutor agreed at trial that witnesses who were hypnotized would not be allowed to point to the defendant and identify him as the person they saw. Defendant has not pointed to any such identification. With respect to an identification or comparison of the car, we found in section I that the identifications or comparisons by those witnesses that defendant identified in his appellate brief were based on facts recalled and related before hypnosis. In defendant's supplemental brief, he does not point to an identification or comparison made by any particular witness. We do not believe an identification or comparison of the defendant's car is inadmissible per se because the testifying witness has been hypnotized. We further do not believe that this is what the Michigan Supreme Court meant in *Lee IV, supra.*

16. *People v Davis,* 343 Mich. 348; 72 N.W.2d 269 (1955); *Frye v United States,* 54 US App DC 46; 293 F 1013 (1923).

17. The prosecution urges this Court to follow *Daubert v Merrell Dow Pharmaceuticals,* 509 US ___; 113 S.Ct. 2786; 125 L Ed 2d 469 (1993), and replace the *Davis-Frye* standard. However, we are bound to continue to follow this standard until the Michigan Supreme Court overrules or modifies its decisions in this area. *Boyd v WG Wade Shows,* 443 Mich. 515, 523; 505 N.W.2d 544 (1993); *People v Bullock,* 440 Mich. 15, 27; 485 N.W.2d 866 (1992). Furthermore, it is unnecessary to assess the DNA evidence in this case under the more relaxed Supreme Court standard because it is determined here to be admissible under even the more rigorous *Davis-Frye* standard.

18. Dr. Adams primarily addressed genetic-population studies, which are only relevant to the resulting statistical information on DNA test results. Defendant has not challenged that portion of the trial court's ruling.

19. See *State v Moore,* 268 Mont. 20, 41-42; 885 P.2d 457 (1994) (PCR analysis is sufficiently reliable for forensic purposes); *State v*

Lyons, 124 Or.App. 598, 602-610; 863 P.2d 1303 (1993), review gtd 319 Or. 406; 879 P.2d 1284 (1994) (PCR test results from FSA ruled admissible under a seven-factor relevancy test, which includes determining if the technique has general acceptance in the field); *Clarke v State,* 813 S.W.2d 654, 655 (Tex App, 1991), aff'd 839 S.W.2d 92 (Tex Crim App, 1992), cert den ___ US ___; 113 S.Ct. 1611; 123 L Ed 2d 172 (1993) (relevancy standard was met for the admission of PCR test results); *Spencer v Commonwealth,* 240 Va. 78, 97-98; 393 S.E.2d 609 (1990), cert den 498 U.S. 908 (1990) (while not applying the *Frye* test, the court held that PCR test results, performed by Dr. Blake and FSA, were sufficiently reliable to be admitted).

20. Because of the concern over such errors, another company is attempting to market another polymerase that is even more accurate. As a result, in future cases this problem may not be an issue.

21. However, we have not been asked to decide if the statistical method used by FSA to compute the frequencies for the twenty-one genotypes appearing in various racial and ethnic populations also meets the *Davis-Frye* standard.

www.ingramcontent.com/pod-product-compliance
Ingram Content Group UK Ltd.
Pitfield, Milton Keynes, MK11 3LW, UK
UKHW020126290926
15471UKWH00003B/320

9 781623 29114